Literature,
Popular Culture,
and Society

Literature,
Popular Culture,
and Society

Leo Lowenthal

A Spectrum Book
Prentice-Hall, Inc.
Englewood Cliffs, N. J.

Leo Lowenthal—sociologist, literary critic, historian, philosopher—is an author of international reputation. Among his works may be found *Literature and the Image of Man*, *Prophets of Deceit* (with Norbert Guterman), and *Culture and Social Behavior* (with Seymour M. Lipset). Dr. Lowenthal (Ph.D., Frankfurt-am-Main, Germany) is now Professor of Sociology and Professor of Speech at the University of California (Berkeley).

Acknowledgments

Thanks are due to the University of Chicago Press for permission to reprint parts of my article "Historical Perspectives of Popular Culture," *The American Journal of Sociology*, Vol. 55 (January, 1950), pages 323–332 (Chapter 1); to the Free Press for permission to reprint the paper "The Debate over Art and Popular Culture in 18th Century England" by Leo Lowenthal and Marjorie Fiske, from *Common Frontiers of the Social Sciences*, edited by Mirra Komarovsky (1957), pages 33–112 and 413–418 (Chapter 3); to Paul F. Lazarsfeld and Frank N. Stanton, owners of the copyright, *Radio Research* 1942–43, Duell, Sloan & Pearce, Inc. (1944), for permission to reprint my essay "Biographies in Popular Magazine," pages 507–548 and 581–585 (Chapter 4); to the University of Illinois Press for permission to reprint my essay "The Sociology of Literature" from *Communications in Modern Society*, edited by Wilbur Schramm (1948), pages 82–100 (Chapter 5); to the Beacon Press for permission to reprint pages 221–229 from my book *Literature and the Image of Man* (incorporated in Chapter 5), and for using some of the material contained in the introduction to this book for the introduction of the present volume. Other parts appeared in the *International Social Science Journal*, Vol. XII, No. 4, 1960; permission for reprint was given by *UNESCO*.

I am indebted for editorial advice to Ina Lawson and my son Daniel K. Lowenthal.

Special acknowledgment is due to my wife, Marjorie Fiske. Her advice has been invaluable in editorial matters; above all she is the co-author (and as such has done more than her share) of the third chapter, which deals with England in the eighteenth century.

Table of Contents

Introduction

I

The essays collected in this volume, though written at various times over the last three decades, have an underlying theme closely relating to my long-term intellectual concerns. These concerns are in turn bound up with my background and experience.

During my university training in Germany, immediately after the end of the First World War, I devoted four years to the study of the social sciences and another four years to that of literature and history; throughout this period I was also engaged in the study of philosophy. By now, I have lived for more than a quarter of a century in the United States, and my professional affiliations both here and abroad have been that of a sociologist. These bare facts of my intellectual life may indicate that I can neither confess nor boast adherence to an unequivocally defined specialization. I believe this to be an advantage. Approaching sociological research humanistically while retaining a sociological view of the humanities can lead to a new awareness of the communion of the Western mind. Unfortunately the stubborn claims of privilege made by single academic specialties have all too often obscured this unity.

Obviously, if we except the genius and the charlatan, no one individual can undertake to apply the generalist's mentality to an infinite number of fields and data. My own work—partly by accident, partly by predilection—has focused over the years on cultural phenomena, particularly on literary productions. In the sociologist's idiom, it is the area of communication; in the parlance of the humanist, it is the area of literature (artistic or otherwise).

The French philosopher and political theorist Charles de Bonald once said:

> Were one to see the literature of a people whose history one does not know, one could tell what this people had been, and were one to read the history of a people whose literature one does not know, one could assume with certainty, which one had been the basic trait of its literature.

That is to say, literature is a particularly suitable bearer of the fundamental symbols and values which give cohesion to social groups, ranging from nations and epochs to special social sub-groups and points of time. Conceived in this sense, literature embraces two powerful cultural complexes: art on the one hand, and a market-oriented commodity on the other.

Popular commodities serve primarily as indicators of the socio-psychological characteristic of the multitude. By studying the organization, content, and linguistic symbols of the mass media, we learn about the typical forms of behavior, attitudes, commonly held beliefs, prejudices, and aspirations of large numbers of people. At least since the separation of literature into the two distinct fields of art and commodity in the course of the eighteenth century, the popular literary products can make no claim to insight and truth. Yet, since they have become a powerful force in the life of modern man, their symbols cannot be overestimated as diagnostic tools for studying man in contemporary society.

Literature as art is another matter. It is the creation of individuals and it is experienced by individuals, qua individuals. It thus seems to be as remote from the concerns of a social scientist as the physician-patient relationship is from the interests of a research biochemist, and it is not surprising that social scientists usually have made a detour around it—at least in their professional work. Yet it is my profound conviction that particularly since the dawn of our era in the Renaissance, creative artistic literature presents one of the essential sources for studying the relation between man and society.

On a previous occasion I compared the creative writer with the authors of personal documents such as memoirs, autobiographies, diaries and letters and commented that: "It is the artist who portrays what is more real than reality itself."[1] This is a broad, if not grandiose statement. My purpose here is to explore it in some detail.

II

Great works of literature enable us to study the way in which people live out their social roles. Political and economic history provide a wealth of data about institutional change, but only in recent times has sociology with its own methods and facts been able to fill in the picture and suggest the significance of these changes to the human being. Sociologists have performed part of their function admirably; they have devised ingenious methods for giving us insightful details about contemporary man living in contemporary social situations. But the study of the change in man's psychic relation to society over long periods has been too much neglected. It is our hope that we can, with the aid of literature, eventually bring this field within the sociologists' perspective.

As Robert K. Merton and others have noted, the American love of technique has often severely limited the scope of inquiries that American sociolo-

[1] See the introduction to my book, *Literature and the Image of Man* (Boston: Beacon Press, 1957).

gists make. Problems are chosen to fit the techniques. Europeans, on the other hand, have tended to the other extreme, often taking the whole of history as their field. Nonsense can, of course, result from either method pushed to the extreme, and it goes without saying that considerable work remains to be done at both ends of this continuum. Much contemporary theory and research goes about its business as if the problems which it sets came into being *ob ovo*—the moment the sociologist turned his attention to them. The study of the history of the individual as portrayed in literature can tell us how we got here and, by so doing, enhance our ability to assess where we are going.

But more important is the question of significance. If we limit ourselves to observable facts and to our own society, there is no way to determine what is important and what is unimportant, what essential and what unessential. Here, a knowledge of the central problems of past societies is of an obvious value. Literature in particular shows not only the socialized behavior of man, but the process of his socialization as well; it speaks not only of individual experience, but of the meaning of that experience. The writer's desire to create the unique and important work forces him to discover those new and telling expressions that often successfully bring hitherto nameless anxieties and hopes into focus. A writer is a specialized thinker about the individual. His work can be a key source to the sociologist, who is a specialist in the relations of the individual to society. Sociological interpretations of literature can become not mere isolated studies of a particular cultural phenomenon, but efforts to put into a sociological framework some of the most valuable evidence about the human being that exists.

The historian must depersonalize social relationships in favor of an emphasis on larger events; at the other extreme, memoirs, autobiographies and letters provide us with more personal data, but the autobiographical "I" fails to give us those generalized portraits that depend for their success upon holding the mirror of reality up to large segments of society. The fictional work, at its best embodying the general in the particular, combines the advantages of these two extremes: it presents the important theme as it is acted out and felt by the individual, and at the same time gives us a wealth of sociologically meaningful detail.

To consider literature in a sociological context immediately brings up the problem of the reliability and typicality of its data. For whom does a writer speak? Does he have in mind, for example, only himself and a limited elite who are his readers? How far beyond this group do his insights extend? By and large, the great dramatists and novelists of the past have only been read by a small minority, while the majority were and are exposed mainly to mass-produced and very largely escapist material. Certainly, all literature whether first or second rate, can be interpreted sociologically, but Flaubert presents problems entirely different from Mary Roberts Rinehart. In short, the most telling truths about society and the individual are contained in a literature that is not read by the broadest strata; the realization of the ideal—

an entire society aware of the profoundest truths about itself—lies still in the future. The writer who achieves greatness does so, we assume, because of the depth of his insight into the human condition, including those aspects of that condition that are, in non-fictional terms, the province of the sociologist. The fact that he is a rare phenomenon and that his readers may be few presents, in itself, a sociological problem, but it in no way detracts from his stature as a reporter or from the breadth and depth of his observations.

Of more importance is the fact that the writer's breadth of observation is dependent on the accessibility of various population groups to him and the opportunities these various groups have for self-expression in ways that permit the writer to speak for them. The muteness of the lower classes about their own experience is an unfortunate limitation only partly compensated for by the depth and penetration of the artist's insights into more fortunately placed individuals. It does, however, tell its own story; the comparative absence of the lower orders from literature is a direct reflection of their social role. Thus the bulk of the fictional characters considered in scociological studies undertaken thus far are from the middle and higher levels of society. Still, the Spaniards to whom Cervantes spoke, the Englishmen who saw Shakespeare's plays, and the French audiences of Corneille, Racine, and Molière had no trouble in recognizing the characters presented to them nor in distinguishing the nuances that mark the various levels they represented. There is, in short, enough evidence to insure that the largely middle-class individuals whom the artists portray are genuine.

In the end, of course, we should have to admit that our science is an historical one and that it suffers from the same lack of certainty as do all historical and therefore non-experimental sciences. Also, only some of the subject matter of any science of man is self-evident. When our topic is the living, full human being, with all of his feelings and attitudes, there can be no guarantees of certainty. Here, as in psychology and sociology in general, we can at best hope that, by a certain finesse and an eye for probabilities, we can sift out the valid and important from the misleading and trivial in much of our data. Ambiguity is inseparable from the study of man.

Direct social observations and the portraits of social "types" in literature speak for themselves; they are what many people have in mind when they think of a "sociological interpretation." Far more illuminating, however, are those larger portrayals of human reaction and expectation that give a greater depth to the study of social influences and allow us to discern the insecurities and frustrations (or the securities and satisfactions) experienced by man in a given society. Indeed, it is often precisely where a writer thinks he is discovering immutable truths about human nature that we can see the process of social change at work most clearly. Thus, for example, Corneille, the spokesman *par excellence* for the French absolute monarchy, viewed man as, by nature, incapable of imposing order on himself and his affairs without the guidance of a powerful state authority. Ibsen, living in the heyday of a highly competitive middle-class society, portrays individuals who are highly competitive in all their affairs, both public and private. In both of these cases, the social origins of character traits thought at the time to be innate are quite apparent.

Since literature deals with all levels of human behavior, an essential task of the sociologist dealing with it is to find that core of meaning which, through artistic images, expresses the many facets of thought and feeling. This seemingly formidable task is made feasible if we note carefully similarities of character and attitude that are taken for granted at one time but not at another. Thus, for example, we find in *Don Quixote* a number of sentiments and forms of behavior which denote extreme personal insecurity—insecurity ranging from fears of starvation and worry about status to deep moral and philosophic doubts. All these fears can be related, more or less directly, to the sudden access of social mobility that followed upon the downfall of the hierarchical feudal world. Cervantes' hero is a highly isolated individual who is sometimes hopeful, more often apprehensive. By Molière's time, the middle class had become entrenched, and the problem of man as he saw it was that of adaptation to this new and powerful but still largely unexplored social order.

Analyses of such works can reveal, in other words, those central problems with which man has been concerned at various times, permitting us to develop an image of a given society in terms of the individuals who composed it. It is in this way that literature tells us not only what a society was like in a past age, but also what the individual felt about it, what he could hope from it, and how he thought he could change it or escape from it. Like the living man of our own times, the fictional character of the past sees and records not only the reality around him, but his hopes, wishes, dreams, and fantasies as well. The social meanings of this inner life of the individual are related to the central problems of social change.

Similarly, large ranges of experience not ordinarily thought to be of concern to the sociologist take on social meaning when viewed in the light of a central problematic context. Thus, we find that nature, for example, has taken on a variety of meanings in the course of time, meanings that depend very largely upon the kind of society in which the writer lived. In various stages of our literary history, nature has meant the non-human world to which one goes for relaxation from the human scene; the source of Utopias that hold up a non-historical, "natural" ideal to an historical society viewed as having grown corrupt; or, as in Romanticism, the goal of a flight from a society viewed as inescapably frustrating to the individual. In fact, most of the "universal values" in literature prove on close analysis to be more intimately related to social change than is often thought.

It is one of the functions of the writer as well as the sociologist to describe and label new experience. Only after such creative tasks have been performed can the majority of people recognize and become articulate about their predicament and its sources. Otherwise, their "opinions" are apt to be mere clichés often reflecting conditions which no longer exist. Literature may justify or defy society but it does not merely passively record it. But whether it is the literary artist or the sociologist who constructs the image for us, that image will rest upon a human—and therefore biased—interpretation.

At first sight, this pace-setting function of literary material and its inevitable limitation might seem to disqualify it for the scientist. But when we turn our attention to the problem of *how* a literary character dissents from a social order or *how* he seeks to justify it, then we have descriptive materials of prime importance. A study of the modes of rejection or acceptance of existing social orders found in literature enables us to fill in the blanks left by political and economic history. Attitudes toward social institutions have changed in the course of time as radically as the institutions themselves. Thus, in the late sixteenth and early seventeenth centuries, the national state and the monarchy were almost universally accepted as ideals by authors who saw in them a cure for the evils of decaying feudalism. Of course, the idea of the kind of monarchical state that was desirable varied from author to author, but generally, the existing structure provided a kind of limit to the aspirations of the time. It was only later that republican ideals appeared in literature, and only later still that the kind of elaborate critique of middle-class society found in Ibsen could make its debut. We find that not only attitudes, but ideals themselves are usually reactions sharply delimited by specific social orders. They may look forward, or backward, to a different age, but they tend to do so from within the confines of an existing reality. Thus, the "bias" of the writer is far from the kind of drawback that it would appear to be at first sight. The writer is not concerned with a bare reality of objects, events, or institutions, but with a *human* reality that involves attitudes and feelings which are never neutral. If this is bias, it is the inevitable result of trying to present a living reality instead of a dead one.

My endeavor, then, is to treat the documents of artistic literature as primary sources for the interpretation of the imagery of self and society as a means of rounding out our understanding of social norms and values in times past.

III

In turning now to popular literature as commodity, we enter a field where social science research has flourished for the last three decades. It has, however, been so preoccupied with research techniques and methodological devices for refined data processing that a paradoxical situation has developed. One of the many professional specialities of our day, dedicated to the study of one of the most visible, audible, and time-consuming social institutions, has not attracted a good deal of interested attention from the literate public at large. I think that this is basically due to the reluctance of the theorists and research specialists to relate their work to the general intellectual discussion of modern mass culture on the one hand and to its historical antecedents on the other.

An investigation does not have to start with a *tabula rasa*. One of the first tasks is to make clear that much has been written on the tablet which now has to be deciphered and read. Modern communications research, like so many other specialized activities in the social sciences, has led an ascetic life—limiting itself to closely defined problems of content analysis, effects, audience stratification, problems of inter- and intra-media relations, and so on. Outside of this world of diligent and conscientious specialized research, a literary discussion has been raging, led by more or less sophisticated contributors to literary and highbrow magazines, by social philosophers, artists, educators, and other agents of institutionalized and non-institutionalized public policy. Both groups, if they ever take note of each other, treat the other side with irony or contempt—the writers by poking fun at the specialists who do not see or do not want to see the forest because of their jargon, and the specialists by denying any dignity of evidence to the theorizing or moralizing literati. The real victim in this battle is not the literary guild which has gone on setting its own standards of proof and speculation unruffled by the methodological headaches of the specializing disciplinarian, but this very social scientist who increasingly has felt the need for locating (and thereby dynamizing) his studies, projects, and plans in a meaningful whole of socially useful and theoretical orientations. Being a scientist and not a theologian or a metaphysician, he will not gain or regain such orientation without recourse to an historical continuum.

Indeed, popular culture has a history of many centuries, and is probably as old as human civilization. We have only to think of the differentiation between esoteric and exoteric religious exercises in early Oriental and Occidental civilization, of the dichotomy between high and low tragedy and comedy on the stages of ancient Greece and Rome, of the gulf between philosophizing elites at the estates of Roman emperors and the circuses promoted by the very same elite, of the organized medieval holidays with their hierarchical performances in the cathedral and the folksy entertainments at popular fairs to which the crowd surrendered immediately after participation in the services.

Popular art as such is not a specifically modern phenomenon. But until the modern era, it did not give rise to intellectual or moral controversies. They arose only after the two domains had come in contact. The process that led to the change was gradual, but there is little doubt that it was associated with broad social and technological changes which ushered in the beginnings of a middle class. The artist, traditionally dependent for his subsistence on the direct consumers of his art, no longer had to please only one rich or powerful patron; he had now to worry about the demands of an increasingly broader, more "popular" audience. Though the process took place in all great European nations with varying speed, there has arisen in each of them, since the end of the eighteenth century, a class of writers and playwrights who cater to the needs of these broader audiences. And during that century the controversies about popular culture began to rage in earnest. We owe an even earlier formulation, in terms that have stayed with us, to Montaigne, who was one of the most profound students of human nature of all times. His psychological analysis of entertainment as a means of meeting a universal human need applied to *both* domains of culture, and he thus unwittingly fired the opening shot in the battle of ideas that followed.

Montaigne's ideas on the psychological and social function of entertainment contrast with those of Pascal. His century—the seventeenth—marks the consolidation of modern national states following the breakdown of the medieval supra-national political, economic, and cultural hierarchies. The intellectual task of the period was to reconcile the individual's religious and moral heritage and his basic human needs with the requirements of the national and capitalist economy which was replacing the feudal system. It is therefore not surprising that the philosophers of this period discussed the individual's cultural efforts and personal needs in relation to his spiritual and emotional well-being, nor is it surprising that it was the philosophers who played leading roles in these discussions. Looked at today, these discussions sometimes present a bewildering play of speculation around the question of whether the individual should ever be allowed to indulge in any leisure-time activities except those which may be construed as contributing to the salvation of his soul. Rambling and general as these philosophical speculations may be, however, they nevertheless juxtapose, for the first time in modern history, serious against relatively frivolous leisure-time pursuits, and in so doing implicitly pose a problem.

Some of the milestones in the history of this debate on popular culture are discussed in the body of this book. It is my hope that the interpretation of the social role of artistic and non-artistic products in literature will eventually be amenable to theoretical formulation. For the time being they remain a series of isolated concepts and basic, as yet largely unresolved, questions.

Let me start by enumerating some considerations (and prejudices) which are likely to turn up in a review of the dimensions of popular culture:

(a) the *sum total* of ideas, concepts, values of a society—in short, "culture" in the anthropological sense;

(b) *popularization* of genuine art and intellectual thoughts and systems;

(c) *residues* of past elite culture adapted to the lower intellectual capacities and less consciously differentiated emotional needs of a population at large;

(d) the *folk art* of the modern middle and lower middle classes who produce and consume the products of the mass media;

(e) the content and the values *inherent* in the mass media themselves;

(f) concepts and values *derived* from mass communications and operative in society as a whole;

(g) the *data* of operational research, i.e., whatever such research shows various samples of the population believe to be the meaning of the term.

While it would certainly be a sterile undertaking to devote much time to a discussion of definitions, it would be helpful if, in the not too distant future, we could at least arrive at a working definition. But even an operational definition will probably be impossible to arrive at before confronting the question of the relationship between "genuine art" and "popular culture."

Among others, the following questions will have to be explored:

(a) *Are we really dealing here with a dichotomy* or are the two concepts simply formed in different logical contexts? Could it not be said when we talk about art, that we reflect upon a specific product, its inner structure, its norms, and the relationship of such structure and norms to those of other individual products? And, in thinking of popular culture, do we not tend to confine our considerations to questions of consumption, dissemination, and effects on large audiences? In the case of art and even of art criticism, are not the criteria (moral and intellectual) concerned mainly with the "truth," the degree of insight provided by the work, while in the case of popular culture, is not the main criterion the nature of "effect"? Many writers illustrate this "dichotomy" point of view; a few will be found who plead for a combination of the two viewpoints.

(b) *Are the equations* art ↔ insight ↔ elite *on the one hand, and* popular culture ↔ entertainment ↔ mass audience *on the other valid?* Do elites never seek entertainment and are the broad strata *eo ipso* alienated from high culture? Does entertainment, on the other hand, preclude insight? The various hypotheses of writers such as Harbage on Shakespeare's mass appeal (*Shakespeare's Audience*, New York: Columbia University Press, 1941), Dwight MacDonald on popular culture, and others on the artistic potential of the contemporary mass media, particularly radio and television, are relevant in this context.

(c) This leads to a further question, namely *whether and under what conditions art can become popular culture.* The etchings of Albrecht Dürer, whose artistic character will hardly be contested, were the popular posters which the partisans of Protestantism in the first half of the sixteenth century used in propagation of their cause. The operas of Verdi served as devices for mass demonstrations for the adherents of the Italian *Risorgimento*, a majority of the population. The music dramas of Richard Wagner were promoted in Nazi Germany as devices for mass identification of the populace with alleged heroism innate in the German soul. Finally, the museums "with" and "without" walls, the mass dissemination and the consumption of motion and still pictures of various forms of the graphic arts, of classical philosophy and history in paperback books, and of serious music on phonograph records in our own society serve as social arrangements to make works of art "popular" commodities.

(*d*) But if we confine ourselves to contemporary expressions, the question remains *whether the gap between art and popular culture will widen* as the mass media spread through modern civilization. Works of art have nearly always been produced by one individual. In this individual's product are encompassed his own artistic and intellectual intentions, and the individual creator carries the full responsibility for both content and form. But under the conditions of the mass market of a democratic industrialized society, a great number of individuals must participate in the production of "goods" designed for a "popular" market. It may well be, then, that the inherent necessities of producing popular culture for a modern society prevent art (as we conceive it in terms of the "equation" above) from penetrating into this realm. In exploring this problem some attention must be paid to the concept of "folk art" and the extent to which the mass media at their best may be evolving art forms which fall between folk and "high" art. Consideration should be given, too, to the question of the direct and indirect effects of this relatively new mass media culture on the contemporary artist.

(*e*) This leads to the important problem, no less familiar to a nineteenth-century historian than to a twentieth-century social scientist: *who makes decisions about the kinds of entertainment and art offered in a given society?* To indicate the scope of the problem briefly, one need only ask: who decides about the form and content of productions which may become, or are intended from the beginning to be, products of popular culture? If one can determine the conditions under which the decisions are made, one has moved at least a step toward answering the question of whether the gap between art and popular culture is unbridgeable. Decisions which are taken by joint conferences of financial groups, advertising agency and media corporation executives, engineers, directors and script writers have become so far removed from the realm of the responsibility of the individual artist that no ready answers suggest themselves.

(*f*) In connection with these questions, there arises the problem of *what is "good" and "bad" in the arts and popular culture?* Some social scientists interested in both areas are convinced that the traditional aesthetic criteria applied to art are not necessarily different from the standards now applied in judging products of popular culture. They assume that such classical aesthetic theories as those of Aristotle or German classicism, centering on various shadings of the concept of catharsis, are essentially theories about the *effects* of products. This problem of standards for criticism should be rather fully explored, because effects as we understand them today ("responses") are essentially psychological data, while the categories of classical aesthetics seem to be directed toward a moral standard which makes the audience (as well as the artist) responsible for the impact of the work of art.[2] Modern effects studies acquit the respondents of any moral or aesthetic responsibility by concentrating only on the psychological aspect of the respondents' experiences. Sample source material for such discussion may be found in the writings of contemporary art and literary critics, the works of professional critics of the mass media such as Gilbert Seldes, John Gould, and John Crosby, and in the few detailed scientific studies on the uses and gratifications of the mass media.

Although I am not prepared even to begin formulating a theory of popular culture, I can sketch a few possible points of view from which it might be surveyed.

(1) For example, one might look at the *patterns of influence* vis-à-vis art and popular culture both on an historical continuum and on a class scale in any given period. An artist is of course influenced by his predecessors, and in turn influences his successors. But he also influences the standards of his audience and is influenced by their standards. In addition, both audiences and artists of one generation or era probably exert considerable influence on the standards and expectations of the audiences in ensuing generations. Finally, the entrepreneur of each period interacts with both artist (or producer) and audience, and may or may not influence succeeding generations.

The content, the intensity, and the direction of such influence all shift over time. Comparatively speaking, the serious artist in the sixteenth and seventeenth centuries was probably somewhat less influenced by audience or entrepreneur than is his counterpart today. Because there were fewer mass media and other communications channels available to influence him (consciously or unconsciously), he was perhaps more likely to set his own standards. Furthermore, since his support came largely from the elite, the intellectual and aesthetic criteria of audience and artist were likely to be not too far apart.

With the development of mass media which have to satisfy the demands of multiplicities of outlets, more and more people who may or may not be artists have come to "produce." The concern of these producers must necessarily be focused more on filling the channels and competing with rivals than on expressing their own ideas. Thus, in producing for the mass media it is probable that the concept of what the audience "wants" becomes increasingly important. This in turn leads to the problems of whether, in a

[2] Edgar Allan Poe in his essay "Exordium" protested against this identification of reaction with standards in 1842: "That a criticism '*now*' should be different in spirit . . . from a criticism at any previous period, is to insinuate a charge of variability in laws that cannot vary—the laws of man's heart and intellect—for these are the sole basis on which the true critical art is established . . . Criticism is thus no 'test of opinion.' For this test, the work, divested of its pretensions as an *art-product*, is turned over for discussion to the world at large. . . ." Edgar Allan Poe, *The Complete Poems and Stories with Selections from his Critical Writings*, Vol. II of two vols. (New York: Alfred A. Knopf, Inc., 1951), pp. 932–33.

society dominated by mass media, there are, in fact, any discernible "programming" standards beyond the needs and choices of the audience, and, if there are, what are they and under what circumstances are they taken into account? Could it be, for example, that the artistic merits of the mass media have suffered from the fact that the philosopher, the modern literary and art historians, and others who serve as critics of "high art" have by and large, not deigned to cast a critical eye on the mass media or other products of contemporary popular culture?

(2) A second point of view that might be used in developing such a framework for a social theory of popular culture would center more on *content* than on channels—on what was and is communicated in various periods—from elite to elite, elite to mass audience, mass media to mass audience. It might be possible to formulate some hypotheses about the relationship between political and social trends and the content and style of popular and "high" art in various periods. In the process, the transitions in critical concern from moral and ethical criteria to problems such as determinism, gratifications, escape, mediocrity, and conformism should be related to changing social, political, and technological conditions.

(3) A third orientation might be centered around the evolution and transmission of *particular standards*. One would have to consider, in this connection, whether the standards of the artist and the critic were or are decisive in some areas (and eras) while motivations of the audience act like standards in others. And one might explore further the pessimistic view that, with the snowballing growth of the mass media brought about by television, the media will allegedly come to be produced by masses and, except for a very few avant-gardists and classicists, people would then be talking to people about their own everyday affairs and there would be no need for, or concern with, standards, artistic or otherwise. Here again one has to pay special attention to the question of who is concerned with which aspects of popular culture.

It is now all too clear that I do not have an all-embracing formula to offer for the study of popular culture. Indeed, I find myself here (more so than in the area of artistic literature) caught between the prerogatives claimed by the social sciences and the humanities. Despite considerable confusion, competition, and occasional bitterness, however, there is probably more agreement among the two groups than either is at present aware of. Students entering one or the other field may have preconceived ideas, sometimes contemptuous ones, about what students in the other area are doing (indeed this is an area which should be well worth exploring), but the fact is that they often speak in each other's terms without knowing it. When social scientists who work in an academic framework draft rationales for studies of the social aspects of the mass media, they are usually guided by the same sense of responsibility and concern for cultural and moral values which are part and parcel of the approach of the humanists to the same problems (a fact which belies the not unheard-of assumption that the social sciences are mere bagatelles of commercial and political merchandising). Actually, both groups share a concern with the role of the arts and their counterparts in modern society, both seek standards and criteria for judgment with regard to media output and its social role, and both believe in the importance of studying the transmission of values through time and space. Such emotional involvement and tension in itself suggests that there are many concerns common to the two fields but that they have not yet worked out efficient means of communicating with each other.

IV

The first four chapters of this volume deal with literature as commodity while the last is concerned with problems of literature as art. There is, however, a certain overlap, since the historical material, in discussing the issues of popular arts, is quite frequently taken from the writings of leading literary figures. An attempt has been made to refer to historical as well as contemporary phenomena and to select sources from a number of countries including England, France, Germany, Norway, Russia, and the United States. The material on popular culture as offered here is centered on the study of intellectual debates over the arts and its popular counterparts, not on an analysis of the popular commodities themselves (with one exception).

Chapter 1, "Popular Culture in Perspective," has a definite polemic slant. In its original form, it was a lecture given some ten years ago at a conference sponsored by the Committee on Communications at the University of Chicago. What I wanted to advocate then and want to restate now is a less parochial approach to the study of communications and popular culture than is frequently practiced in the profession of social research. Here the reader can find a first and short reference to the historical antecedents of concerns with popular culture, as well as some suggestions for a broader orientation in social research strategy.

It is this perennial intellectual interchange of ideas which is outlined in its general historical and systematic aspects in Chapter 2, "The Debate over Art and Popular Culture: A Synopsis." The reader will find here the broad outlines of the problems the European intellectuals in England, France, and Germany had to face once a literary mass market began to threaten in earnestness the status and social acoustic of the artist.

While the second chapter tries to convey in rather bold strokes a secular development, Chapter 3 is a close analysis of a specific time and place. "The Debate over Art and Popular Culture in Eighteenth-Century England" is a "case study" dealing with the uncertainties, hopes and frustrations of the artist and the professional critic under the impact of a literary mass market and mass public in one era and in one country. It was precisely during this period that the painful process of the separation of literature into art and commodity came for the first time into the light of full intellectual awareness. It was a complex process to be sure, since in a number of instances writers in a quasi-schizoid mood practiced both crafts, and some even took a stand on both sides of the issue simultaneously.

Chapter 4, "The Triumph of Mass Idols: The Popular Biography," is entirely concerned with the present, and it also represents an instance where popular commodities themselves are dealt with. The section on American biographies in popular magazines tries, with some recourse to established research procedures in content analysis, to analyze magazine features as symptoms of certain trends in the aspirations of the American public at large in the first four decades of the century. The reader will notice that this content analysis is used as a diagnostic tool—different literary materials are interpreted as indicators of change in the sociopsychological habitudes of American society over a period of time.

With Chapter 5 we turn to literature as art. "Literature and Society" attempts to state the main issues with which I think a humanistically conceived sociology of literature as one aspect of a sociology of culture has to deal. The problem areas enumerated are fairly exhaustive but the examples are sketchy, and I must refer the reader interested in more details to my *Literature and the Image of Man*.

None of these essays is written for the specialist, and I have therefore in many cases limited myself to quotes from original sources and omitted the listing of secondary material. By and large, the papers are presented here in their original form with only minor editorial changes, and the reader should bear in mind the contexts within which the various papers originated, for these contexts often explain variations in style and argumentation. I have already intimated the origins of Chapter 1. Chapter 2 owes its existence to a commission by an *ad hoc* committee of the Ford Foundation, which for several years had considered the feasibility of sponsoring research on television programming and policy; the specific task assigned to me was to present a working paper on the general cultural and historical framework of the mass media to this committee, which consisted largely of leaders in American cultural public policy. Chapter 5 also originated in an historically determined situation. When in 1947 the University of Illinois inaugurated an Institute for Communications Research its first director, Wilbur Schramm, invited me to outline the principles underlying my claim that literature is a communications medium in its own right. Chapter 3 has the following origin. The most outstanding sociologist of communications in this country, Paul F. Lazarsfeld of Columbia University, aware of my humanistic orientation though not necessarily sharing it in his own scholarly approach, generously encouraged me to contribute a research monograph to a collection of papers dealing with *Common Frontiers of the Social Sciences*, a book which appeared under the editorship of Mirra Komarovsky, Chairman of Barnard College's Department of Sociology.

CHAPTER 1

Popular Culture in Perspective

A blind spot that limits contemporary analyses of mass culture was anticipated by Tocqueville's remarks on the fact-finding obsession of the American
mind a century ago:

> The practice of Americans leads their minds to fixing the standard of their
> judgment in themselves alone. As they perceive that they succeed in resolving
> without assistance all the little difficulties which their practical life presents,
> they readily conclude that everything in the world may be explained, and that
> nothing in it transcends the limits of the understanding. Thus they fall to denying
> what they cannot comprehend; which leaves them but little faith for whatever
> is extraordinary and an almost insurmountable distaste for whatever is super-
> natural. As it is on their own testimony that they are accustomed to rely, they
> like to discern the object which engages their attention with extreme clearness;
> they therefore strip off as much as possible all that covers it; they rid themselves
> of whatever separates them from it, they remove whatever conceals it from sight,
> in order to view it more closely and in the broad light of day. This disposition of
> mind soon leads them to condemn forms, which they regard as useless and incon-
> venient veils placed between them and the truth.[1]

My plea on behalf of these "veils" takes the form of five unsystematic
groups of observations: I shall indicate that (1) the discussion of popular
culture has a century-old tradition in modern history; (2) the historical locus
of popular culture today will be fixed; (3) an attempt will be made to evaluate the over-all approach of empirical research to the social function of
contemporary popular culture; (4) the current philosophical, qualitative,
nonresearch analysis of popular culture will be summarized briefly; and (5)
some programmatic notes will be offered on the relationship between social
criticism and social research.

The first published version of this chapter appeared as "Historical Perspectives of Popular
Culture" in *The American Journal of Sociology* (January 1950). Copyright 1950 by the
University of Chicago.
[1] Alexis de Tocqueville, *Democracy in America* (New York: Alfred A. Knopf, Inc., 1945),
p. 4.

I

I

POPULAR CULTURE—AN OLD DILEMMA

In a survey of radio-listening habits in a foreign country, one of those interviewed remarked:

> Radio is the companion of the lonely. It has made gigantic strides for almost half a century. Women in particular, especially those with small pensions and without other resources, who are completely isolated, are now in touch with the whole world thanks to the radio. They have undergone a regular transformation; they have found a kind of second youth. They are up-to-date and they know the stars of the headlines, of the theatre, of the movies, the world of sports, etc. I have heard village people, discussing the merits of Mozart and Chopin, refer to what the radio had said.

In the opposite vein another woman revealed that she did not have a radio set in her home. Asked to explain why, she answered:

> Because once there is a set in the house, one cannot resist. Everybody listens idiotically, the kids and the others too. When we stay with my friend G., my husband plays with the radio all the time.

Her view was supported by a male respondent, who also refused to permit a radio in the house. He believed that studies, conversation, and activity around the house provide enough interest, that the indiscriminate outpouring of music and talk over the radio lowers everyone's intellectual level.

These spontaneous remarks accent two themes which have run continuously through the modern era: on the one hand, a positive attitude toward any device that further socializes the individual; on the other hand, a concern about the mental and moral condition of the individual laboring under the levelling weight of massive institutional forms of leisure-time activity.

Beyond the requirements of biological and material survival, the vital question has become: how to live out that stretch of life which is neither sleep nor work? The question asked on every social and cultural level of modern society—what can we do with ourselves now that we have time on our hands?—found its most exquisite intellectual formulation in a philosophical dialogue that never took place. Montaigne in the sixteenth century took stock of the situation of the individual after the breakdown of medieval culture. He was particularly struck by the loneliness that envelopes men who must live in a world without faith, in which tremendous pressures were being exerted on everyone under the conditions of a postfeudal society. To escape destruction by these pressures, to avoid becoming lost in the horrors of isolation, Montaigne suggested distraction as a way out since "Variety always solaces, dissolves, and scatters." And a few basic concepts which we have been accustomed to regard as very modern emerge as early as the sixteenth century: escape, distraction, and "borrowed emotions."

> Is it reasonable that even the arts should take advantage of and profit by our natural stupidity and feebleness of mind? The barrister, says Rhetoric, in that farce they call pleading, will be moved by the sound of his own voice and his feigned emotion, and will suffer himself to be cozened by the passion he is acting. He will affect a real and substantial grief in this mummery he is playing, to transmit it to the jury who are still less concerned in the matter than he. Like those men who are hired at funerals to assist in the ceremonial of mourning, who sell their tears and grief by weight and measure; for, although they are stirred by borrowed emotions, it is certain that, through the habit of settling their countenance to suit the occasion, they are often quite carried away and affected with genuine melancholy.[2]

A reply worthy of being matched against Montaigne's came a century later. Meanwhile, commercial culture had developed; the waning influence of religion—pre- or post-Reformation—had made itself felt much more strongly in the average way of life. Restlessness, the pursuit of happiness as relief from whatever one was committed to doing, everywhere and anywhere had become a major social issue. It was then that Pascal spoke up against the complete surrender of man to self-destroying restlessness:

> Men are entrusted from infancy with the care of their honor, their property, their friends, and even with the property and the honor of their friends. They are overwhelmed with business, with the study of languages, and with physical exercise; and they are made to understand that they cannot be happy unless their health, their honor, their fortune and that of their good friends be in good condition, and that a single thing wanting will make them unhappy. Thus they are given cares and business which make them bustle about from break of day. —It is, you will exclaim, a strange way to make them happy! What more could be done to make them miserable?—Indeed! what could be done? We should only have to relieve them from all these cares; for then they would see themselves: they would reflect on what they are, whence they came, whither they go, and thus we cannot employ and divert them too much. And this is why, after having given them so much business, we advise them, if they have some time for relaxation, to employ it in amusement, in play, and to be always fully occupied. How hollow and full of ribaldry is the heart of man![3]

Again and again he warned against what he called "diversion" as a way of life which could lead only to permanent unhappiness:

> When I have occasionally set myself to consider the different distractions of men, the pains and perils to which they expose themselves at court or in war, whence

[2] E. J. Trechmann, trans., *The Essays of Montaigne* (New York: Modern Library, Inc., 1946), p. 729ff.
[3] Blaise Pascal, *Pensées*, Everyman's Library ed. (New York: E. P. Dutton & Co., Inc., 1931), p. 44.

arise so many quarrels, passions, bold and often bad ventures, etc., I have dis-
covered that *all the unhappiness of men arises from one single fact, that they cannot stay
quietly in their own chamber.*
. . . They have a secret instinct which impels them to seek amusement and
occupation abroad, and which arises from the sense of their constant unhappiness.[4]

Thus, the attitude toward leisure which, for Montaigne, guarantees survival means self-destruction to Pascal. And the controversy is still going on.
Each side has its partisans on all intellectual levels in everyday life, as
illustrated in the study on radio as well as in learned treatises. On one side
there is the benevolent analyst of a mass medium who seems to say that,
while everything is not yet wonderful, it is getting better every day.[5] On the
other hand, we find the nonconformist social critic who connects the loneliness of modern man with his interest in mass media as a setup of utter
frustration.[6]

Obvious differences in the language used to frame the dilemma measure
the span of three centuries. The sixteenth- and seventeenth-century philosophers cannot escape sociological jargon; the nonprofessional radio listeners
or non-listeners cannot escape the psychological self-interest that pervades
everyday life and makes every man his own Montaigne—if not his own
Freud. But beneath these differences in nomenclature the dilemma remains
the same: perhaps it could be called a conflict between the psychological
and the moral approaches to popular culture.

II

THE HISTORICAL LOCUS OF POPULAR CULTURE

The counterconcept to popular culture is art. Nowadays artistic products
having the character of spontaneity more and more are being replaced by a
manipulated reproduction of reality as it is; and, in so doing, popular culture sanctions and glorifies whatever it finds worth echoing. Schopenhauer
remarked that music is "the world once more." This aphorism exhibits the
unbridgeable difference between art and popular culture: it is the difference between an increase in insight through a medium possessing self-
sustaining means and mere repetition of given facts with the use of borrowed
tools.

A superficial inventory of the contents and motivations in the products of

[4] *Ibid.*, pp. 39–42.
[5] See, for example, Coulton Waugh, *The Comics* (New York: The Macmillan Company,
1947), p. 354.
[6] See, for example, James T. Farrell, *The League of Frightened Philistines* (New York:
Vanguard Press, n.d.), pp. 276–277.

the entertainment and publishing worlds in our Western civilization will include such themes as nation, family, religion, free enterprise, individual initiative; and in the Eastern orbit, higher production achievements, national cultures, Western decadence. The topical differences are not decisive and, in any case, considerably smaller than the political differences which keep these two worlds apart. The great French pre-Marxian socialist philosopher Saint-Simon, whose life extended from the *ancien régime* through the Revolution and the Napoleonic era into the days of the reactionary Bourbon restoration, once remarked that, while he had experienced the most contradictory political systems, he realized that consistent, deeply rooted social tendencies which were completely impervious to political change made themselves felt in those decades. The very concept of society rests in this insight. Rigidly and consistently different as political systems are from one another today, there is also a complete inconsistency in the content of popular culture within a given political system—and popular culture is an element of society of the first order. The yardstick is expediency, within the total social situation, of course, and particularly the distribution of power.

A matchless critical analyst of modern popular culture, if not its discoverer, formulated its relativism with respect to content. "Those modern counterfeit practices in the arts, . . . ," Nietzsche wrote,

> are regarded as necessary—that is to say, as fully in keeping with the needs most proper to the modern soul. . . .
> Artists harangue the dark instincts of the dissatisfied, the ambitious, and the self-deceivers of a democratic age: the importance of poses. . . . The procedures of one art are transferred to the realm of another; the object of art is confounded with that of science, with that of the Church, or with that of the interests of the race (nationalism), or with that of philosophy—a man rings all bells at once, and awakens the vague suspicion that he is a god. . . .
> Artists flatter women, sufferers, and indignant folk. Narcotics and opiates are made to preponderate in art. The fancy of cultured people, and of readers of poetry and ancient history, is tickled.[7]

What Nietzsche expressed in the general terms of the philosopher of culture has its spokesmen today. In an analysis of cartoon films a modern writer has pointed to the criterion of social expediency in the selection of their materials:

> It is just Disney's distinguishing characteristic that he is uncritical of what he reflects. He is quite artless. If the values by which the society lives are still serving, if the prevailing outlook is relatively brightfaced, and aggressive, he will improvise from that—and give us Mickey Mouse. If the time is one of crisis, and these values will no longer serve but are in conflict and in question, if the prevailing state of mind is in deep bewilderment, he will improvise with equal

[7] Friedrich Nietzsche, *The Will to Power*, Vol. II, *Complete Works* (London: T. N. Foulis, 1910), pp. 265–66.

lack of inhibition. His particular talent is that he does not embarrass himself. This makes his dreams sometimes monstrous. But it gives them a wide reference.[8]

In the present postwar period, disillusionment over the lack of compelling cultural and moral solutions has become prevalent. It finds expression in manufactured resonances built into entertainment products: particularly in the manipulation of trappings and clichés of institutional religion. In the average movie the pursuit of love means the appearance of the clergyman. Nietzsche had already commented on the artificial respiration administered to religion in an era of decadence and nihilism. When he said, "God is dead," he meant that the frenzied activities of modern life produce popular culture in an attempt to fill a vacuum which cannot be filled. Nietzsche linked the precarious role of religion with the pressure of civilization:

> The sum of sensations, knowledge and experiences, the whole burden of culture, therefore, has become so great that an overstraining of nerves and powers of thought is a common danger, indeed the cultivated classes of European countries are throughout neurotic, and almost every one of their great families is on the verge of insanity in one of their branches. True, health is now sought in every possible way; but in the main a diminution of that tension is feeling, of that oppressive burden of culture, is needful, which, even though it might be bought at a heavy sacrifice, would at least give us room for the great hope of a *new Renaissance*.[9]

With this quotation we return to the differences between popular culture and art, between spurious gratification and a genuine experience as a step to greater individual fulfillment (this is the meaning of Aristotle's catharsis). Art lives on the threshold of action. Men free themselves truly from the mythical relation to things by stepping back, so to speak, from that which they once worshipped and which they now discover as the Beautiful. To experience beauty is to be liberated from the overpowering domination of nature over men. In popular culture, men free themselves from mythical powers by discarding everything, even reverence for the Beautiful. They deny anything that transcends the given reality.[10] This is exactly what Tocqueville meant, I think, in our opening quotation. From the realm of beauty man walks into the realm of entertainment, which is, in turn, integrated with the necessities of society and denies the right to individual fulfillment.[11] Men no longer surrender to illusions.

[8] Barbara Deming, "The Artlessness of Walt Disney"; first published in *Partisan Review* (Spring 1945), p. 226.
[9] Friedrich Nietzsche, *Human All-Too-Human: A Book for Free Spirits*, Vol. VII in *op. cit.*, p. 227.
[10] For a comprehensive theory on myth and art see Max Horkheimer and Theodor W. Adorno, *Dialektik der Aufklärung* (Amsterdam: Querido Verlag, 1947), *passim*.
[11] See Tocqueville, *op. cit.*, Vol. I, p. 264.

III

SOCIAL RESEARCH AND POPULAR CULTURE

To what extent, if at all, is modern social science equipped to deal with modern social culture? The instruments of research have been brought to a high degree of refinement. But is this enough? Empirical social science has become a kind of applied asceticism. It stands clear of any entanglements with foreign powers and thrives in an atmosphere of rigidly enforced neutrality. It refuses to enter the sphere of meaning. A study of television, for instance, will go to great lengths in analyzing data on the influence of television on family life, but it will leave to poets and dreamers the question of the actual human values of this new institution. Social research takes too much of modern life, including the mass media, at face value. It rejects the task of placing them in an historical and moral context. In the beginning of the modern era, social theory had theology as its model, but today the natural sciences have replaced theology. Such a change in models has far-reaching implications. Theology aims at salvation, natural science at manipulation; the one leads to heaven and hell, the other to technology and machinery. Social science is today defined as an analysis of painstakingly circumscribed, more or less artificially isolated, social sectors. It imagines that such horizontal segments constitute its research laboratory, and it seems to forget that the only social research laboratories that are properly admissible are historical situations.

This has not always been the case. Popular culture, particularly as represented by the newspapers, has been a subject of discussion for about a hundred and fifty years. Before the naturalistic phase of social science set in, the phenomena of popular culture were treated as a social and historical whole. This holds true for religious, philosophical, and political discussions from the time of Napoleon to Hitler. Our contemporary social science literature seems barren of any knowledge of, or at least of any application and reference to, the voluminous writings produced on both the left and the right wings of the political and cultural fronts in the nineteenth century. It seems to ignore Catholic social philosophy as well as Socialist polemics, Nietzsche as well as the great, but completely unknown, Austrian critic, Karl Kraus, who tried to validate the notion of the crisis of modern culture by a critique of popular culture. Kraus focused attention on the analysis of language. The common denominator of his essays in his thesis that it is in the hollowing-out of language that we can see the disintegration, and even the disappearance, of the concept and existence of the autonomous individual, of the personality in its classical sense.

Students of the role of the contemporary press, even of such specialized problems as readership figures, would do well to read nineteenth- and early twentieth-century analyses of the press. There they would find, in the different political and philosophical camps, illustrations of the fruitfulness of studying social phenomena in context—in the case of the press, the relationship of the modern newspaper to the history of the economic, social, and political emancipation of the middle classes. A study of the modern newspaper is meaningless, in the very exact sense of the word, if it is not aware of the historical framework, which is composed of both critical materials like those of Karl Kraus, writing at the end of an epoch, and optimistic attitudes like the following, from the work of the German publicist, Joseph Goerres, at the beginning of the nineteenth century:

> What everybody desires and wants shall be expressed in the newspapers; what is depressing and troubling everybody may not remain unexpressed; there must be somebody who is obliged to speak the truth, candid, without reservation, and unfettered. For, under a good constitution the right of freedom of expression is not merely tolerated but is a basic requirement; the speaker shall be looked upon as a holy person until he forfeits his right by his own fault and lies. Those who work against such freedom leave themselves open to the charge that the consciousness of their own great faults weighs heavily upon them; those who act justly do not shun free speech—it can in the end lead only to "honor be to whom honor is due"; but those who are dependent on dirt and darkness certainly like secretiveness.[12]

This is not to say that the whole field of sociology has been given over to an ascetic rejection of the historical meat from the contemporary gravy. A number of leading scholars in social theory and social history have kept alive the conscience of a historical civilization. It is worth our while to read again the following remarks by Robert E. Park:

> In fact, the reason we have newspapers at all, in the modern sense of the term, is because about one hundred years ago, in 1835 to be exact, a few newspaper publishers in New York City and in London discovered (1) that most human beings, if they could read at all, found it easier to read news than editorial opinion and (2) that the common man would rather be entertained than edified. This, in its day, had the character and importance of a real discovery. It was like the discovery, made later in Hollywood, that gentlemen prefer blonds. At any rate, it is to the consistent application of the principle involved that the modern newspaper owes not merely its present character but its survival as a species.[13]

His point of view finds confirmation in an excellent study in the history of mass culture by Louis B. Wright:

[12] Joseph Goerres, *Rheinischer Merkur*, July 1 and 3, 1814.
[13] Introduction to *News and the Human Interest Story*, by Helen MacGill Hughes (Chicago: University of Chicago Press, 1940), pp. xii–xiii. Copyright 1940 by the University of Chicago.

If it is desirable to trace the pedigree of the popular culture of modern America, it is possible to find most of its ideology implicit in the middle-class thought of Elizabethan England. The historian of American culture must look back to the Renaissance and read widely in the forgotten literature of tradesmen.[14]

One of the difficulties which have occasionally arisen in intellectual intercourse between people of American and European backgrounds is perhaps due to the antihistorical allergy of the former and the historical oversensitivity of the latter. I can illustrate this point: when I received the first two volumes of the outstanding work by Samuel A. Stouffer and his staff, *The American Soldier*, I was curious to learn how the authors would place their research within the context of the social theories about the soldier that have been developed from Plato on. But, I could find no historical reference beyond a solitary quotation from Tolstoy, who wrote in one place in *War and Peace:* "In warfare the force of armies is a product of the mass multiplied by something else, an unknown X." The authors added the following comment: "Thus for perhaps the first time in military history, it is possible to present statistical evidence relating to the factor X described in the quotation from Tolstoy's *War and Peace* at the beginning of this chapter."[15] They seem to have been fascinated by the mathematical symbolism of Tolstoy's sentence, but they successfully resisted the temptation to compare the social situation of armies in the time of Napoleon with modern conditions. In the face of such heroic restraint, it seems appropriate to quote the following flippant remark of a fellow-sociologist: "In this respect I speak of the failure of modern psychology. I firmly believe that one can learn more about the *ordre du coeur* from La Rochefoucauld and Pascal (who was the author of this term) than from the most up-to-date textbook on psychology or ethics."[16]

It seems to me that the splendid isolation of the social researcher is likely to reinforce a common suspicion, namely, that social research is, in the final analysis, nothing but market research, an instrument of expedient manipulation, a tool with which to prepare reluctant customers for enthusiastic spending. Only twenty years ago, social scientists were well aware of the dangers in the mass media, and they did not consider it beyond their duty to concern themselves with the negative, as well as the positive, potentialities of these mass media.[17]

[14] Louis B. Wright, *Middle-Class Culture in Elizabethan England* (Chapel Hill, N. C.: University of North Carolina Press, 1935), pp. 659–69. Edwin Miller's *The Professional Writer in Elizabethan England* (Cambridge, Mass.: Harvard University Press, 1959) is a significant example of an historical framework used to illuminate a study of the beginnings of mass culture.

[15] Samual A. Stouffer *et al.*, *The American Soldier: Adjustment during Army Life*, Vol. I (Princeton, N. J.: Princeton University Press, 1949), p. 8.

[16] J. P. Mayer, *Sociology of Film* (London: Faber & Faber, 1945), p. 273.

[17] See the pioneering article on "The Agencies of Communication" by Malcolm A. Willey and Stuart Rice in *Recent Social Trends in the United States*, Vol. I (New York: McGraw-Hill Book Co., Inc., 1933), p. 215.

Today, manipulation is taken for granted as an end of social science. A publisher can now dare to praise an outstanding sociological work with the following blurb on the jacket of the book:

> For the first time on such a scale an attempt was made to direct human behavior on a basis of scientific evidence, and the results suggest the opening of a new epoch in social studies and in social management.

> It is the editor's hope that the value of social science will prove to be as great as to the military, for whom the original research was undertaken. . . .

> The problems were Army problems, for the most part peculiar to wartime. But the implications are universal.[18]

Expediency and the lack of a historical or philosophical frame of reference make a sorry marriage of convenience.

IV

SOCIAL CRITICISM OF POPULAR CULTURE TODAY

The social criticism of popular culture today lacks any systematic body of theories. The situation has been characterized aptly by Frederick Laws:

> It will hardly be denied that the *condition of criticism today is chaotic*, especially when it is applied to the products of these immense distributing machines, *the new media*. Much reviewing is unselective in its enthusiasm and can with difficulty be distinguished from advertising copy. . . . *There is a lack of clearly expressed and generally recognized standards of value*. We believe that this confusion is partly due to a failure to realize or accept the fact that *the social framework in which works of art are produced and judged has changed fundamentally*. It is nonsense to suppose that the means of distribution or the size of social origin of the audience wholly determines the quality of art or entertainment, but it is stupid to pretend that they do not affect it. . . .[19]

There is a literature on mass culture today which is thoroughly critical. Some of this criticism is directed against the product, but more of it is turned against the system on which the product depends. In special analyses, as in studies of a purely philosophical and sociological character, most authors concur in their final characterization of the products of popular culture.

The decline of the individual in the mechanized working processes of modern civilization brings about the emergence of mass culture, which re-

---

[18] Jacket of Vols. I and II of Samuel A. Stouffer *et al.*, *op. cit.*
[19] Frederick Laws, *Made for Millions: A Critical Study of the New Media of Information and Entertainment* (London: Contact Publications Limited, 1947), p. xvii.

places folk art or "high" art. A product of popular culture has none of the features of genuine art, but in all its media popular culture proves to have its own genuine characteristics: standardization, stereotype, conservatism, mendacity, manipulated consumer goods.

There is an interdependence between what the public wants and what the powers of control enforce upon the public in order to remain in power. Most students are of the opinion that the habit of advertisement is the main motivating force in creating receptivity to popular culture and that the products themselves eventually take on the character of advertising.

There is no consensus on the taste of the populace. Whereas some have confidence in the people's instinct for what is good, the prevailing view seems to be that only the bad and the vulgar are the yardsticks of their aesthetic pleasure.

There is considerable agreement that all media are estranged from values and offer nothing but entertainment and distraction—that, ultimately, they expedite flight from an unbearable reality. Wherever revolutionary tendencies show a timid head, they are mitigated and cut short by a false fulfillment of wish-dreams, like wealth, adventure, passionate love, power, and sensationalism in general.

Prescriptions for improvement run from naïve proposals to offer aesthetically better merchandise, in order to create in the masses a taste for the valuable in life, to the theory that within the present set-up of social power there is no hope whatsoever for improvement and that better popular culture presupposes a better society.

Finally, there is considerable speculation about the relations between the product of mass culture and real life. The radio, the movies, the newspapers, and the best sellers are, at the same time, models for the way of life of the masses and an expression of their actual way of life.

V

SOME THESES ON CRITICAL THEORY AND EMPIRICAL RESEARCH

What follows are some notions about the direction in which, I believe, research into popular culture might fruitfully take.

(1) The theoretical starting point for study of the mass media ought not to be market data. Empirical research continues to labor under the false hypothesis that the consumers' choice is the decisive social phenomenon from which one should begin further analysis. The first question is: What are the functions of cultural communication within the total process of a society?—followed by such specific questions as these: What passes the censorship of the socially powerful agencies? How are things produced under the dicta of formal and informal censorship?

(2) These studies would not be psychological in the narrow sense. They should aim rather at finding out how the objective elements of a social whole are produced and reproduced in the mass media. This implies the rejection of the "taste of the masses" as a basic category but would insist on finding out how taste is fed to the consumers as a specific outgrowth of the technological, political, and economic conditions and interests of the masters in the sphere of production. What do "likes" or "dislikes" really mean in social terms? While it is true, for example, that people today behave as if there were a large free area of selection according to taste and while they tend to vote fanatically for or against a specific presentation of popular culture, the question remains as to how such behavior is compatible with the actual elimination of free choice and the institutionalized repetition characteristic of all media. This is probably the theoretical area in which one would have to examine the replacement of taste—a concept of liberalism—by the quest for information.

(3) Other tacit assumptions of empirical research—as, for example, the differentiation into "serious" and "nonserious" written, visual, or auditory communications—need scrutiny. The problem of whether we are faced with serious or nonserious literature is two-dimensional. One would first have to furnish an aesthetic analysis of qualities and then investigate whether the aesthetic qualities are not subject to change under the conditions of mass reproduction. I would challenge the assumption that a higher increase in so-called "serious" programs or products automatically means "progress" in educational and social responsibility, in the understanding of art, and so on. It is still unsafe to assume that one cannot decide what is right and what is wrong in aesthetic matters. A good example of the establishment of aesthetic criteria will be found in the works of Benedetto Croce, who tries to show concretely that works of art have immanent laws which permit decisions about their "validity." It is neither necessary nor sufficient to supplement a study of the reaction of respondents by a study of the intentions of art producers in order to find out the nature and quality of the artistic products, or vice versa.

(4) The acceptance at face value of such concepts as "standardization" do not advance insight into popular culture, for it is clear that standardization means different things in different contexts. We want to know what standardization means in industry. Probably the specifically psychological and anthropological character of popular culture is a key to the interpretation of the function of standardization in modern man—but this too is an assumption. In connection with the latter point, I am particularly interested in the trajectory of psychological regression. But I wish I knew whether the consumption of popular culture really presupposes a human being with pre-adult traits or whether modern man has a split personality: half mutilated child and half standardized adult. There is enough evidence to indicate mechanisms of interdependence between the pressures of professional life and

the freedom from intellectual and aesthetic tension in which popular culture seems to indulge.

(5) As for the problem of the stimulus and its nature, here the connection with European philosophical heritage is particularly noticeable. My own thinking has its roots in the concept of understanding (*Verstehen*) as it was established philosophically and historically by Dilthey and sociologically by Simmel. Too often empirical research conceives the stimulus to be as devoid of content as a color stimulus in a psychological laboratory. But the stimulus in popular culture is itself in historical process and the relation between stimulus and response is pre-formed and pre-structured by the historical and social fate of the stimulus as well as of the respondent.

CHAPTER 2

The Debate over Art and Popular Culture: A Synopsis

The purpose of this chapter is to single out some of the significant elements of the historical discussions which have centered around the problem of art versus entertainment, as a first step toward providing a broader base for the study of contemporary mass media, particularly television. To present a systematic inventory of this material, which extends over several centuries, would require the long-range and cooperative efforts of historians, philologists, and social scientists.[1] But since our purpose is not to trace the history of the great cultural change marking the modern era, we shall begin at a point where the controversy was formulated in terms that have stayed with us. (This may be an appropriate point, too, to remind the reader that we are, in this chapter, concerned with the *discussions* which surrounded the problems of art versus popular media rather than with an historical review and analysis of the products themselves.)

Of the many individuals who have made notable contributions to the discussion of popular culture, an effort has been made to select those who were not limited to a narrow area of intellectual activities. For the first period, as we have already indicated in our Introduction, Montaigne and Pascal were the outstanding figures: the former an essayist, lawyer, politician, and a civil servant in addition to being a philosopher; the latter a mathematician, theologist, and spiritual leader of a religious movement. For the turn of the eighteenth and nineteenth centuries, German authors have seemed most representative as well as most eloquent: Goethe—poet, statesman, theater manager, and natural scientist; Schiller—philosopher, aesthetician, professor of history as well as great creative writer; Lessing—dramatist, historian, theologician, and theater critic all in one. For the latter part of the nineteenth century, we have paid particular attention to the poet, critic, and school administrator, Matthew Arnold, and to Walter

Parts of this chapter appeared in *International Social Science Journal*, Vol. XII, No. 4, 1960, pp. 532–542.

[1] An ideal framework would be very broad indeed, encompassing not only relations of art and entertainment but all elements of popular culture such as manners, customs, fads, games, jokes, and sports, on which even greater masses of material exist.

Bagehot, who was an outstanding public and political figure, and have included some material from the English quarterly magazines. Tocqueville's range of interest is by now also well known—diplomat, political writer, essayist; the other Frenchman in our group is Hippolyte Taine—historian, sociologist, and literary critic. Taine's German contemporary, Gervinus, who could be included in this discussion, was an active liberal politician as well as historian of note and literary critic.

I

DIVERSION AND SALVATION IN THE 16TH AND 17TH CENTURIES

The Need for Diversion (Montaigne)

Our review begins with two literary figures who, although separated by no more than sixty years in time are, in some respects, poles apart in viewpoint: Montaigne, the founder of modern skepticism, and Pascal, the forerunner of modern religious existentialism. These two philosophers had in common, however, a quest for certainty in a world which was no longer circumscribed and governed by one church, one empire (the Roman-German), and by the almost unchanging economy of feudal society. With other intellectuals of their times, they sought a philosophy for the governing of man's spiritual and emotional life in this period of painful transition. Montaigne's concern was with how man could *adapt* himself to increasing societal pressures; Pascal's was with how man could *save his soul* in the face of the temptations to which he is subjected in periods of profound change. Both philosophers were concerned for the individual's development and security, but their differences in approach are apparent in their analyses of many problems of life, including, as we shall see, the problems of art and entertainment. These two fundamental themes, adaptation versus salvation, have persisted through most discussions of popular culture down to the present day.

The traumatic nature of the realization that the standards of the Middle Ages had broken down is suggested by the extent to which Montaigne and his contemporaries felt compelled to attribute to man a universal and inherent unhappiness. Montaigne believed that a painful inner state resulting from spiritual, social, and economic insecurity made it necessary for man to run away from himself. He even uses the word so often applied in interpreting the gratifications in the consumption of modern mass media—*escape:*

A painful fancy takes possession of me; I find it shorter to change than to subdue it; if I cannot replace it by another contrary idea, I replace it at least by a different one. . . . If I cannot combat it, I run away from it. . . . By changing place, occupation, company, I escape. . . . It loses my trace and leaves me safe.[2]

But in order to be successful in the alleviation of inner pain, the escape must be into diversified materials and activities. Montaigne believed that nature has endowed man with a capacity for great variety, and that this capacity provides him with the wherewithal, if not for saving, at least for soothing his soul:

> In this way does Nature proceed . . . for Time, which she has given us for the sovereign physician of our passions, chiefly obtains its results . . . by supplying our imagination with other and still other matters. . . .

The inner suffering attendant upon the deep moral and spiritual uncertainties of the transition from feudal to modern society, then, resulted in a need to escape into a variety of diversions. Montaigne thus asks himself whether the arts, particularly the literary arts, can serve as instrumentalities for this kind of escape, and his answer is affirmative. Even though they may not believe in fictional tales, Montaigne finds that his countrymen can escape into and be carried away by "the laments of fiction; the tears of Dido and Ariadne. . . ." He believes (unlike his successors in later centuries) that these fictional emotions move the writer, the actor (and the barrister) just as they do the audience, because the writers and actors share with their audiences the need to escape from their own woes.

In a tentative and exploratory way, Montaigne turned his attention to the problem of the various levels of art, and, as many social philosophers after him (including our contemporaries), finds much in common between folk and high art, if not in essence then in form. He seems to imply that honesty and spontaneity have a beauty all their own, and that this beauty is to be valued nearly as much as the highest forms of art. Both are true, and therefore beautiful expressions. He goes on, then, to castigate the in-betweens, those who despise folk art but are not capable of great art—dangerous, foolish, troublesome people whose products "disturb the world." These are the producers of mediocrity, the "halfbreeds, who despise the first stage (folk art) . . . and have not been able to join the others (great artists), with their seat between two stools." Montaigne thus tentatively established standards for primitive and high art, and places what might be called the forerunners of the mass media into a kind of limbo in-between. His criterion for judgment can probably best be labelled as moral, growing out of the Renaissance ideal of the intertwining of the true and the beautiful.

The Dangers of Diversion (Pascal)

One of Montaigne's greatest admirers and searching critics is Blaise Pascal, the great seventeenth-century French philosopher, who, in his most famous

[2] Montaigne, *Essays, passim.*

work, *Pensées*, often takes issue with his sixteenth-century predecessor. Pascal has no quarrel with Montaigne's conviction that man needs diversion, and he too realizes that this need springs from the lack of spiritual belief and other uncertainties of the post-feudal era, "the natural poverty of our feeble and mortal condition."[3] As mentioned earlier, no more than Montaigne does Pascal minimize the force of this drive: men "have a secret instinct which impels them to seek amusement and occupation abroad, and which arises from the sense of their constant unhappiness."

But whereas Montaigne justified entertainment and art (high and low, if not middle), or at least accepted it as an inevitable response to a deep-seated human need, Pascal finds this kind of escape something to be fought against. Man is impelled to continuous motion, to "noise and stir." But he should fight it, for he is driven to run away from the inner contemplations which can lead to his salvation. We heard before about his "discovery" that "all the unhappiness of men arises from one single fact, that they cannot stay quietly in their own chamber." If they did, they "would reflect on what they are, whence they came, and whither they go"; but men are so frivolous, he fears, that "though full of a thousand reasons for weariness, the least thing such as playing billiards" is sufficient to amuse them.

Most dangerous diversion of all, in Pascal's view, is the theater. It absorbs all our senses and therefore has a great capacity for deceiving man into believing he has all those noble qualities he sees portrayed on the stage: "All great diversions are a threat to the Christian life, but among all those which the world has invented, none is to be feared more than the theater." In a way, Pascal's critique of entertainment (and so far as we know he includes even great art under this category), prefigures one of the most important themes in modern discussions on popular culture: the view that it is a threat to morality, contemplation, and an integrated personality, and that it results in a surrender to mere instrumentalities at the expense of the pursuit of higher goals.

The difference between Montaigne and Pascal, insofar as their ideas have a bearing on those modern discussions, may be summed up as follows: Montaigne stands for a pessimistic conception of man—the demands of human nature cannot be changed, and we must make the best of them; there is no point in denying them gratifications (illusory or real). All we can do is try to raise somewhat the quality of the cultural products we offer man. Pascal, his inspiration and motivation deeply religious, stands for spiritual progress: the need for entertainment and escape is not ineradicable, man's nobler impulses must be mobilized against it, and heightened consciousness of our inner selves, which we can achieve only in solitude, away from the distractions of entertainment, opens the way to salvation. Pascal's language naturally lends itself to translation into a language of modern reformers and champions of social and cultural change; Montaigne's superficially resembles that of the modern box office manager—"The public wants or needs it";

[3] Pascal, *Pensées, passim.*

actually, Montaigne's attitude is more profound. He has a keen sense of the audience as participant, and his conception of the function of entertainment leaves no room for the possibility of manipulation or passivity, which later are to become serious problems.

II

THE ARTIST AND HIS PUBLIC

The lively disputes which played so great a role in French intellectual life between 1650 and 1750, often centered around the question whether the theater, of, e.g., a Corneille, a Racine, or a Molière, was a frivolous pursuit incompatible with the requirements of morality and religion. By 1800, the problem was obsolete. All over Europe, and especially in Germany, the theater had become an accepted institution. But partly as a result of this firm entrenchment, a new dilemma developed: What should be the relationship between playwright and audience?

Goethe

The seriousness with which this problem was viewed is attested by the fact that Goethe found it necessary to precede his great metaphysical tragedy *Faust* with a "Prelude on the Stage," which deals precisely with the questions whether and to what extent an artist should make concessions to the taste of the populace and its predilection for mere entertainment and relaxation. The "Prelude on the Stage" is presented in the form of a dialogue between two characters identified as the Manager and the Poet. The matter at issue is the character of the works to be presented to the public, and the Manager, who is interested only in box office receipts, has some definite ideas about "art." According to him, the secret of success is quite simple: "a hash, a stew—easy to invent" will do the trick. The public, the Manager observes cynically, is stupid, and you win its favor by "sheer diffuseness":

> Only by mass you touch the mass; for any
> Will finally his bit select.

When the Poet objects that "such a trade debases," and that to produce "botching work" is inconsistent with the artist's pride and love of truth, the Manager invokes the age-old principle that the end justifies the means, and form and content must be adjusted to the audience:

> A man who some result intends
> Must use the tools that best are fitting.

The material on which the Poet works is the public, says the Manager, and the public is passive: "soft wood is given you for splitting." People come

THE DEBATE OVER ART AND POPULAR CULTURE 19

to the theater bored, exhausted, or worst of all "fresh from reading the daily papers." They come "as to a masquerade," their sole motive is curiosity, or (this refers to the ladies) to display their finery. He invites the Poet to have a look at his patrons' faces—"The half are coarse, the half are cold."

> Why should you rack, poor foolish bards,
> For ends like these, the gracious Muses?
> I tell you, give but more—more, ever more. . . .[4]

This dialogue shows how the basic components of the discussions about entertainment changed from the times of Montaigne and Pascal to that of Goethe. The two French writers looked upon entertainment as a means for satisfying the need to escape from inner suffering, a need to be gratified (on a high artistic plain) according to the one, and to be denied gratification in favor of spiritual pursuits according to the other. Here in *Faust* we find the discussion divested of its religious and moral overtones, and three new elements introduced: consciousness of the manipulative factors inherent in entertainment; the role of the business intermediary between artist and public, whose criterion is success and whose goal is economic; and a sense of conflict between the needs of the true artist and the wishes of a mass audience. The Manager implies that the audience will take anything so long as there is sufficient quantity and variety, and he endeavors to convince the Poet that the audience is putty in his hands. But unlike Montaigne, the Manager does not advise the Poet to give his audiences variety because it is psychologically wholesome, but because by providing something for everyone, success is insured (if he thought more money could be earned by moral sermons, the Manager would not hesitate to exhort the Poet to write accordingly). Finally, whereas Montaigne makes no clear-cut distinction between the psychological motives of artist and audience, Goethe seems to see the artist as the spokesman for the high standards of his "trade," and the public in the passive role of consumers. Similarly, when the Poet resists the Manager's exhortations, he does not do so in the name of religious or spiritual values, but in terms of the artist's mission.

This divergence between the interests of the artist and those of the public was later to lead to complete cleavage between the two. But with Goethe, we are only at the beginning of the period which witnessed both the spread of popular newspapers and magazines and an unprecedented flowering of great literature. At this stage, the artist and his audience were still on speaking terms. It is not surprising, then, that we find Goethe, not in any systematic and sustained way, but in passages scattered throughout his writings and extending over his long lifetime, considering such problems as the character of the audience, the nature of the mass media, the problem of artistic standards, and the responsibilities of the artist.

On the Character of the Modern Audience. Goethe both echoes Pascal and

[4] Goethe, *Faust* (New York: Modern Library, Inc., 1950), p. 5.

foreshadows a fundamental theme in modern criticism of organized entertainment when he complains of the restlessness, the continuous desire for
change, novelty, and sensation which characterizes the modern audience.
"The theater," he says, "like the world in general, is plagued by powerful
fashions," and fashion (we might call it fad) consists in adoring something
with great abandon, only to "ban it later forever."[5]

Not only the theater, but the newspapers reflect this restlessness:

> We have newspapers for all hours of the day. A clever head could still add a few
> more. This way everything, what everybody does, wants, writes, even what he
> plans, is publicly exposed. One can only enjoy oneself, or suffer, for the enter-
> tainment of others, and in the greatest rush, this is communicated from house to
> house, from town to town, from empire to empire and at last from continent to
> continent.

This restless urge for novelty does not seem to disturb Goethe in itself, but
rather because it prevents the kind of ripening that is essential to the creative
process—that in the constant reading of newspapers about the events of
yesterday, for instance, one "wastes the days and lives from hand to mouth,
without creating anything."[6]

A second characteristic of the modern audience noted by Goethe is its
passivity. He refers to it in the above-quoted passage from *Faust*, when he
has the Manager say to the Poet that the audience "is soft wood given you
for splitting." The audience wants to be given pleasure for their money, they
have no genuine interest in the message of the play offered them. They
"throng into the theater unprepared, they demand what they can enjoy
directly. They want to see something, to wonder at something, to laugh, to
cry. . . ."[7]

Another characteristic of modern mass culture singled out by Goethe is
that of conformism. He hints at it in his ironical remarks on the fashionably
dressed theater goers, and he anticipates Tocqueville and other social critics
such as Toennies in Germany, Ward and Cooley in America, Karl Kraus in
Austria, by his insight into the role of newspapers in producing conformism;
the so-called free press, he says, is actually contemptuous of the public;
seemingly everything is acceptable except dissenting opinion:

> Come let us print it all
> And be busy everywhere;
> But no one should stir
> Who does not think like we.[8]

[5] Goethe, "Weimarisches Hoftheater" in *Sämtliche Werke*, Jubiläumsausgabe, Vol.
XXXVI (Stuttgart, Berlin: Cotta), p. 193.

[6] Goethe, *Maximen und Reflexionen*, Schriften der Goethe Gesellschaft, Vol. 21 (Weimar:
Verlag der Goethe Gesellschaft, 1907), p. 102.

[7] Goethe, "Weimarisches Hoftheater," *loc. cit.*, p. 192.

[8] Goethe, *Zahme Xenien* in *Sämtliche Werke*, Vol. IV, p. 47.

On the Nature of the Mass Media. For Goethe, the art which appeals to the lower instincts of the public is not generically different from esoteric art, but merely "botching work." His characterizations of such artistically inferior products anticipate many of the elements of the modern social critic's characterization of the popular art produced for the mass media. Inferior art, he suggests, aims only at entertainment. "All pleasures, even the theater," Goethe writes in a letter to Schiller dated August 9, 1797, "are only supposed to distract, and the strong affinity of the reading public to periodicals and novels arises out of the very reason that the former always and the latter usually bring distraction into distraction." He understands well the urges of the audience, but refuses to condone those who capitalize on them by offering inferior products; "everyone who fools the public by swimming with the current can count on his success" (letter to Schiller, January 3, 1798). The works of these manipulators of popular taste are indiscriminate in their content; they reproduce the world mechanically, in all of its details, and appeal to the public's lower instincts.[9] The lack of creativity in the common man is partly their fault.[10]

At one point in his career, Goethe planned a project with Schiller which was to involve cataloguing the distinctive characteristics of such inferior art, which they designated as dilettantism. In another letter to Schiller, dated June 22, 1799, Goethe refers to this study of dilettantism as a "project of the greatest importance."

For the extent to which artists, entrepreneurs, sellers, buyers, and amateurs of every art are steeped in dilettantism, is something I discover to my horror only now, after we have reflected so much on the matter and given the child a name. . . . When we open the sluice gates, we will cause the most unpleasant rows, for we shall flood the whole lovely valley in which quackery has settled so happily. But since the main feature of the quack is *incorrigibility*, and since the

[9] Schiller elaborated this theme, emphasizing the unrealized potentialities of the audience: "The assertion so commonly made, that the public degrades art, is not well founded. It is the artist that brings the public to the level of his own conceptions; and, in every age in which art has gone to decay, it has fallen through its professors. The people need feeling alone, and feeling they possess. They take their station before the curtain with an unvoiced longing, with a multifarious capacity. They bring with them an aptitude for what is highest—they derive the greatest pleasure from what is judicious and true; and if, with these powers of appreciation, they deign to be satisfied with inferior productions, still, if they have once tasted what is excellent, they will, in the end, insist on having it supplied to them." See, "The Use of the Chorus in Tragedy" in *The Works of Frederick Schiller: Historical Dramas* (London: Bohn, 1872), p. 439.

[10] Compare this concept, for instance, with the castigations which the great American sociologist, E. A. Ross, formulated in his *Social Control*, published around the turn of the century: ". . . the great agencies of Law, Public Opinion, Education, Religion and Literature speed to their utmost in order to fit ignoble and paltry natures to bear the moral strains of our civilization, and perhaps by the very success of their work cancelling the natural advantage of the noble over the base, and thereby slowing up the development of the most splendid qualities of human nature." Edward Allsworth Ross, *Social Control: A Survey of the Foundations of Order* (New York: The Macmillan Company, 1939), p. 437.

contemporary quacks are stricken with a quite bestial arrogance, they will scream that we are spoiling their gardens, and after the waters recede, they will restore everything as it was before, like ants after a downpour. But never mind, they shall be condemned once and for all.

The result of this enterprise is a "Schema on Dilettantism" drafted by Schiller. It consists of a table of all the arts, from poetry to the dance; the usefulness and harmfulness of each are indicated in separate columns. A glance at this table reveals at once that the writer had a hard time trying to fill the "useful" column. For instance, under music, the beneficent effects include "whiling away the time," "sociability," "gallantry," whereas the corresponding "harmful squares" are filled out with phrases such as "emptiness of thought," "lack of neighborliness," "strumming." Under poetry we find in the "harmful" column such descriptions as "platitudes," "awkwardness," and "mediocrity." The "Schema" never went beyond the draft stage, but it is clear from the context that it represents an attempt to judge what we would today call popular culture from the point of view of classical humanistic aesthetics.

On Artistic Standards. In the eighteenth century the artist produced for a relatively small, cultivated public whose needs and tastes were fairly uniform; at the beginning of the nineteenth century, a new, much larger public, which foreshadows the modern audience for the mass media, is clamoring for attention, and this fact confronts the artist with new problems, the most important of which is that of "true" standards. As Goethe remarks in *Xenien,* "Formerly there was one taste, now there are many tastes. But tell me, where are those tastes tasted?"

The problems of standards occupies a central place in modern discussions about popular culture, and it is invariably connected with the problem of the influence of public taste on the character of the mass products. We find in these discussions some of the arguments advanced by Goethe's Manager. Some tend to believe that prevalent standards originate in the dispositions and needs of the public, and seek to determine some invariable elements in the public taste, elements that reflect basic unchangeable features of human nature. Others claim that public taste is not a spontaneous but an artificial product, and that it is determined by political or economic vested interests which, via the mass media, manipulate the consumers' fantasies and frustrations for specific selfish purposes. There are also those who defend an intermediate position: standards of taste, according to them, are determined as a result of an interplay of these two sets of forces.

Goethe speaks for the artist—and his own position with regard to standards is quite clear: he represents the humanistic tradition which places responsibility for the fate of culture and individual morality in the hands of the intellectual elite. This elite betrays its mission when it plays up to the cheap instincts of the populace by producing inferior books and vulgar plays. In other words, Goethe does not ask how the writer could go about gaining the attention of a large public, but the opposite: how can the public be persuaded to undertake the intellectual effort required by true art, and what can the artist himself do to facilitate the process? Like many artists and theoreticians since the Renaissance, Goethe felt that the specific function of art, as contrasted with religion, philosophy, and the sciences, is to stimulate productive imagination. One of the implications of his criticism of cheap art as being too literal, as catering to specific emotional needs, is precisely, as we have seen, that it hinders creativity. In his essay on the Weimar Court Theater, he insists that the public "should not be treated as rabble," and that in selecting plays for performance the guiding purpose should not be catering to the public's *needs*, but encouragement of imagination and contemplation:[11] the playgoer should be made to feel, Goethe says, "like a tourist, who does not find all the comforts of home in the strange places which he visits for his instruction and enjoyment."[12]

In his emphasis on this function of art, Goethe is in agreement with his countryman Lessing, the poet, dramatist, and critic, who was also keenly interested in the development of the German theater. In his *Laocoön*[13] and *Hamburg Dramaturgie*,[14] Lessing devoted several pages to a discussion of the differences between genuine art and the imitative art. He explicitly condemns artistic works that fail to leave scope for the audience's imagination. He attacks the conception (ascribed to an ancient writer) according to which painting should be silent poetry, and poetry, speaking painting. Such a conception, he observes, would paralyze the imagination of temporal relationships in the case of poetry and the imagination of spatial relationships in the case of painting. Realizing that it is more difficult for the painter and sculptor to appeal to the imagination than it is for the writer or playwright, Lessing recommends that they portray "the most fertile moment," i.e., the moment that affords an optimum of free scope for imagining what precedes and what follows the action represented in a painting or a sculpted figure. "The more we see, the more we must be able to add by thinking. The more we add by thinking, the more must we believe to see." Similarly, according to Lessing, dramatists who, like Racine or Voltaire, portray rigid types, are inferior to the ancients and to Shakespeare, who portray characters in the process of development and enable the spectator to identify himself with them.

[11] Compare this with Schiller's comment on theater audiences: "Their object is relaxation, and they are disappointed if mental exertion be required when they expected only amusement. But if the theater be made instrumental toward higher objects, the pleasure of the spectator will not be interested, but ennobled. It will be a diversion, but a poetical one." "The Uses of the Chorus in Tragedy," *loc. cit.*, p. 439.

[12] Goethe, "Weimarisches Hoftheater," *loc. cit.*, p. 294.

[13] Lessing, "The Limits of Painting and Poetry," 1766.

[14] Lessing, "Collection of Theater Reviews," 1767–9.

Needless to say, the danger discerned by Lessing and Goethe has become more acute with the advent of the more modern media.[15] In fact, a little epigram by Goethe could be applied almost verbatim to television:

> Talking a lot of nonsense,
> Or even writing it,
> Will kill neither body nor soul,
> Everything will remain unchanged.
> But nonsense, placed before the eyes
> Has a magical right:
> Because it fetters the senses
> The mind remains a vassal.[16]

Goethe believes, then, that the more a given work of art occupies the senses of the audience, the less scope is left for the imagination; in this respect, the impact of a bad book is infinitely less than the impact of a bad spectacle that appeals simultaneously to the eye and the ear, and that reduces the spectator to almost complete passivity.[17] In sum, he is uncompromising in his standards for art and the artist; his suggestions are confined to efforts to improve the repertoire of the theater and to raise the intellectual level of the audience. Unlike later writers, such as the French novelist Gustave Flaubert, who view the rising influence of the populace with despair and expect the end of civilization, Goethe implicitly condemns the artist who withdraws to his ivory tower. He once said in a conversation that only in decadent ages do artists and poets become self-centered, while in ages of progress the creative mind is always concerned with the outer world (*Conversations with Eckermann*, January 29, 1826). At no point, however, must the artist stoop to

---

[15] To modern critics, the stultifying effects of popular art on the imaginative faculty are no longer a matter for speculation. One of these critics, Randall Jarrell, observes that "the average article in our magazines gives any subject whatsoever the same coat of easy, automatic, 'human interest.'" He contrasts the attitude of Goethe who said that "the author whom a lexicon can keep up with is worth nothing," with that of Somerset Maugham who says that "the finest compliment he ever received was a letter in which one of his re aders said: 'I read your novel without having to look up a single word in the dictionary.'" And Jarrell concludes that "popular writing has left nothing to the imagination for so long now that imagination too has begun to atrophy." Randall Jarrell, *Poetry and the Age* (New York: Alfred A. Knopf, Inc., 1953), pp. 18–19.

[16] Goethe, *Zahme Xenien, loc. cit.*, p. 47.

[17] The American sociologist, William Albig, in his extremely stimulating book, *Modern Public Opinion* (New York: McGraw-Hill Book Co., Inc., 1956), pp. 424–426, has discussed this problem by contrasting the possible effects of reading versus motion picture viewing. In his analysis of modern man's "need for more and more stereotypes," he believes that stereotypes presented in the movies "influence opinions about real persons" to a very high degree while "printed descriptions are rarely so vivid." He believes that "superficiality may be disarmingly convincing when provided in pictorial forms. In reading, even at the lowest levels, one may stop to think, or just stop at any point. In the picture the tempo of portrayal is mechanically controlled outside the individual. And he is thereby discouraged and, indeed, often frustrated. The individual is a more passive recipient than is the case in other means of communication."

the public; he serves it best by retaining full freedom, by following only his own inner voice. In his essay on experimentation, Goethe compares the artist with the scientist, whose conclusions must be continually submitted to the public, while "The artist may be well advised to keep his work to himself till it is completed, because no one can readily help him or advise him with it."

Schiller and the Social Role of Aesthetic Experience

Throughout his discussions of the problems of the artist in relation to society, Goethe, as we have seen, maintained an olympic detachment toward immediate social and political problems. Friedrich Schiller, on the other hand, was a true son of the French revolution, and in both his artistic and theoretical works he paid enthusiastic tribute to its political achievements. His central concern was with the development of a "moral" society, and his studies on aesthetics, as well as his analysis of the roles of art and popular culture, are all concerned with the problems to be overcome in the attainment of such a society. While a detailed, systematic analysis of Schiller's writings would be most rewarding for our purposes, we must confine ourselves here to a mere outline of his conception of the central role of artistic experience in attaining an ideal state.[18]

The Experience of Beauty as the Means to the "Good" Life. Schiller did not believe that the individual is caught in a struggle between evil and good forces within himself, but rather that man in all cases would "prefer the good because it is good"—providing it does not entail trouble or exclude the agreeable. Man knows within himself what moral goodness is, and it is not innate evil forces but simply our sensuous desires for comfort and pleasure which prevent us from attaining it.

> Thus in reality all moral action seems to have no other principle than a conflict between the good and agreeable; or, that which comes to the same thing, between desire and reason; the *force* of our sensuous instincts on one side, and, on the other side the feebleness of will, the moral faculty; such apparently is the source of all our faults.[19]

Schiller did not believe that this conflict could or should be resolved by a victory of one of these forces over the other; if, for instance, human life was organized only on the basis of the gratification of instincts, we would achieve the state described by Hobbes which (according to Schiller) would "only

[18] Lest this over-simplified review unwittingly distort Schiller's breadth of vision, we should perhaps here remind the reader that he was an outstanding student of Kant and an exponent of the German idealistic philosophical school; a notable professional historian; an outstanding dramatist and poet and an intimate associate of Goethe. He has written voluminously on the problems with which we are here concerned.

[19] Schiller, "The Moral Utility of Aesthetic Manners" in *Works of Frederick Schiller*, Cambridge Edition (New York: John D. Williams, 1840), Vol. 8, p. 128.

make society possible by subduing nature through nature." On the other hand, he did not believe a moral state such as that of Rousseau, which orders the individual to subordinate himself to the general will, could be achieved, for such a state, though on a higher plane, would negate individual freedom. The only acceptable state would be one in which the freedom of each individual is fully preserved without destroying the freedom of others, and this state, Schiller believed, can come into being through an aesthetic experience which utilizes and reconciles the two forces in man—namely the experience of beauty.

> Art has for its object not merely to afford a transient pleasure, to excite to a momentary dream of liberty; its aim is to make us absolutely free; and this it accomplishes by awakening, exercising, and perfecting in us a power to remove to an objective distance the sensible world; (which otherwise only burdens us as rugged matter and presses us down with a brute influence); to transform it into the free working of our spirit, and thus acquire a dominion over the material by means of ideas.[20]

This experience of beauty can be enjoyed through great art and it produces, Schiller believed, both individual and social blessings. On the individual level, the perception of beauty involves and unifies man's sensuous and spiritual beings, aspects of himself which are otherwise often conflicting and unreconcilable.

> All art is dedicated to pleasure, and there can be no higher and worthier end than to make men happy. The true art is that which provides the highest degree of pleasure; and this consists in the abandonment of the spirit to the free play of all its faculties.[21]

On the social level, genuine aesthetic experience is the only form of communication which has a unifying rather than a dividing effect (all other forms of communication grow only out of self-interest and appeal only to self-interest):

> Taste alone brings harmony into society, because it establishes harmony in the individual. . . . All other forms of communication divide society, because they relate exclusively either to the private sensibility or to the private skilfulness of its individual members, . . . only the communication of the Beautiful unites society, because it relates to what is common to them all.[22]

Today, with inferior artistic products dominating our communications, this seems an almost utopian idea. Even for Schiller the dangers threatening genuine art (which he believed to be the only source of true beauty) by the

[20] Schiller, "The Uses of the Chorus in Tragedy," *loc. cit.*, p. 440.
[21] *Ibid.*, pp. 439–440.
[22] Schiller, *On The Aesthetic Education of Man.* Translated from the German with an Introduction by Reginald Snell (London: Routledge & Kegan Paul Ltd., 1954), p. 138.

increasing demands of an industrialized society were a matter for great concern.

The Problem of Mediocre Art. Schiller recognized that as society became more mechanized, it made harsher demands on the life of the individual. These demands exhaust both mind and body, and man therefore requires rest and relaxation in his leisure time:

> Now labor makes rest a sensible want, much more imperious than that of the moral nature; for physical nature must be satisfied before the mind can show its requirements.[23]

Beauty, it is true,

> . . . addresses all the faculties of man, and can only be appreciated if a man employs fully all his strength. He must bring to it an open sense, a broad heart, a spirit full of freshness.[24]

Mediocre art, however, makes no such demands, he goes on. It does not quicken but merely suspends thought:

> After this can one wonder at the success of mediocre talents . . . ? or the bitter anger of small minds against true energetic beauty? They reckon on finding therein a congenial recreation, and regret to discover that a display of strength is required to which they are unequal.[25]

Here Schiller describes what might be called the tired businessman's conception of art and foreshadows those more recent critics who are concerned about the extent to which mediocre artistic products lull the reader, listener- or viewer into passivity. Such passivity, in turn, is conducive to the experience and appreciation of form but not of substance.

The over-development of taste (Schiller uses the word as synonymous with a sense for form) can grow out of aesthetic sensualism or from a more elevated appreciation along the lines of the formalistic theory of art (in which beauty consists only in proportion, or in the suitability of the means employed by the artist to the end he pursues). The danger here is that "good taste becomes the sole arbiter," and men merely indulge in an amusing game, becoming "indifferent to reality and finish by giving value to form and appearance only." Man realizes his highest potential only when he gives free play to all of his forces. He must not let himself become beguiled into thinking that because taste (or sense for form) has successfully replaced or suppressed his instinctual drives that he is free. "Taste," he says, "must never forget that it carries out an order emanating elsewhere."

[23] Schiller, "On Simple and Sentimental Poetry" in *Works*, Cambridge Edition, *op. cit.*, Vol. 8, p. 336.
[24] *Ibid.*
[25] *Ibid.*, p. 337.

In discussing the ever-new forms offered by a developing culture, Schiller in a way anticipates the modern mass media and the danger that they will, by creating new demands for form, crowd out creative and moral thinking:

> So far from setting us free, culture only develops a new want with every power that it bestows on us; the bonds of the physical are tightened ever more alarmingly, so that the fear of loss stifles even the burning impulses towards improvement.[26]

While recognizing the danger, however, Schiller remains much more optimistic than we are today. Whereas we are inclined to believe that the experience of true art and beauty is reserved for exclusive groups, he is still able to envisage an "aesthetic" state or a state governed by the concept of beauty, through which all men become free:

> In the midst of the awful realm of powers, and of the sacred realm of laws, the aesthetic creative impulse is building . . . a . . . joyous realm. . . . *To grant freedom by means of freedom* is the fundamental law of this kingdom.[27]

Here, in essence, is the eighteenth- and nineteenth-century liberal-idealistic concept of the potentialities of man, where political, philosophical and aesthetic theories all converged on the potential of every man for a spontaneous, productive, and creative existence. Schiller, in short, was aware of, but did not succumb to, the stirrings of modern skepticism about the opportunities for individual development in a mass society which were soon to prevail.

III

"CULTURE WORKS DIFFERENTLY"

In Germany the reaction to the tide of popular literature was largely confined to academic dismay and a sense of futility but a different attitude came to the fore in other countries, one reflecting a broader social outlook and greater political freedom. Particularly in England, critics of popular art, while rejecting it on aesthetic grounds, tended to see in it only one of many manifestations of deeper social forces.

This new attitude was formulated as early as 1800—the tide of popular writing hit England several decades before it had reached Germany—in William Wordsworth's famous preface to the second edition of his *Lyrical Ballads*. The great English poet voiced his alarm about the extent to which the "beauty and dignity" represented in true art was threatened "frantic by

---

[26] Schiller, *Aesthetic Education, op. cit.*, pp. 36–37.
[27] *Ibid.*, p. 137.

novels, sickly and stupid German tragedies and the deluge of idle and extravagant stories in verse." In analyzing the spread of this popular literature, he makes use of a psychological construct which by now has become familiar to us: the need of modern man for "gross and violent stimulants," tends "to blunt the discriminating powers of the mind," whereas the function of true art is to stimulate these powers. Popular literature reduces people to an attitude of passivity or, in the words of Wordsworth, to "a state of almost savage torpor." He finds these predispositions activated by social change, by "the great national events which are daily taking place, and which the increasing accumulation of intelligence hourly gratifies."[28] In the same context, Wordsworth says that his own works are a modest endeavour to "counteract the new degrading" tendencies.

The few sentences quoted here contain in embryo almost all the themes that characterize English criticism as compared with nineteenth-century German criticism of popular culture: the concern about art is subordinated to the concern about culture as a whole; attention is focused on institutionalized social pressures; the threat of conformism is particularly emphasized; and an attempt is made to account for the audience's attitude not on the basis of some kind of inborn tendency to passivity, inertia, or debased instincts, but as the natural result of social pressures. Finally, these critics believe that great art can counteract the bad effects of increasing industrialization.

Matthew Arnold is a most eloquent spokesman among these English critics. In contrast to Wordsworth, and reminiscent of Pascal, his concern is more with spiritual than with aesthetic values: what for Wordsworth is "beauty and dignity" is for him "spirituality and sweetness and light."[29] Where Wordsworth evokes Shakespeare and Milton, Arnold points to Lessing and Herder as writers who broaden the basis for life by diffusing "sweetness and light to make reason and the Will of God prevail." He is deeply troubled lest the rapid spread of industrialization overwhelm "culture," which for him is the "idea of perfection as an inward condition of the mind and spirit." This role of true culture, he believes, is more essential to mankind than ever before.

> This function is particularly important in our modern world of which the whole of civilization is, to a much greater degree than the civilizations of Greece and Rome, mechanical and external and tends constantly to become more so . . . faith in machinery . . . is our besetting danger.

Having thus juxtaposed cultural goals against concern with industrial progress, Arnold goes on to deal with specific phenomena of popular culture.

[28] Quoted from: *An Oxford Anthology of English Prose* (Oxford University Press, Inc., 1944), p. 393ff.
[29] These and the following quotations are from Matthew Arnold, *Culture and Anarchy* [first published in 1869] (New York: Cambridge University Press, 1950). See particularly, pp. 22–23; pp. 60–61; pp. 69–71.

Not unlike Pascal (or, for that matter, the social critics in modern "little" magazines), he deals with the games, sports, and mass media as various manifestations of the same trend away from the true essence of life.

> . . . the result of all the games and sports which occupy the passing generation of boys and young men may be the establishment of a better physical type for the future to work with . . . our generation of boys and young men is in the meantime sacrificed.

In the same context, he attacks the producers of literature for mass consumption.

> Plenty of people will try to give the masses, as they call them, an intellectual food prepared and adapted in the way they think proper for the actual condition of the masses. The ordinary popular literature is an example of this way of working on the masses.

Such manipulation, he believes, is incompatible with culture which "works differently." He, too, singles out the newspaper (particularly the American newspaper) for special attack, and finds its pragmatism the very opposite to culture.

> Because to enable and stir up people to read their Bible and the newspapers and to get a practical knowledge of their business does not serve the higher spiritual life of a nation so much as culture, truly conceived, serves; and the true conception of culture is . . . just what America fails in.

Walter Bagehot, in his treatise on *The English Constitution*, written in 1867, says that the English inclination toward "the outward show of life," its remoteness from "true philosophy," exposes the nation more and more to a style of superficiality and adoration of success. He is concerned lest the values of British aristocracy go completely astray under the pressure of the sorry alliance between professional politicians and professional money-makers, and he deplores the extent to which this modern idolatry will also be reflected in the writings of the nation.

> It is not true that the reverence for rank—at least for hereditary rank—is as base as the reverence for money. As the world has gone, manner has been half hereditary in certain castes, and manner is one of the fine arts. It is a style of society; it is in the daily spoken intercourse of human beings what the art of literary expression is in their occasional written intercourse.[30]

He isolates newspaper reading as the only intellectual activity which still finds a broad audience. Just as the classical European or American sociologists (Toennies, Max Weber, Ward, or Ross), he points at the newspapers

[30] Walter Bagehot, *The English Constitution*, The World's Classics ed. (New York: Oxford University Press, Inc., 1944), pp. 80–81.

as reinforcements of public opinion, deliberately subservient to specific political and business interests: "Even now a dangerous distinction is given by what is exclusively called public life. The newspapers describe daily and incessantly a certain conspicuous existence; they comment on its characters, recount its details, investigate its motives, anticipate its cause." Referring to the world of politics, he complains that the newspapers "give a precedent and a dignity to that world which they do not give to any other," whereas "the literary world, the scientific world, the philosophical world, not only are not comparable in dignity to the political world but in comparison are hardly worthy at all. The newspaper makes no mention of them and could not mention them." Bagehot, quite in line with German idealistic thinking as developed by Schiller, believes that the source of this inclination rests with the producers, not with the consumers, who, however, are eventually seduced.

> As are the papers, so are the readers; they, by irresistible sequence and association, believe that those people who constantly figure in the papers are cleverer, abler, or, at any rate, somewhat higher than other people. . . . English politicians . . . are actors on the scene, and it is hard for the admiring spectators not to believe that the admired actor is greater than themselves.[31]

Bagehot is completely steeped in the traditional discussion about the irreconcilable contrasts between true culture and art, on the one hand, and popular products which lower the intellectual and moral standards of a people on the other. In his *Literary Studies*, most of which were written in the fifties, we find an essay on the Waverly Novels (the German critics too were keenly aware of the entertainment functions of the novels of Scott) in which Bagehot, after having paid oblique praise to the successful manufacturer of novels, comments as follows:

> On the whole, and speaking roughly, these defects in the delineation which Scott has given us a human life are but two. He omits to give us a delineation of the soul. . . . We miss the consecrating power. . . . There are perhaps such things as the love affairs of immortal beings, but no one would learn it from Scott. His heroes and heroines are well-dressed for this world, but not for another; there is nothing even in their love which is suitable for immortality. As has been noticed, Scott also omits any delineation of the abstract unworldly intellect. This too might not have been so severe a reproach, considering its undramatic, unanimated nature, if it had stood alone; but taken in connection with the omission which we have just spoken of, it is most important. As the union of sense and romance makes the world of Scott so characteristically agreeable— a fascinating picture of this world in the light in which we like best to dwell on it—so the deficiency in the attenuated, striving intellect, as well as in the supernatural soul, gives to the "world" of Scott the cumbrousness and temporality, in short, the materialism, which is characteristic of the world.[32]

[31] *Ibid.*, p. 42.
[32] Walter Bagehot, *Literary Studies*, Introduction by George Sampson, Everyman's Library ed., Vol. II (New York: E. P. Dutton & Co., Inc., 1932), pp. 160–161.

Schiller said that a literature which served only to gratify the reader's need for relaxation could not be called art. Bagehot expresses the same idea in different terms; popular literature is to him a literature that lacks moral and intellectual values. He criticizes Scott's novels on the ground that they fail to show the tension between the human soul and the real world, that they remain on the level of the sensuous and agreeable, instead of stressing immortality. Bagehot thus comes close to the point of view of Pascal: art which excludes spiritual and intellectual struggle is not art.[33]

Arnold, Bagehot, and the other critics of the times did not view esoteric artistic production on the one hand and substitute products seeking the market or popularity on the other as alternatives. Rather, they formulated a concept of art which made it neither exclusive nor condescending—but, at the same time, it granted no living space to the products of popular culture. What these thinkers believed was the basic function of art, and particularly of literature, is to bring about the universal liberation of mankind.[34]

Such a concept of art, particularly of literature, as a liberating force, goes far beyond that of the classical humanists of the late eighteenth and early nineteenth centuries whose first concern was the individual, organized society being viewed as an agglomerate of autonomous moral subjects. This newer concept came to the fore after the boundless optimism about the potentialities of the individual had begun to recede, and it was rooted in the idea of superimposed social change which in turn would benefit the individual. This newer concept, curiously enough, writers as different in national origin and literary style as Matthew Arnold and Leo Tolstoy expressed in almost the same way when they elaborated on the capacity of the arts and literature to provide the basis for man's emancipation from any sort of social manipulation by conveying ideas of truth and freedom. Their texts are rich, as well as astonishingly similar, in the expression of this concept.[35]

[33] It is interesting to note that John Stuart Mill, whose social and political views are completely opposed to those of Bagehot, also condemned an art dominated by utilitarian values. In his literary essays he praises Coleridge for being "ontological, conservative, religious, concrete, historical and poetic," and attacks Bentham for being "experimental, innovative, infidel, abstract, matter of fact, and essentially prosaic." [See *Mill on Bentham and Coleridge*, with an Introduction by F. R. Leavis (London: Chatto & Windus, Ltd., 1950).]

[34] Lionel Trilling once observed: "In the nineteenth century, in this country as in Europe, literature underlay every activity of mind. The scientist, the philosopher, the historian, the theologian, the economist, the social theorist, and even the politician, were required to command literary abilities which would not be thought irrelevant to their respective callings." *The Liberal Imagination: Essays on Literature and Society*, Anchor Book (New York: Doubleday & Company, Inc., 1953), p. 99.

[35] Cf. Matthew Arnold, *Culture and Anarchy* (New York: Cambridge University Press, 1950), pp. 69–71, and Leo Tolstoy, *What Is Art?* (London: Walter Scott Publishing Co., Ltd.), pp. 192–93, translated from the original Russian manuscript, with an introduction by Aylmer Maude. This is the extreme all-or-nothing concept of art, implying that what is merely liked by the people is likely to be no art. In the contemporary discussion of the mass media one can find a quite opposite view, one which sometimes brushes off the art Tolstoy

The crucial question of the role of "public taste," that is to say, the impact of the market place on public opinion, in a liberalistic if not democratic society becomes a recurrent topic in pre-Victorian and Victorian discussions. One could arrange most of the literati of this era on a continuum ranging from strong agreement to strong disagreement with the following statements of William Hazlitt (1778–1830).

> The highest efforts of genius, in every walk of art, can never be understood by the generality of mankind.[36]

> The public taste hangs like millstone round the neck of all original genius that does not conform to established and exclusive models.[37]

It is on these premises that Hazlitt becomes apprehensive about the denigration of art. His concept of popular culture is one of the decay of high culture under the dictates of the buying customers' taste.

> The public taste is, therefore, necessarily vitiated, in proportion as it is public; it is lowered with every infusion it receives of common opinion. The greater the number of judges, the less capable must they be of judging, for the addition to the number of good ones will always be small, while the multitude of bad ones is endless, and thus the decay of the arts may be said to be the necessary consequence of its progress.[38]

He comes very close to using our contemporary categories in describing mass culture and mass leisure by pointing at the social configuration of official pontificators in matters artistic, the role of money, and the eagerness of the general public to keep up appearances whenever they make for social success. To quote from an article in the *Examiner* (1816), in which he takes the selection policy of the British Museum to task:

> . . . the Royal Academy are a society of hucksters in the Fine Arts who are more tenacious of their profits as chapmen and dealers, than of the honour of Art. . . . A fashionable Artist and a fashionable hair-dresser have the same common principles of theory and practise; the one fits his customers to appear with *éclat* in a ball-room, the other in the Great Room of the Royal Academy.[39]

It should be noted that the status problem of the artist which, at least in England, had seemingly been solved in the eighteenth century is now raised

---

and Arnold discussed on the grounds that it was *not* for the people. Such a viewpoint is quite expressly stated, for example, in Coulton Waugh's book on the comics. See Chapter 1, footnote 5.

[36] Hazlitt, *The Round Table* (1817) in *The Complete Works* (London: J. M. Dent & Sons, Ltd., 1930), Vol. 4, p. 164.

[37] Hazlitt, *Lectures on the English Poets* (1818) in *op. cit.*, Vol. 5, p. 96.

[38] *Ibid.*, pp. 45–46.

[39] Hazlitt, *op. cit.*, Vol. 18, pp. 105–108.

again as the artists or their spokesmen take a second look at the new "patron," the market place. Hazlitt takes an extreme negative position by inferring that an author as such has no social standing whatsoever.

> To be at all looked upon as an author, a man must be something more or less than an author—a rich merchant, a banker, a lord, or a ploughman. He is admired for something foreign to himself. . . . To be well spoken of, he must enlist under some standard; he must belong to some coterie.[40]

Hazlitt's contempt for the public culminates in the following statement:

> It reads, it admires, it extols only because it is the fashion, not from any love of the subject or the man.[41]

The last quotation may remind us of Goethe. At times they seem to quote from each other. Hazlitt, when speaking about going to the opera or a play, writes:

> The boxes, splendid as they are, and splendid as the appearance of those in them is, do not breathe the spirit of enjoyment. They are rather like the sick wards of luxury and idleness, where people of a certain class are condemned to perform the quarantine of fashion for the evening. The rest of the spectators are sulky and self-important. . . .[42]

Goethe's theater Manager explains to the Poet:

> If one comes bored, exhausted quite,
> Another, satiate, leaves the banquet's tapers,
> And, worst of all, full many a wight
> Is fresh from reading of the daily papers.
> Idly to us they come, as to a masquerade,
> Mere curiosity their spirits warming:
> The ladies with themselves, and with their finery, aid
> Without a salary their parts performing.
> What dreams are yours in high poetic places?
> You're pleased, forsooth, full houses to behold?
> Draw near, and view your patron's faces!
> The half are coarse, the half are cold.[43]

The following quotation, in singling out the United States as the crassest example of the devaluation of taste within a democratic society, reminds us of Stendhal and Tocqueville:

> *Macbeth* is only tolerated in this country for the sake of the music; and in the United States of America, where the philosophical principles of government

[40] Hazlitt, *Table Talk* (1821–1822) in *op. cit.*, Vol. 8, pp. 210–211.
[41] *Ibid.*, p. 99.
[42] *Ibid.*
[43] Goethe, *Faust*, Prelude, *op. cit.*

are carried still further in theory and practice, we find that the *Beggar's Opera* is hooted from the stage. Society, by degrees, is constructed into a machine that carries us safely and insipidly from one end of life to the other, in a very comfortable prose style.[44]

In an article in the *Examiner* (1816) he indicts "the petulance of public opinion" coupled with "public ignorance" which will "debauche" rather than "reform" bad taste. To sum up: "The diffusion of taste is not the same thing as the improvement of taste."[45]

Leigh Hunt (1784–1859) was probably the first professional theater critic, and definitely one of the initiators of authoritative and influential newspaper reviews of the stage. His basic concerns seem to be identical with those of Hazlitt.[46] Hunt, too, was concerned with what he considered the vitiate state of the theater. In 1807 he wrote a series of articles in the *News* on the position of comedy in England (which at times sounds like a paraphrase of Oliver Goldsmith's satire of the English stage in *The Citizen of the World*, 1762), in which he deplored the new extravagances of the comic writers, who use tricks and artifices for effect. The new comic writer is interested in quick success, in attaining applause in the easiest possible manner. The incidents and characters are either "of very manifest commonplace," or they depend on "the most monstrous disguises to gain the appearance of novelty; they remind us of the tricks practised . . . at some of our country fairs. . . ."[47] In short, the art of the modern comic writer consists of a series of deceptions aimed at astonishing the audience. And what part of the audience is responsible for encouraging this display of vulgarity?

> [The modern writer] . . . accordingly writes for the galleries, or, in other words, for that part of the audience which is the least capable of judging, but the noisiest in declaring its judgment.[48]

With Sir Walter Scott (1771–1832) we encounter a radically different attitude toward the relation between the artist and the public. First of all, he considers the trade of writing a legitimate business which deserves its

---

[44] Hazlitt, *Lectures on the English Poets* (1818) in *op. cit.*, Vol. 5, p. 10.

[45] Hazlitt, *op. cit.*, Vol. 18, pp. 102–103.

[46] It turns out, however, that Hunt represents a type of writer who, in the course of a literary career, comes to terms with conformist standards. Forty years later Hunt published his *Autobiography* (London: Smith, Elder and Company, 1850) in which he commented on his theatrical criticism as a young man. His views now have softened considerably; he displays now an almost complete reversal of his previous opinion: "Not that I mean to say that their comedies were excellent, or that my commonplaces about the superior merits of Congreve and Sheridan were not well founded; but there was more talent in their 'five-act farce' than I supposed; and I mistook, in great measure, the defect of the age—its dearth of dramatic character—for that of the writers who were to draw upon it."

[47] Leigh Hunt, "An Essay of the Appearance, Causes and Consequences of the Decline of British Comedy" in *Critical Essays* (London: J. Hunt, 1807), p. 132.

[48] *Ibid.*, p. 131.

monetary rewards: "I care not who knows it—I write for general amusement."[49]

In an intimate journal entry he very frankly confesses that "the public favor is my only lottery" and he proudly adds that "I have long enjoyed the foremost praise."[50] We might perhaps say that he formulates the credo of the middle-brow in assuming a pre-stabilized harmony between books which sell and the healthy tastes of the reading public.

> . . . it has often happened, that those who have been best received in their own time, have also continued to be acceptable to posterity. I do not think so ill of the present generation, as to suppose that its present favour necessarily infers a future condemnation.[51]

In strict contrast to the esoteric concept of art defended by Hazlitt or the early Hunt—not to speak of Coleridge, Wordsworth, and Shelley—Scott advocates a "cultivation" of literature "useful" for the business of society.

> A taste for poetry . . . is apt if too much indulged, to engender, a fastidious contempt for the ordinary business of the world, and gradually to unfit us for the exercise of the useful and domestic virtues, which depend greatly on our not exalting our feelings above the temper of well-ordered and well-educated society. . . . Cultivate, then, sir, your taste for poetry and the belles lettres, as an elegant and most interesting amusement, but combine it with studies of a more serious and solid cast.[52]

What Scott has done is to turn art into a residual category of activity which is to rob it of aesthetic principle. For Scott there are no critical rules by which to judge the adequacy or beauty of artistic works. Different classes derive pleasures from different types of artistic production and Scott allows this distinction to stand. He is alarmed however when he decides that the standards of his class are being lowered by the popularity of certain types of art—again a conventional moral standard is substituted for an aesthetic one. Scott implicitly washes his hands of the problem of maintaining or establishing artistic standards by concluding that if art is residual, and if the standards of society prevail, then the audience to whom it is directed is the legitimate critic.

The Edinburgh Review

As one makes one's way through the volumes of such periodicals as *The Edinburgh Review, The Quarterly Review, Blackwood's*, and others, one becomes

[49] Scott, Introductory epistle to *Fortunes of Nigel* (1822), Vol. I (London: W. Scott, Ltd., 1892), p. xxxviii.

[50] *Journal of Sir Walter Scott* (1826), ed. J. G. Tait (Edinburgh: Oliver and Boyd, 1950), p. 73.

[51] Scott, Introductory epistle to *Fortunes of Nigel, op. cit.*, p. lii.

[52] *Letters of Sir Walter Scott*, Vol. II of twelve vols., ed. H. J. C. Grierson (London: Constable and Co., Ltd., 1932), p. 278.

increasingly aware of the prevailing though implicit sociological orientation of many of its contributors, the prominent as well as those less well known. Almost any category relevant to conceptualizing the area of culture and communications may be found in this huge body of writing. They contain, e.g., various theories of the social role of literature, high and low; of the changing public taste; of the reinforcing role of different media; of inter-relations between social coteries and literary fads; of the intertwining of politics, big business, and promotion. Within the scope of this essay, I can only convey a feeling for this wealth of data.

The *Edinburgh Review*, founded in 1802, is perhaps the most fruitful source for locating the main topics in the debate on culture, popular and otherwise, and its relationship to society at large throughout the century. Although the review articles which form the almost exclusive subject matter of this maga-zine are unsigned, it is well known that practically all major figures in English literary life at one time or another were fairly regular contributors. The prevailing attitude displayed over the years is one of friendly compro-mise—balancing quality against the needs and justifiable claims of the reading public at large. Here are a few examples of topics discussed and positions taken.

In Volume 65 (1837) we find the review of an historical book, the article subtitled "Newspaper Literature." It praises "the universal empire to which modern civilization seems advancing." While it is admitted that "the English picture is a great deal less poetical" than the genius of antiquity, still "our own age and country" can be proud of "the numbers who can share the advantages of the convenience of life."

> The cheap and rapid journey by railroad or steam-boat, the warm glass-windowed home, the clean shirt and cotton stockings, the far-brought luxuries of the tea-table and the pipe, his small shelf of well-adapted knowledge, and, above all, his newspaper.[53]

This is the key word, indeed. The writer continues to say that newspapers are:

> an essential element and symbol of the peculiar spirit and tendency which char-acterize our civilization. There is no place to which they do not penetrate; no object which they may not serve; no description of person to whom they are not welcome.[54]

[53] *Edinburgh Review*, Vol. 65, 1837 (No. CXXXII), p. 197. All contributions to the *Edinburgh Review* are anonymous. Wherever possible, the contributor is supplied. The writer of the article quoted above is William Empson. For research on authorship, I am indebted to Ina Lawson of the Department of English, University of California, Berkeley.

There is a project now in progress at Wellesley College under the editorship of Walter E. Houghton. Known as *The Wellesley Index to Victorian Periodicals*, it will eventually give us, among other things, the authors' names.

[54] *Ibid.*

The author does not hesitate to engage in some sort of sociological aesthetic by ascribing to the newspaper of today the function of the epic of past periods.

> As far as our contemporary civilization rests upon them, their immediate influence in favour of the sublime and excellent, may fall short of the flight attempted by epic poems; but they will probably prove, in their humbler way (and we are sure to speak of it with all due reverence for poets), as good securities for freedom.[55]

The crucial dilemma of, on the one hand, a public opinion dependent on newspapers, and, on the other, the need of the writers to satisfy the newspaper public is evaded. The article states in the same breath that as far as the "writer for the daily press" is concerned, "the public have no choice but to submit." But at the same time "a writer is very unfavorably situated for truth."[56]

The overriding note, however, is one of optimism, particularly the thesis that "the only adequate standard at any given period [namely for the measurement of the moral and intellectual level of a society] would be the style of its popular writings and of its domestic buildings."[57] This means:

> Under a free and cheap press, newspapers are perhaps the best representative, at any given time, of the real moral and intellectual state of the greater part of a population.[58]

It may be noted in passing that this article touches upon two important concerns of John Ruskin. For him, too, architecture was a basic criterion for judging the cultural level of a society; but his adamant anti-liberalistic position did not allow him any kind of friendly and balanced evaluation of cultural goods produced for a large mass of people, and very much in contrast to this article, he postulates art itself as the sole criterion for the moral and intellectual state of a period.

That this was a lively debate was borne out by another article which appeared about ten years later. It speaks about the "unfortunate effects" produced by "dependence on periodical literature."

[55] *Ibid.*, p. 148.
[56] *Ibid.*, p. 201.
[57] See also, Vol. 61, 1835 (No. CXXIII), p. 184: "Books, how cheap soever, and however popularly written, are not likely to be read by the uninformed. To buy, or to get, and to begin reading a volume, indicates a certain progress in improvement to have been already made. But all men will read THE NEWS; and even peasants, farm servants, country day-labourers, will look at, nay pore over the paper that chronicles the occurrences of the neighbouring market-town. Here then is a channel through which, alongside with political intelligence and the occurrences of the day, the friends of human improvement, the judicious promoters of general education, may diffuse the best information, and may easily allure all classes, even the humblest, into the paths of general knowledge."
[58] *Ibid.*, Vol. 65, p. 203.

The constantly recurring demands of Periodical Literature are fatal to all deliberation of view—to all care, or study, or selection or materials; in the case of those who engage in it as a Profession.[59]

The article comments scathingly on the need to offer "novelty," "artificially fretted into foam," which prevents the public from learning to appreciate the "calmness and repose of manner, and to that breadth and evenness of composition which are the distinguishing characteristics of those works which we regard as the classics of our language."[60] Again, America looms on the horizon as the most telling example of the debasement of culture when the author goes on to say:

We hope that Mr. Dickens is mistaken as to the degree in which the Press in the United States impresses and influences the general feeling. We cannot but think that, if his description of it be just, the strength of the poison must act as an antidote. Does any well-educated man in America read these papers *with respect?*[61]

The pages of the magazine are full of arguments, pro and con, of press and magazine features such as the "feuilleton," serialized and digested novels. There is, however, one issue of crucial interest, namely the comparative social role of the newspaper in the world of print. An interesting article, five years later, not only reiterates the thesis that the newspaper is the most appropriate yardstick for the state of culture, but also declares that the newspaper is superseding the book.

It is a well-known fact, which any leading book-seller will verify with a sigh, that whenever public events of importance occur, or great changes are under discussion, it is useless to publish books.[62]

An article in 1843 discusses the state of the theatre. Not unlike the attacks of the German classic writers (particularly of Schiller), the preference of the public at large for unworthy melodramas and comedy is ascribed to the weakening of artistic sensibility under the impact of the demands made by modern civilization.

The present excessive taste for gorgeous scenery on the stage, and profuse illustration in books, seems to us very like yielding to that prosaic tendency of a feeble mind, which, unwilling to realize pictures for itself, demands scenic representations to flatter its idle incompetence.[63]

This topic of the castrating effect of modern civilization on the productive imagination, is resumed in an article which appeared in dealing with poetry.

[59] *Ibid.*, Vol. 83, 1846 (No. CLXVIII), p. 383.
[60] *Ibid.*
[61] *Ibid.*, Vol. 76, 1843 (No. CLIV, Art. VIII), p. 520 [James Spaulding, author].
[62] *Ibid.*, Vol. 88, 1848 (No. CLXXVIII, Art. II), p. 342 [A. Hayward, author].
[63] *Ibid.*, Vol. 78, 1843 (No. CLXVIII, Art. V), pp. 384–385.

The aids and appliances which are now multiplied round men, enfeeble them. The shield of law renders it no longer necessary that every man should be competent to his own defence; and the division of labour has forestalled the necessity of intellectual self reliance, and of that large yet minute development of faculties which was produced when, for the work of one man, the most opposite qualities were required. Industrialism, likewise—while the prosperity which is its just reward too often betrays it into selfishness—is a sedative to the passions.[64]

This article, by the way, anticipates modern categories of social criticism such as those used by Riesman and others, categories which suggest that an individual's values must be neutralized if he is to remain an accepted member of a social team.

A certain social uniformity ensues, exercising a retarding force like the resistance of the air or the attrition of matter, and insensibly destroying men's humours, idiosyncracies, and spontaneous emotions. It does so, by rendering their concealment an habitual necessity, and by allowing them neither food nor sphere. Men are thus, as it were, cast in a mould. Besides—the innumerable influences, intellectual and moral, which, at a period of diffused knowledge like the present, co-exist and cooperate in building up our mental structure, are often completely at variance with each other in origin and tendency: so that they neutralize each other's effects, and leave a man well stored with thoughts and speech, but frequently without aim or purpose.[65]

The article ends by stating that art can only retain "but a feeble hold on the true and real" in a period which is characterized "by subserviency to Opinion—that irresponsible life which makes little things great, and shuts great things out from our view. But, without simplicity, ideality cannot exist.[66]

A critical evaluation of an important French publication dealing with popular literature appeared in 1858. The book is *Histoire des livres populaires, ou de la littérature du colportage, despuis le XV siècle*, par M. Charles Nisard, Secrétaire-adjoint de la Commission de l'examen des livres du colportage, Paris 1854. For fifteen pages the reviewer deals with this book because "it is impossible not to regard it as full of significance in reference to the same important class of publications in England." He gives a number of examples of this "*substratum* of publications" in England. I know of no other nineteenth-century formulation which so clearly states the issue of popular culture as far as mass-market productions are concerned. When speaking about contemporary "hawkers" of literature he states:

This, no doubt, is one of the great social problems of the age, hardly, if at all, inferior in interest to that of primary education itself; because it involves the success of that self-education, which bears even more directly on the practical

[64] *Ibid.*, Vol. 89, 1849 (No. CLXXX, Art. III), p. 360 [Aubrey de Vere, author].
[65] *Ibid.*
[66] *Ibid.*

formation of character of the individual, and the determination, for good or evil, at the outset, of the moral principles which, whether unfelt or openly avowed, are destined to be his guide of action throughout life.[67]

Being a magazine with a stated social purpose, the *Edinburgh Review* again and again permits its contributors to come back to the deplorable level of popular entertainment. A number of remedial measures are proposed at various times and by various contributors, such as increased and free education, legal measures against trash, a classification of the theaters, and a deliberate effort on the part of intellectuals to raise the standards of the general public so that their "casting vote" will be for works of "good taste."[68]

Throughout the nineteenth century, the writers who viewed the new developments with alarm were seldom contradicted. While the public continued to buy bestsellers, the champions of higher culture seemed to dominate the theoretical discussions. However, some limited opposition to this stance of purity appeared, and there were writers who took up the cudgels in defense of an art for and of the people. This attitude is well expressed in the *Edinburgh Review* of 1896. This question is posed: is it true that increased moral and material welfare of the masses "can only be obtained by making it more difficult for the man of intellect to make his mark on the age," that "the levelling up of the masses inevitably leads to the levelling down of genius?"[69] If it be true, "the interests of the many must, we fear, prevail over the requirements of the few. . . ."[70] But, it is not true:

. . . material prosperity has been accompanied by moral progress; the life of our people is, on the whole, more healthy than it was fifty years ago . . . their homes are brighter, the conditions of toil easier, and their opportunities for sensible recreation greater. . . . there is no proof that, in levelling up the masses, we have levelled down genius. We have, on the contrary, argued that, though genius may be devoting itself to new pursuits or new inquiries, there is no evidence of decay in our intellectual growth; and that an age which has done more to dominate nature, and to explain nature, than all the preceding centuries, cannot rightly be charged with inferiority of intellect.[71]

It is on this note of optimism that the *Edinburgh Review* summarizes the achievements of the century, and carries forward with new momentum the growing triumph of science and technology. Here are Arnold's Philistines, relating popular culture to the grand march of Victorian progress. This article is a high point in the history of the *Review*. Until roughly 1860, it displayed an enormous interest in literary matters such as taste and style, and it contained a great deal of programmatic pronouncements on cultural

[67] *Ibid.*, Vol. 107, 1858 (No. CCXVII, Art. VIII), p. 246.
[68] *Ibid.*, Vol. 65, 1837 (No. CXXXII), p. 204.
[69] *Ibid.*, Vol. 183, 1896 (No. CCCLXXV), p. 20.
[70] *Ibid.*
[71] *Ibid.*

and particularly aesthetic affairs which led to many a controversy. Later on, the contributions are less vigorous, the style becomes flat and the level of discussion vague and at times trivial. One might hypothesize that the intellectual history of the magazine reflects the declining role of art as the key concern of public intellectual and educational policy which had its heyday in the Romantic schools of European writers.

IV

The Sociological Approach

For all their differences, the academic and the cultural reactions to the rise of mass culture have one important feature in common: both are essentially moralizing, both, that is, hark back to Pascal's religious condemnation of entertainment. The more modern condemnations differ from Pascal's in that they substitute art for religion, but art is here conceived as a kind of divine service to truth and beauty, essentially moral and spiritual in nature. Thus while popular art is depicted as the pursuit of relaxation or the attempt to escape reality, higher art is assumed to be a legitimate and spiritually fruitful pursuit, which ennobles the soul, and raises it to an ideal realm. The causes that induce men to engage in the inferior, non-spiritual activities and the nature of that higher art which is opposed to these activities are conceived in various ways, but in each case, explicitly or implicitly, the spokesmen for the academic and for the cultural approach formulate an injunction, a moral judgment, which amounts to a condemnation of popular art.

It is perhaps no accident that another, third attitude to the new phenomenon was for the first time formulated and applied in the country of Pascal and Montaigne. This new attitude, which we shall call the "sociological," marks, in a sense, a return to Montaigne, to his method of dispassionately studying all human phenomena, with moral judgment suspended. The French intellectual tradition of exploring each new idea to its ultimate consequences and to formulate it in its most extreme form is not alone responsible for the fact that the phenomenon of popular culture was studied in a spirit of dispassionate objectivity in France before any other country. There is also the historical circumstance that in France the political and social struggles of the nineteenth century were fought with the greatest intensity and ideological movements achieved the greatest measure of articulate expression. The numerous upheavals which France underwent after the French Revolution from the Napoleonic dictatorship to the Communist experiment of the Commune of 1871 favored the development of that ironic detachment in the face of social phenomena which is the precondition of a scientific approach.

Alexis de Tocqueville, one of the precursors of the modern social scientist, as early as 1835 analyzed the phenomenon of popular culture and its relationship to literary art in just such a detached scientific spirit. He does not ask whether popular art is good or bad, he merely states that so-called superior forms of art do not find a favorable soil in modern capitalist democracies because men "engaged either in politics or in a profession" have neither time nor mind to allow them more than "to taste occasionally and by stealth the pleasures of mind" which "are considered as a transient and necessary recreation amid the serious labors of life." Men in the American democracy, for instance, "can never acquire a sufficiently intimate knowledge of the art of literature to appreciate its more delicate beauties." Members of an industrialized society are inured "to the struggle, the crosses and the monotony of practical life." Like many sociologists of the pre-research era, he proceeds to infer that predispositions conditioned by the means of earning a living in turn give rise to the need for excitement in leisure time, in order to offset the boredom of the job. Thus he believes that modern man "requires strong emotions, startling passages, truths and errors brilliant enough to rouse them up and to plunge them at once, as if by violence, into the midst of the subject." After having rooted the psychological needs in the groundwork of the economic situation, Tocqueville describes (without, by the way, giving any concrete examples) the literature of the democratic age in terms of the satisfaction of social needs. He believes that no true art or respect for form will be possible, but that:

> Style will frequently be fantastic, incorrect, overburdened, and loose, almost always vehement and bold. Authors will aim at rapidity of execution more than at perfection of detail. Small productions will be more common than bulky books; there will be more wit than erudition, more imagination than profundity; and literary performances will bear marks of an untutored and rude vigor of thought, frequently of great variety and singular fecundity. The object of authors will be to astonish rather than to please, and to stir the passions more than to charm the taste.[72]

His conclusion is pessimistic. He believes that only mass communications will be successful in modern societies, and that they can only be products of popular culture, unrelated to valid intellectual, artistic, or moral criteria. The writer, then, becomes part and parcel of a business civilization and is, in his way, just as much a manufacturer of commodities as any other businessman.

> Democratic literature is always infested with a tribe of writers who look upon letters as a mere trade; and for some few great authors who adorn it, you may reckon thousands of idea-mongers.[73]

About two decades later, Tocqueville's countryman, Hippolyte Taine, elaborated on these concepts. The five volumes of his *History of English*

---

[72] Alexis de Tocqueville, *Democracy in America*, Vol. II (New York: Alfred A. Knopf, Inc., 1945), p. 59.
[73] *Ibid.*, p. 61.

Literature, shot through with observations about the relationship of the writer and his public, could be reread today as a sociological classic. The differences between pure art and popularly accepted literature are not as important to him as to his colleagues at home and abroad, and he finds fault with English criticism because it is "always moral, never psychological, bent on exactly measuring the degree of human honesty, ignorant of the mechanism of our sentiments and faculties."[74] This approach to literature comes close to being "applied science." Take, for instance, his analysis of Dickens which consists of three chapters: the first analyzes the life and character of the author, the third, the characters of his novels, while the intermediary chapter is devoted to a phenomenology of the public of Dickens. A few lines from his chapter on "The Public" will illustrate how he goes about describing public receptivity for popular literature:

Plant this talent on English soil; the literary opinion of the country will direct its growth and explain its fruits. For this public opinion is its private opinion; it does not submit to it as to an external constraint, but feels it inwardly as an inner persuasion; it does not hinder, but develops it, and only repeats aloud what it said to itself in a whisper. The counsels of this public taste are somewhat like this; the more powerful because they agree with its natural inclination, and urge upon its special course:

"Be moral. All your novels must be such as may be read by young girls. We are practical minds, and we would not have literature corrupt practical life. We believe in family life, and we would not have literature paint the passions which attack family life. We are Protestants, and we have preserved something of the severity of our fathers against enjoyment and passions. Amongst these, love is the worst. Beware of resembling in this respect the most illustrious of our neighbors. Love is the hero of all George Sand's novels. Married or not, she thinks it beautiful, holy, sublime in itself; and she says so. Don't believe this; and if you do believe it, don't say it. It is a bad example. . . ."[75]

With Taine we have nearly reached the threshold of modern times. Going on to the turn of the century, we find the discussion on art and popular culture centered around two schools: that of Nietzsche and that of Karl Marx. We cannot analyze the approaches of these two schools in any detail, but what both have in common is an attitude of negativism with regard to present-day political and cultural civilization. In a way (at least within our frame or reference), Nietzsche and his school are more radical than the Marxists because of their belief that all intellectual life (including the great work of the past) is besmirched by the pragmatic utilitarianism of modern civilization. In the interests of a higher type of intellectuality and vitality, Nietzsche and his students, above all the Austrian writer, Karl Kraus, reject practically all literary products of the present, finding that their style and

[74] H. A. Taine, *History of English Literature*, translated from the French, Vol. IV (London: Chatto & Windus, Ltd., 1886), pp. 142, 143.
[75] *Ibid.*

language reveal nothing but commercialism, immorality, and untruth. Marx himself, who never more than occasionally referred to literature, was still very much steeped in humanistic tradition, differentiating between genuine artists such as Shakespeare, Goethe, and Balzac who are devoted to truth, and what he would call lackey literature in the service of the interests of ruling groups.

V

TOWARD A CLARIFICATION OF THE DISCUSSION

In reviewing the historical background of the controversies on popular culture, we find that the field tends to have been dominated by the Pascalian condemnation of all entertainment. Because most authors we have so far considered have consistently equated popular literature with entertainment, their attitude toward popular culture is, by and large, negative. Even the representatives of what we have called the sociological approach are far from defending popular culture, which at best is considered a necessary evil. How is the other side of the controversy represented?

Because of the intellectual tradition of most critics, we probably cannot expect to discover any champions of "inferior" art as such. A theoretical defense of popular art seems to be possible only in the form of rebuttal, or in the form of questioning of the basic assumptions of the defenders of "genuine" art. For example, one might question prevalent assumptions about the function of high art; one might question the implicit assumptions stemming from Montaigne and Pascal that popular productions serve only to gratify lower needs; finally, since the condemnation of popular products has always been associated with a condemnation of the mass media as such, one might ask whether the mass media are irrevocably doomed to serve as vehicles of inferior products.

Have any of these three potential lines of defense ever been manned? When we try to answer this question, we feel the lack of historical studies most acutely. Not only is there no comprehensive work on the subject, but even those small analyses which do exist are generally unsatisfactory, unsystematic, and often superficial. In this section, then, even to a greater extent than in the preceding chapters, we can only hint at the kind of insights and formulations that might be developed in the light of serious historical research.

If the Pascalian idea had been adopted in its original form, not only popular art but all art would have been condemned as distractions which block man's path to individual salvation. Many critics of popular art assume that high art fulfills a purpose other than that of entertainment or escape and belongs on an exalted plane. There are, however, social philosophers (as well as champions of popular art) who have questioned this assumption.

If high art is not entertainment, what, they ask, is it? What is its content, its function, its value? No general agreement on these matters has ever been achieved, although a great many philosophies of art have been formulated.

Especially in France, where the most extreme theories of art for art's sake were developed in reaction to the rise of popular art, esoteric art was under attack throughout the nineteenth century, and many French critics regarded movements such as naturalism as a healthful return to popular art. It was certainly awkward to defend so-called art for art's sake on the ground that it performed a moralizing or educational function. In 1901, George Sorel, the French social philosopher whose *Reflections on Violence* profoundly influenced political thought in the twentieth century, wrote a book entitled *La Valeur sociale de l'art* [*The Social Value of Art*] in which he suggests that it would be difficult to defend great art on the grounds of its educational function.

> It would be impossible to find two persons who agree on the educational value of famous works by our contemporaries. This is also true of past works. Thus M. Brunetiere [famous French literary historian and critic] even wonders whether *Bajazet* and *Rodogune* [classical tragedies by Corneille] do not contain adventures whose proper place would be in the chronicles of crime and licentiousness.[76]

Arguing in the same book against another French critic, Guyot, who maintained that "true artistic beauty is moralizing in itself and expresses true sociability," Sorel asks ironically: "Should we then assume that there is a true beauty and a false beauty?"[77]

Whether such arguments against high art are valid is beside the point here. No doubt, they were often based on superficial views that took too literally the pronouncements of the defenders of such art. But it is pertinent that writers such as Flaubert, who are generally regarded as champions of the esoteric and who were extreme in their rejection of popular entertainment, held views on art that by no means coincide with those of the academic critics. In his private correspondence where he expresses himself freely, Flaubert often complained about the existing cleavage between the artist and the public. He regarded modern art, including his own, as inferior to Greek art precisely because it reflected this cleavage, and he fervently hoped that some day the situation would change.

> The time for Beauty is over. Mankind may return to it, but it has no use for it at the present. . . . It is beyond the power of human thought today to foresee in what a dazzling intellectual light the works of the future will flower. Mean-

---

[76] G. Sorel, *La Valeur sociale de l'art*, quoted by Henri Poulaille in *Nouvel Age Litteraire* (Paris: Valois, 1930), p. 13.

[77] *Ibid.*, p. 14.

while we are in a shadowy corridor, groping in the dark. We are without a
lever. . . . We all lack a basis—literati and scribblers as we are. What's the
good of all this? Is our chatter the answer to any need? Between the crowd and
ourselves no bond exists. Alas for the crowd; alas for us, especially. . . . But
we must, regardless of material things and of mankind, which disavows us, live
for our vocation, climb into our ivory tower, and dwell there along with our
dreams. . . . [From a letter to Louise Colet, April 24, 1852.][78]

Such views were alien to the classical age, to Goethe and Schiller, for
example, who did not by any means believe that genuine art was incompatible with a function of entertainment. Schiller, for instance, in his *Letters
on the Aesthetic Education of Mankind*, to which we have referred earlier in this
chapter, saw the art of the future as the manifestation of what he called
the "play instinct," and spontaneity as one of its main characteristics.

The French critics of the naturalistic school, and some of its branches such
as the so-called populist movement whose avowed aim was to work toward
a new literature that would adequately express modern mass culture, turned
against esoteric art the arguments its champions used to condemn popular
art—namely, that its main function was to serve entertainment and escape.
Art for art's sake, esoteric art—in short, non-popular art—was, in the eyes of
those naturalistic critics a luxury, a means of escape—"the private property
of a kind of caste of mandarins which jealously defends it in order to safe-
guard its privileges," wrote Henri Poulaille, a novelist who led the populist
movement in the late 1920's and early 1930's. He championed an art of the
people, for the people, and by the people, an art that would tell the truth,
and according to him such an art had a respectable tradition, including
such names as Balzac, Hugo, Zola. He condemned popular trash as the
means of escape of the poor classes, and was optimistic about the possibilities
of a new non-escapist art and the potentialities of the new mass media,
which he believed would eventually release literature as a means of escape.

A simple gramophone record transports us to the Hawaiian Islands, to China,
to Mexico. We can see on the screen, at a moment's notice, the Fiji Islands,
India, Siam. The entire symphony of the world is available to our eyes, to our
ears, if we just choose to look or to hear. . . .

Our literature is a thing of the past. It no longer gratifies the need of escape that
summons man at every moment. At least it cannot gratify it as well as the modern
mechanical discoveries. . . .[79]

As far as the merits of popular art are concerned, we are confronted with
a welter of opinions and arguments, which have never been systematized,
and we must confine ourselves to a random sampling. A strong case for at

[78] Gustave Flaubert, *Correspondance, deuxième série* (Paris: Conard, 1926), pp. 395–396.
[79] Henri Poulaille, *op. cit,* p. 433.

least the historical *study* of popular art has been made by a renowned scholar, Louis B. Wright, who thoroughly analyzed the Elizabethan age in England. Unlike Gervinus, who refused to admit popular art to his history of literature, Wright thinks that it is an important and fruitful subject of study, and criticizes previous works on Elizabethan England on the ground that "in all that welter of books one subject has been comparatively neglected: the important matter of the average citizen's reading and thinking, his intellectual habits and cultural tastes.[80] According to Wright, and this is another important argument in favor of popular art, entertainment is not the sole function of this art.

> The bourgeois reader liked to be amused, but more important than the desire for amusement was the demand for information of every conceivable sort.

Other authors have pointed out the possibilities of development inherent in popular art, and even singled out some of its products as equal in value to those "major arts." In 1924, Gilbert Seldes made a strenuous and sophisticated effort to introduce the popular arts—comics, movies, vaudeville—into the Parnassus of respectable, time-honored art. Referring to comics, for example, he says:

> It happens that in America irony and fantasy are practiced in the major arts by only one or two men, producing high-class trash; and Mr. Herriman, working in a despised medium, without an atom of pretentiousness, is day after day producing something essentially fine. It is the result of a naïve sensibility rather like that of the *douanier* Rousseau; it does not lack intelligence, because it is a thought-out, a constructed piece of work. In the second order of the world's art it is superbly first rate—and a delight![81]

This appraisal of Krazy Kat was echoed by Robert Warshow, in an essay on "Krazy Kat" in the November-December 1946 *Partisan Review*, who finds that while most phenomena of "mass art forms" can be dismissed as "Lumpen Culture," "Krazy Kat is as real and important a work of art as any other." It is interesting that in neither case are any serious analyses made within the broader social and moral contexts which we have met in the earlier discussions of these problems.

As early as 1930, that is fifteen years before the television era, Henri Poulaille, the populist writer, observed that:

> The motion pictures are in the process of destroying the old prejudice of written art, on which all literatures are based. . . . Thanks to the motion pictures, the

---

[80] This and the following quotations are from Louis B. Wright, *Middle Class Culture in Elizabethan England.* (Chapel Hill, N. C.: University of North Carolina Press, 1935). See particularly, pp. vii; 83; 659; 660.

[81] Gilbert Seldes, *The Seven Lively Arts* (New York: Harper & Brothers, 1924), p. 231. Reprinted by permission of Harper & Brothers.

reader of books restores his contact with objective reality, and soon we shall be able to see the effects of television, which will further continue the training of the senses that was begun by the motion pictures.[82]

More recently René Sudre, another Frenchman, has dealt with the same problem in a provocative study on the potentialities of radio, which deserves somewhat more lengthy discussion because it deals with a great number of relevant problems. It is entitled *The Eighth Art*, and it was published in 1945, when television was still in its infancy. The primary purpose of this book is to show that radio has the potentialities of a new *artistic* medium and that it can create new artistic values. He begins by making radio an instrument with which to challenge traditional philosophy and psychology.

> The radio confuses the philosophers. What is it that I am not present for the speaker at the microphone while he is present for me? Does presence itself split itself up? This is a very serious psychological problem which Pierre Janet has posed when he analyzes the troubles of inner thought.[83]

He then plunges into an ode to the listener.

> *Beatus solus!* Happy is the solitary man. Less secluded than the man of Pascal, he retreats in order to meditate about his salvation; your (radio's) devotee lets the world enter into his chamber whenever he pleases. Without removing him from the world you favor this contemplative attitude which becomes a refuge from modern restlessness for an ever growing number of refined people. If he has a family you wisely isolate it by keeping it at home. One assembles around you protecting tubes.

This is indeed a remarkable passage. Without being aware of the controversial aspects of his statement, this French author outlines in a rudimentary form a conceptual framework for some much needed research to explore the socializing or individualizing, integrating or isolating, the family conserving or family destroying aspects of residential, electronic entertainment. Furthermore (perhaps unknowingly) he repeats within the context of modern entertainment institutions the concerns of the sixteenth- and seventeenth-century philosophers about the salutary or damaging effects of diversion. To the best of my knowledge, this is the only instance in our time where an author has echoed Pascal's worries about the potential deterioration of the individual under the impact of post-medieval, leisure-time activities.

For our purposes the specific value of Sudre's essay comes to the fore when it is scrutinized for its apparent inconsistency and arbitrariness. After having defended radio for two hundred pages out of two hundred and two in philosophical, phenomenological, psychological, technical, esthetic terms,

---

[82] Poulaille, *op. cit.*, p. 437.
[83] This and the following quotations are from René Sudre, *Le Huitième Art: mission de la radio.* (Paris: Juillard, 1945). See pages 8, 11, 56, 85, and 196–97.

he turns about on the last two pages and vehemently attacks the universe of radio programs.

> If there are frivolous books, pernicious books, there are also heroic books and sublime books and this compensates. As far as radio is concerned, one hardly notices any balance. The performance of the Ninth Symphony or the presentation of some noble literary production does not expiate for the disturbing stupidity, the chronic lawlessness of many radio programs.

He goes on to propose a device for improvement which is halfway between the tradition of a French enlightener and an American, tradition-minded social reformer.

> We would wish for radio a permanent observer who would give us something to think about every day. Actuality is an inexhaustible material for education if one looks upon it from a moral angle. What one would need is not a sceptic or pessimistic philosopher, but a man of good will, smiling and nevertheless manly, who would understand everything but who would not leave us in despair.

Of television at the time of the writing of this book, relatively little was known. Still, the alert author throws out in a naïve, involved, and partisan fashion some quick judgments on the future of television without being quite sure that it would ever come to pass. In principle, what he says here belies everything he has previously expounded as a raison d'être for a modern, technological instrument of popular culture. While radio seems not to be the enemy of imagination, television is.

> Will television give us the photographic beauty of certain cinematic productions? We must recall that true art is based on the principle of the economy of means, namely, to suggest and not to show, not to say everything but to leave much to the imagination.

The possibility for developing genuine arguments about mass culture which may lead to some conclusive answers exists, but by and large the discussion has been unreal, in the sense that the pros and cons for the most part miss each other, and that the concepts used in those arguments remain vague, usually because a historical perspective is lacking. Take, for instance, the last-mentioned argument advanced by Sudre to justify his pessimistic view of television, and which seemingly goes back to Lessing's and Goethe's theory on creative imagination. What Sudre fails to see is that the concept of imagination is itself relative and determined by the historical context. Otherwise, if he were consistent he could just as well argue against the use of color in painting and advocate a return to the cave drawings. In other words, the principle of artistic economy in question is defensible only in the relative sense that good art achieves a maximum effect with minimal means, and not in the absolute sense that good art is *defined* by paucity of means.

Similar confusions can be detected all along; the very concept of popular literature or art has been used in a variable sense, without regard for historical determinants, as we had occasion to hint before. And it would seem fair to say that the present discussion on popular culture and on the possibilities of the mass media will continue to turn in circles until a new and systematic effort is made to clear the field from confusions, and to make real discussion possible.

The Debate Over Art and Popular Culture: English Eighteenth Century as a Case Study

I

THE LITERARY MEDIA

If one takes the term "mass" media to mean marketable cultural goods produced for a substantial buying public, the eighteenth century in England is the first period in history where it can be meaningfully applied. During the first few decades of the eighteenth century, the growing industrialization and urbanization of England, together with the cheaper production of paper and improved methods for producing and distributing literary goods, made reading matter less costly and more easily accessible than it had ever been before. Those who were literate read considerably more than their counterparts in the previous century; women were proving themselves to be particularly avid readers, and literacy was becoming a professional prerequisite for the merchant and shopkeeper classes. By the last quarter of the century even remote villages hired their own schoolmasters, or at least maintained Sunday schools in which the rudiments of reading were taught.

Magazines

Despite the fact that new literary products were developing and that commercial competition became intense, each new form, or variation on an old form, found a ready market. The magazine, as distinct from pamphlets supported by religious or political groups, was the newest and most characteristic medium of the age. In the fifty-year period between 1730 and 1780, at least one new magazine a year was presented to the London public, the

The first published version of this chapter appeared in *Common Frontiers of the Social Sciences*, ed. Mirra Komarovsky (Chicago: The Free Press of Glencoe, Illinois, 1957). Copyright 1957 by The Free Press; reprinted by permission of the publisher.

majority bearing the "something for everyone" format, including questions and answers on all spheres of personal life (with heavy doses of advice to the lovelorn), news, gossip, and fiction. Prototypes of nearly all forms of modern magazines were introduced and for the most part flourished: women's journals, gossipy theatrical monthlies, true and love story magazines, news digests, book reviews, and even book condensations.

Popular Novels

While the single essay (the *Spectator*, the *Tatler*, *The Rambler*, *The Bee*, and the miscellany *Gentleman's Magazine*) periodicals represented new literary forms, the novel, though not a new genre, found a new popularity, particularly after the middle of the century. Although early best sellers were likely to be reprints of seventeenth-century romances, the publication of Richardson's *Pamela* in 1740 marked a major change. For thirty years after *Pamela*, novels were characterized by a mixture of middle-class realism and sentimentality which the four major authors, Richardson, Fielding, Smollett, and Sterne, expressed in varying proportions. With them the eighteenth-century novel reached its peak; after them came a period of imitation, repetition, and poor craftsmanship so bleak the writers feared that this form was dying out altogether. Not so the audience, however, for whom this entertainment continued to be popular even when it consisted mainly of patch-works of several old volumes issued under catchy new titles. It was not until the closing decades of the century, with the advent of the tremendously popular Gothic novel, that there was a return to more craftsmanlike work. The increase in juvenile books, too, became apparent by the late 1780's, when works, more amusing if not less didactic than such a standard children's book as *Pilgrim's Progress*, became available in ever-increasing quantities.

As more people joined the ranks of the literate, novel writing became increasingly lucrative. During the 1790's, even a relatively unknown writer could draw a comfortable income by writing serialized novels for enthusiastic publics. The three-volume novel format was especially popular with the ladies, it was said, because one section could be conveniently perused in a single sitting at the hairdresser's.[1] Small-sized books of all kinds were much in evidence throughout the latter half-century, both consequence and reinforcement of the interests in abstracts, abridgements, and anthologies. The growing taste for what Dr. Johnson called "general and easy reading" seems to have been satisfied by these small and light books. He himself highly approved of the development: books, after all, should be held readily in the hand and should be easy to carry about; heavy books give a discouraging appearance of erudition and may succeed in frightening away the public altogether.[2]

[1] A. S. Collins, *The Profession of Letters: Study of The Relation of Author to Patron, Publisher, and Public*, 1780–1832 (London: George Routledge & Sons, Ltd., 1928), p. 98.

[2] *Ibid.*, p. 65.

Changes in the Theater

At the beginning of the eighteenth century the stage had long since been an English institution, rising and falling in popularity and prestige with changes in politics and religion, but always a major arena in which a writer could present his works.

Restoration drama, with its mirroring of the manners and mores of the aristocracy, had been sufficiently uninhibited to provide reforming pastors and laymen with ample reason for attack. Assaults against the English stage were nothing new, and the moralistic and theological arguments brought to bear on them changed very little between the sixth and the eighteenth centuries. As the Restoration play gave way to middle-class themes, play-going became more respectable and, with the licensing of the two patented theaters at Drury Lane and Covent Garden in 1737, the stage once more became a legitimate means of entertainment for the pious as well as the worldly—which is not to say that the zealots ceased to attack it.

It was the Drury Lane theater which, under Garrick's management, reached a new peak in popularity and quality of production. Despite this, both patented theaters were forced to resort to pantomimes, "spectacular" operas, ballet operas, and a variety of sensational devices to insure high attendance. The practice of dividing the evening's entertainment into two parts, the first performance serious and the second light, had its effect on the audience, since it was inconvenient for working people to attend the earlier presentation. Financial records of the major theaters show that while many members of the audience who attended the first performance sat through the second, an even larger group customarily came only for the latter part of the evening. The attempt to abolish the prevailing custom of cutting the admission price in half after the first piece of the evening was over met with public demonstrations and even riots.[3]

The audience increased considerably in the course of the century. Not only did smaller playhouses begin to flourish in the city and in the provinces, but theaters themselves were enlarged. The two patent theaters together could accommodate fourteen thousand persons per week in 1732, over fifteen thousand in 1747, and twenty-two thousand in 1762.[4] Actual attendance, however, may have averaged considerably less than capacity.

Newspapers

The prototype of the modern newspaper appeared soon after the lapse of the Licensing Act in 1695. Within a year or two, the Whigs and the Tories sponsored political newspapers, and by 1700 several papers circulated about

[3] H. W. Pedicord, *The Theatrical Public in The Time of Garrick* (New York: King's Crown Press, 1954), pp. 14–15.

[4] *Ibid.*, p. 16.

London and were delivered to the provinces three times a week when the posts went out. In 1709 eighteen newspapers were published once a week or more in London, amounting altogether to some fifty issues. By 1730 the coffee house owners complained that it was impossible to suscribe to them all. And in 1776 approximately twelve million copies were sold in the entire year.

In the course of the century, the daily newspaper became self-supporting and self-respecting: self-supporting because of the spread of literacy, self-respecting because of a successful struggle against religious and political control.[5] Although the reactions to this growing literary market were mixed, on the whole those who paid attention to it were more concerned with its potentialities for the intellectual and aesthetic development of the country than with the dangers of its possible influences on public opinion. Only in the early decades of the nineteenth century, when there were some four hundred newspapers in England and Ireland, did the problem of the newspaper as a manipulative device become a major concern to the intellectual.

II

AUDIENCE BUILDING

The eighteenth century in England had no "mass" audience in the modern sense; that was to come only in the next century. But the eighteenth century was modern in the sense that, from that time on, a writer could support himself from the sale of his works to the public. In effect what took place was a shift from private endowment (usually in the form of patronage by the aristocracy) and a limited audience to public endowment and a potentially unlimited audience. At the same time, the production, promotion, and distribution of literary works became profitable enterprises. These changes affected the content as well as the form of literature, and therefore gave rise to many aesthetic and ethical problems. Not all of these problems were new; some had their origins deep in the seventeenth or even in the sixteenth century when there existed a popular audience for the theater. But in the eighteenth century, questions of the potentialities and predispositions of the audience assumed new urgency for the writer because his audience became now the exclusive source of his livelihood.

Despite the lack of reliable literacy figures, there seems little doubt that two upsurges in reading took place among the English public during the eighteenth century. The first was in the thirties and forties, as popular magazines and presently novels began to flood the market. This spurt was due more to the fact that the literate were reading more material than to an increase in the numbers of people who could read. In the last two decades of

[5] W. T. Laprade, *Public Opinion and Politics in Eighteenth Century England* (New York: The Macmillan Company, 1936), pp. 13–14.

the century, on the other hand, when the Bible societies, the political pamphleteers, and the reformers produced reams of inexpensive literature in a concerted attempt to counteract the influence of revolutionary writers such as Tom Paine, the increased consumption was due to a growth in the reading public itself. In between, the village schoolteachers and the Sunday schools, the former in order to make a living, the latter in order to spread the Good Word, had gone about the business of teaching children of the clerical, working, and farming classes their ABC's.[6] Printing presses in London, according to contemporary estimates, increased from seventy-five in 1724 to one hundred and fifty to two hundred in 1757; the annual publication of new books quadrupled in the course of the century;[7] and the profession of letters became established as a respectable (and often very profitable) livelihood, indeed so well established that as early as 1752 Samuel Johnson labelled his the "Age of Authors."[8]

Part cause and part consequence of the increase in reading and the professionalization of the author, a number of channels for expanding the market for literary products sprang into being or took a new lease on life after the first quarter of the century—notably the circulating libraries, the bookselling and publishing trade, and the book-review periodicals. These institutions were closely related to each other as well as to the authors whose works they promoted or exploited and, as today, friction between authors and those responsible for the channels of distribution was not a rarity. Several non-commercial devices also served to promote the consumption of literary goods. Literary societies and reading groups spread throughout London and were eventually imitated in the provinces. The coffee houses in the city and in the towns continued to be centers where people gathered to read or to hear newspapers and magazines read aloud, and lingered to discuss what they had read or heard.

Some coffee houses were primarily literary hangouts. Pope, for example, spent a great deal of time talking with fellow-writers in his favorite coffee house, until he found that the consumption of wine was beginning to get the better of his health. Among the more notable literary coffee clubs in the earlier part of the century was the Kit-Cat Club, which counted numerous leading writers of the period among its members and had Tonson, the outstanding bookseller of his time, as secretary. This club consisted mainly of Whigs, but it went out of its way to encourage young writers, presumably regardless of political persuasion, with financial prizes, particularly for comedies. Swift helped to found the Brothers' Club, whose members were

[6] Richard D. Altick suggests, in *The English Common Reader* (Chicago: University of Chicago Press, 1957), that while the consumption of reading matter certainly increased steadily throughout the eighteenth century, it was only after the 1790's that the structure of the reading audience became democratic. On the whole, he feels, the seventeenth century may have had a more representative, and not necessarily a smaller, reading audience than the eighteenth.

[7] Ian Watt, *The Rise of the Novel* (London: Chatto & Windus, Ltd., 1957), p. 37.

[8] *Adventurer*, No. 115. *British Essayists*, XXI, 137–38.

mainly Tories, but whose interests were largely literary—and they, too, contributed to the support of promising younger writers.[9]

The bluestocking clubs, organized in mid-century by a group of literary-minded upper-class women, determined to substitute talk of letters for card games, were eventually imitated by middle-class women both in London and in the provinces. If nothing else, these groups did much to make reading (and writing) among women socially acceptable, even desirable. By the latter part of the century, informal book-discussion and book-buying clubs throve in every part of the country. How these clubs promoted the sale of books is described by Lackington in his *Memoirs*.

> A number of book-clubs are also formed in every part of England where each member suscribes a certain sum quarterly to purchase books: in some of the clubs the books, after they have been read by all the suscribers, are sold among them to the highest bidders, and the money produced by such sale is expended in fresh purchases, by which prudent and judicious mode each member has it in his power to become possessed of the work of any particular author he may judge deserving a superior degree of attention. . . .[10]

Although would-be purchasers in the provinces sometimes complained that the metropolitan dealers ignored their mail orders, enterprising bookseller visited the clubs in outlying districts, sent them catalogues, and in other ways offered moral if not material encouragement.

Circulating Libraries

The principal audience-building efforts of the book dealers (who were publishers as well) were, however, directed to commercial channels. The first circulating library in England was founded in 1740, the same year in which Richardson's *Pamela* was published. The establishment of one of the major institutions for accelerating the spread of reading in the middle class thus coincided with the first important novel of that class.

It was customary for the libraries to charge an annual membership fee which entitled a subscriber to access to all books and magazines carried by the particular establishment to which he belonged. By the turn of the century, approximately one thousand of these profit-making institutions were scattered throughout the country, and their customers included members of the working classes as well as of the middle classes. Free public libraries, however, were noticeably lacking. The library of the Royal Society accumulated only a fair collection, and the British Museum, already distinguished for its collection of original manuscripts, made a poor showing in printed

[9] Leslie Stephen, *English Literature and Society in the Eighteenth Century* (London: Gerald Duckworth & Co., Ltd., 1904), pp. 37–38.

[10] James Lackington, *Memoirs of the Forty-Five First Years of the Life of James Lackington, Written by Himself* (London: By the Author, 1803), p. 250.

books. Edward Gibbon had reason to complain that "the greatest city of the world was still destitute of a Public Library."[11]

The booksellers at first viewed the development of circulating libraries with suspicion; but they soon recognized that, far from cutting off the sale of books, these outlets promised to constitute both an important market and a major advertising medium.[12] Not only did the circulating libraries provide books for families which could not afford to buy them, but they gave readers a chance to preview a book before investing in it.[13]

The ladies took to the new institutions with delight. Toward the end of the century, there is scarcely a popular novel whose heroine does not in the course of her transports or travails select a novel from her circulating library or send her maid to fetch one. By that time, the booksellers were enthusiastic. Lackington was convinced that, along with his own bookshop of course,

> . . . circulating libraries have also greatly contributed towards the amusement and cultivation of the sex; by far the greatest part of ladies now have a taste for books. . . . Ladies now in general read, not only novels, although many of that class are excellent productions, and tend to polish both the heart and the head; but they also read the best books in the English language, and may read the best authors in various languages; and there are some thousands of ladies who frequent my shop, and that know as well what books to choose, and are as well acquainted with the works of taste and genius as any gentleman in the kingdom, notwithstanding they sneer against novel readers, etc.[14]

While some of the literati toward the latter part of the century blamed the circulating libraries for whetting the apparently insatiable appetite for novels which the booksellers were eager to feed by all manner of means, and while many writers poked light fun at the institution in their own fictional works, few serious attacks on this audience-building device were forthcoming in the course of the century.[15]

Bookselling

The conscientious man of letters was rather less tolerant of the booksellers. Possibly his newly acquired financial dependence on the publisher and dealer occasioned some degree of nostalgia for the days of aristocratic

[11] William Lecky, *History of England in the Eighteenth Century*, Vol. I (New York: D. Appleton, 1888), p. 165.
[12] Collins, *op. cit.*, Ch. I (v) *passim*.
[13] Lackington, *op. cit.*, p. 225.
[14] *Ibid.*, p. 259.
[15] Coleridge was later to speak scathingly of "devotees of circulating libraries" whose reading he considered to be on a par with reading word for word "all the advertisements of a daily newspaper in a public house on a rainy day."

patronage; certainly the practices of a good many booksellers provided him with good reason for intolerance.

The Messrs. Tonson and Curll represent the two extremes of prestige and notoriety the bookseller could achieve in the days of Alexander Pope. Tonson, the afore-mentioned secretary of the Kit-Cat Club, left his mark on the history of the book trade as the esteemed publisher of *Paradise Lost* and numerous works by Dryden and Addison. He commanded the admiration of most of his authors, to whom he was generous in his commercial dealings and stimulating in his intellectual contacts.

Edmund Curll, one of the infamous names in the history of commerce, neither got nor deserved a modicum of respect from the literati. Unscrupulous and clever, he displayed a kind of stupid adroitness which repeatedly landed him in jail and encouraged him, on his discharge, to resume with redoubled vigor the very activities for which he had been imprisoned. He had a special knack for exploiting the scandalous, a thriving business in his as in more recent days, and while he did publish some useful works, given the length of his publication lists, he could hardly have avoided it. He dedicated most of his energy to a search for attractive titles and intimately personal (often scurrilous) advertisements for biographies and pornographic pamphlets which were thrown together willy-nilly by hacks to whom he paid starvation wages.[16] He came in for a lot of scathing criticism in Pope's *Dunciad*, and the reasons are not far to seek.

By 1800 the bookselling and publishing trade was one of the major industries in the country. Needless to say, both Tonson and Curll had their share of descendants. Lackington was the most successful as well as the most self-conscious book dealer of the latter part of the century: he went into business in 1774; in 1779 he published his first catalogue of twelve thousand titles and estimated that some thirty thousand people a year made use of it. It was Lackington who first hit upon the idea of remainder sales, and by the turn of the century he was selling over one hundred thousand volumes a year.[17] While he conceded that he made a substantial amount of money, he also took credit for making books available to groups who might not otherwise have been able to afford them.

. . . when I reflect what prodigious numbers in inferior or *reduced* situations of life, have been essentially benefited, in consequence of being thus enabled to indulge their natural propensity for the acquisition of knowledge, on easy terms: nay, I could almost be vain enough to assert, that I have thereby been highly instrumental in diffusing that general desire for READING now so prevalent among the inferior orders of society.[18]

16 Ralph Straus, *The Unspeakable Curll* (New York: Robert M. McBride Co., Inc., 1928).
17 Lackington, *op. cit.*, p. 224.
18 Collins, *op. cit.*, pp. 63–64.

After 1780 the cost of books, already high, rose further.[19] Well-established publishers were making their formats ever more elaborate and costly, in part because the etiquette of the more elegant members of the feminine audience demanded ostentatious bindings. But new booksellers soon entered the lists and issued reprints, including small, modestly priced pocket editions of the classics. Another successful sales device adopted by the booksellers was the publishing of the classics, poetry, and fiction in newspaperlike serials, printed in weekly installments at sixpence each.[20] After allowing a suitable period for the reader to forget the first version, the less scrupulous booksellers did not hesitate to reissue the trashier of these works, particularly the novels, under new titles, but otherwise unchanged.

Advertising methods ranged from the spectacularly absurd to the eminently reasonable and included, in fact, most of the devices which have remained the stock-in-trade of the publisher's business to this day. There was first the matter of the title. If it was catchy, slick, and sensational, it could not go very far wrong. There were *Beauty Put to Its Shift*, *Adultery Atomized*, *Female Falsehood*, and a thousand other titles like them. Old books in new titles were not limited to the folios; the salvation of many a hard-cover work came about by the simple expedient of removing the title page, replacing it with a more vivid or salacious one, and offering the renovated product as "Second Edition, corrected and improved."[21] A particularly successful device was to endow the author (or authoress) with qualities of fame, mystery, or notoriety, and writers said to have been "banished from the realm" were promoted with special avidity. Endorsements by "men of distinction," too, were a commonplace. On the whole the booksellers maintained close and friendly relations at least with their leading writers, and only one writer seems to have found his dependence on the bookseller sufficiently restraining to endeavor to free himself. In 1765, one John Trusler founded a Literary Society intended to eliminate the middleman and to secure all profits for the author by enabling him to bring out his own works independently. This society probably helped nobody but Trusler himself who managed, at most, to sell only one of his books.[22] Until the middle of the century, a great many books continued to be financed by advance subscriptions, but these were solicited by the bookseller himself, except for an occasional penurious and unknown author who went knocking from door to door.

Despite the thriving enterprises of the leading booksellers in London in the second half of the century, their influence was not particularly strong

[19] Some indications of the comparative cost of books and other leisure activities may be found in the following figures given by H. W. Pedicord, and applicable for the mid-century decades: a seat in the first gallery at the Drury Lane, 24 pence; a pot of beer, 3 pence; cheapest dinner, 3½ pence; a small book, 36 pence.

[20] Collins, *op. cit.*, p. 58.

[21] J. M. S. Tompkins, *The Popular Novel in England: 1770–1800* (London: Constable & Co., Ltd., 1932), p. 7.

[22] *Ibid.*, p. 10.

in the provinces, except indirectly through the circulating library and the itinerant pedlar. Lackington describes a journey to Edinburgh in 1787 during which he made it his business to stop at every town with the twofold objective of keeping his finger on the pulse of his trade and picking up scarce or valuable books. His trip, on the latter count, was a notable failure: not only did he find depressingly few valuable books, but the shelves of the provincial bookshops were littered mainly with trash.[23] When he repeated his trip a few years later, he reported the situation very little changed.

Although an unscrupulous bookseller like Curll might arouse almost unanimous expressions of antagonism, the writers were rather less in agreement on the institution of book publishing itself. Both Samuel Johnson and Oliver Goldsmith, for example, were highly dependent on their publishers; but while Johnson was the nearest thing to grateful, Goldsmith—at best— viewed the situation with one auspicious and one drooping eye. Perhaps, as Krutch suggests,[24] Johnson's favorable disposition was the result of a very happy early experience he had with a bookseller who lent him enough money to keep him from starving. In any case, Johnson was not sparing of his commendations. In one of his *Idler* papers, for instance, he credits the booksellers rather than the schools with "popularising knowledge" among the common orders of England.[25]

In his early career as a writer, Johnson suffered from much keener poverty than did Goldsmith, whose main problem was that his money slipped through his fingers. Johnson's poverty was of a more spartan kind. We know how he wrote *Rasselas:* the book was dashed off in a few days to pay for his mother's funeral expenses. And Boswell reports that even when Johnson was finally paid for his *Dictionary* (first published in 1755) there was scarcely any money left after his expenses in compiling it had been met. Yet he countered Boswell's commiserations with a stout defense of the bookseller, justifying the lack of profit to the author by citing the risks to which the publisher exposed himself.[26]

Goldsmith was no party to this kind of defense. In his *Enquiry into the Present State of Learning* and in two of the letters in *The Citizen of the World*, one of which is devoted entirely to the dubious practices of the bookseller, he examines the bookseller's role in a forthrightly critical spirit. In his *Enquiry* he notes at the outset that the interests of the writer and those of the publisher are diametrically opposed:

> The author, when unpatronized by the great, has naturally recourse to the bookseller. There cannot perhaps be imagined a combination more prejudicial

[23] Lackington, *op. cit.*, p. 286.
[24] Joseph Wood Krutch, *Samuel Johnson* (New York: Holt, Rinehart and Winston, Inc., 1944), p. 35.
[25] A. S. Collins, "The Growth of the Reading Public during the Eighteenth Century," *Review of English Studies*, Vol. II (London: Sidgwick and Jackson, Ltd., 1926), p. 429.
[26] James Boswell, *Life of Samuel Johnson* (London: Oxford University Press, 1953), p. 217.

to taste than this. It is the interest of the one to allow as little for writing, and of the other to write as much as possible.[27]

And he directly attacks some of the more underhanded promotional techniques, particularly the device of attaching impressive status, real or invented, to the authors of books in the process of being promoted.

> [Booksellers] . . . seem convinced, that a book written by vulgar hands, can neither instruct nor improve; none but Kings, Chams and Mandarines can write with a probability of success.[28]

But it is in Letter LI of *The Citizen of the World* that we find the most biting sarcasm. Here Goldsmith describes a bookseller's visit to the ironically ingenious Citizen. The bookseller begins by noting the seasonal appetites of his readers: "I would no more bring out a new work in summer than I would sell pork in the dog days." He next boasts that his works are always new and that at the end of every season the old ones are shipped off to the trunkmakers. If he should have a scarcity of new books, there is no dearth of new title pages: "I have ten new title-pages now around me which only want books to be added to make them the finest things in nature." He is quite willing to make a virtue of his lack of cultural pretensions, modestly confessing that he has no desire to lead the public; on the contrary, the public—and the lowest stratum of the public at that—leads him.[29] Such was the writer's plight vis-à-vis the bookseller trade.

Book Reviews

Book reviewing came into being at the end of the seventeenth century largely as a professional service. The review journals of that time were limited to scientific and philosophical works, and at first their principal purpose was to provide scholars with convenient summaries, in English, of the works of their colleagues abroad. One of the earliest of the eighteenth-century reviews, the *Memoirs of Literature* (1710–1714) published by the Huguenot refugee LaRoche, served as protoytpe for the scholarly review. This periodical contained abstracts of English and foreign works in about equal proportions. Critical comments were rare. In 1725, reputedly with the help of a book publisher, LaRoche produced a second journal, *New Memoirs of Literature*, in which he proved to be more enterprising: this review —usually running to some seventy-five pages an issue—not only abstracted but added comment to the works selected for review. *The Literary Magazine*,

[27] Oliver Goldsmith, *An Inquiry into the Present State of Polite Learning in Europe* (1759) in *The Works of Oliver Goldsmith*, Vol. II of four vols., ed. Peter Cunningham (New York: Harper & Brothers, 1881), pp. 56–57.

[28] Oliver Goldsmith, *The Citizen of the World*, Letter XCIII (London: J. M. Dent & Sons, Ltd., 1934), p. 255.

[29] *Ibid.*, Letter LI, p. 142.

first published in 1735 under the editorship of Ephraim Chambers, covered a wider range of works, though it still limited itself to the "serious." It went further in comment and biographical background than had its predecessors, but was reluctant to set itself up as judge. In the words of its editor, the responsibility of the reviewer is

> . . . to give a faithful account of books which come into his hands. . . . When he affects the air and language of a censor or judge, he invades the undoubted right of the public, which is the only sovereign judge of the reputation of an author, and the merit of his compositions. . . .[30]

The first book review journal to move into the field of popular literature and thus to qualify as an audience-building institution was *The Compendious Library*, a one-hundred page bi-monthly publication printed in Dublin (1751–52). Its steps in this direction, however, were both rare and gingerly. In introducing Fielding's *Amelia*, for example, the reviewer first notes that romances and novels have no place in literary journals, but in this instance he justifies the exception on the grounds that fiction which serves "the reformation of manners and the advancement of virtue" may be allowed, and goes on to remark that "This seems to be one, if not the chief, point from which Mr. Fielding's performance ought to be considered. . . ."[31]

With the founding of the *Monthly Review* by Ralph Griffith in 1749, the book review purporting to cover all releases from the presses got its start. The *Monthly*, which at first had the reputation of being hostile to state and church, soon provoked the founding of a rival journal, the *Critical Review*, published by Archibald Hamilton, edited by Tobias Smollett from 1756–1763, and laying claim to Tory and Church support. Both reviews boasted eminent contributors: Goldsmith contributed twenty pieces to the *Monthly* and Johnson as well as Smollett wrote for the *Critical*. Each journal dealt with the more important books of the month in considerable detail; in a "catalogue" appended to each issue, all other publications of the month were covered in three- or four-page reviews. The objective proclaimed by the *Critical* could be applied to the *Monthly* as well:

> To exhibit a succinct plan of every performance; to point out the most striking beauties and glaring defects; to illustrate remarks with proper quotations, and to convey those remarks in such a manner as might best conduce to the entertainment of the public.[32]

The *Critical* successfully competed with the *Monthly* until 1790, but the *Monthly* managed to survive it well into the middle of the nineteenth century. Although criticized by authors for high-handedness on some occasions, these

[30] Quoted in Walter Graham, *English Literary Periodicals* (New York: Thomas Nelson & Sons, 1930), pp. 204–205.
[31] *Ibid.*, p. 208.
[32] *Ibid.*, p. 213.

reviews and their competitors were inclined rather more to praise than to criticize. Witness, for instance, the prospectus of the *New London Review*, a short-lived publication of the years 1799 to 1800.

> The Plan is suggested, and will be executed in the conviction, that few performances are wholly destitute of merit; that it is more useful to disclose latent excellence, than to exaggerate common faults; that the public taste suffers less from inaccurate writing than from illiberal criticism.

Criticism was to be reserved for the works of writers who went off any one of a number of beaten tracks.

> Though no arrogance will be indulged in this Publication, whatever disturbs the public harmony, insults legal authority, . . . attacks the vital springs and established functions of piety, or in any respect clashes with the sacred forms of decency, however witty, elegant, and well written, can be noticed only in terms of severe and unequivocal reprehension.[33]

The task of covering all new books as they were released became more and more unmanageable. One of the *Monthly* reviewers in 1788 complained:

> The Reviewer of the modern novel is in the situation of Hercules encountering the Hydra—One head lopped off, two or three immediately spring up in its place.[34]

The less conscientious journals solved the problem by a process of selection calculated to please the chief suppliers of their advertising revenue, the booksellers, who distributed review copies only to the journals in which they advertised. These books were reviewed first; time and space permitting, a reviewer might then send his "collector" around to other houses for books possibly deserving of his notice. Thus books often were reviewed months after they were released; in the case of particularly popular publications which were sold out by the time a collector arrived, no reviews appeared at all.[35]

As to the reviewers themselves, the *Monthly* and *Critical* and a number of similar journals had, in addition to eminent or well known contributors, other conscientious ones as well. More often, however, they were poorly paid devisers of makeshift who filled up page after page with direct quotations, selected, as one report has it, after first reading the preface, closing the book, sticking a pin between the leaves at random, opening and transcribing the page so chosen, or even a few pages, and then repeating the operation. One novelist of the 1770's accused the reviewers of passing on the merits and demerits of an author on the basis of the title-page alone. A correspondent

---

[33] *Ibid.*, pp. 224–25.
[34] Quoted in Tompkins, *op. cit.*, p. 15.
[35] *Ibid.*

to the *Gentleman's Magazine* in 1782 accused the reviewers of praising the works of those booksellers who owned shares in their journals and running down all others. Yet another novelist accused them of taking bribes from authors, sometimes even going so far as to let them write their own reviews.[36]

Samuel Johnson, as we might expect from his more favorable attitude toward booksellers, was considerably more indulgent toward the reviewers than was Oliver Goldsmith, who devoted a substantial portion of another of his *Citizen of the World* letters to a castigation of their practices. Goldsmith links the undiscriminating nature of the book reviewer's work to the fact that he is being paid by the bookseller, or, worse still, to the fact that the bookseller himself sometimes writes reviews.

> There are a set of men called answerers of books who take upon them to watch the republic of letters, and distribute reputation by the sheet . . . and to revile the moral character of the man whose writings they cannot injure. Such wretches are kept in pay by some mercenary bookseller, or more frequently, the bookseller himself takes this dirty work off their hands, as all that is required is to be very abusive and very dull.

The Chinese visitor goes on to ask his host whether this is the fate of every writer, to which the Englishman replies:

> Yes . . . except he happened to be born a Mandarin. If he has much money, he may buy a reputation from your book answerers.[37]

Such was the ambiguous state of book-reviewing in the second half of the century. Only with the founding of the *Edinburgh Review* and the *Quarterly* in the early nineteenth century did the book reviewers begin to be free of publisher influence. If they kowtowed at all, it was likely to be in response to political party rather than to publishing house pressures.

III

STAGES OF REACTION

The acid comments of writers about the devices used to promote book sales did not then, as it does not now, effect the development of a literary market. Alexander Pope made dire prophesies about the low level to which literature was sinking; but though he was later to be looked back upon by Henry Fielding as "King Alexandre," the despotic ruler of the literary kingdom, Pope's "subjects" did not join in his protest against changes in the literary scene until much later. On the contrary, many literary figures in the first half of the century founded periodicals especially designed for the

---

[36] *Ibid.*, pp. 15–16.
[37] Goldsmith, *Citizen of the World*, Letter XIII, *op. cit.*, p. 34.

growing middle-class readership, and all of them contributed to magazines or newspapers at one point in their careers.

Their predecessors had been writing for a more homogeneous group; the nobility, the landed gentry, and scholars had composed the bulk of their readers. These readers debated about the "rules" and about good and bad writing along with the writers, just as they debated about good and bad music, architecture, and painting; but they did not distinguish between "high" and "low" art, nor did they discuss differences in aesthetic appreciation among different social segments of the audience. The growth of a broader market did not at first change the nature of these discussions. Each form was presumed to have its own special means of providing pleasure, but the accepted function of all writing remained similar to that summarized by the critic John Dennis in his discussion of "greater" and "less" poetry.

> 1. The greater Poetry is an Art by which a Poet justly and reasonably excites great Passion, that he may please and instruct. . . .
> 2. The less Poetry is an Art by which a Poet excites less Passion for the fore-mention'd Ends. . . .[38]

Not all of John Dennis' contemporaries in the world of letters would have agreed with him that the excitation of great passion is the *sine qua non* of great poetry, but his view that the objective of all writing is to instruct would have evoked little controversy. The writer has a social task; he must use his gift as a means of contributing to the elevation of his readers. And just as the writers' creative gifts were assumed to go hand-in-hand with high moral responsibility, so was it assumed that a public which is responsive to moral teachings must also be capable of aesthetic appreciation. But as writers, readers, and literary products multiplied, initial optimism gave way to a mood very close to pessimism.

Optimism

Very early in the century, the English public had begun to display a powerful bent for reform of manners and morals, not the least manifestation of which was its wide-spread support of organizations such as the Society for the Propagation of Christian Knowledge and the Society for the Reformation of Manners—groups with far-flung networks through which numerous pamphlets and books of a moralizing, neo-Puritan nature were distributed.[39] The ideal of the "gentleman" to which tradespeople and aristocrats alike aspired was not the exaggeratedly ornamental and rakish figure which had become the stereotype of Restoration comedy, but the virtuous Christian

---

[38] John Dennis, *The Grounds of Criticism in Poetry, Critical Works of John Dennis*, Vol. I of two vols., ed. Edward Niles Hooker (Baltimore: The Johns Hopkins Press, 1943), p. 338.
[39] George Sherburn, *The Restoration and the Eighteenth Century*, Pt. III of *A Literary History of England*, ed. Albert C. Baugh (New York: Appleton-Century-Crofts, Inc., 1948), p. 826.

citizen. In such an atmosphere it was taken for granted that the new literary forms would edify and elevate; an aristocrat, such as the Earl of Shaftesbury, and Defoe, a writer who saw himself as the very conscience of the middle and lower-middle classes, could agree with the crusading Sir Richard Blackmore that the responsibility of the writer is to "cultivate the mind with instruction of virtue."[40] To be sure, early magazines and newspapers were often attacked for their political bias—the fittest punishment Pope could conjure up for one of the "low" writers he attacked in the early *Dunciad*, for example, was to have him "[end] at last in the common sink of all such writers, a Political News-paper."[41] And Addison puffed his own journal at the expense of the newspapers, which he gently chided for emphasizing "what passes in Muscovy or Poland," rather than the "knowledge of one's self."[42]

The belief that the inclination for moral uplift so apparent in the audience presupposed a capacity for aesthetic advancement was at first reinforced by the success of the single-essay type of magazine, which combined elegant writing with social and cultural purpose, and which first came into its own with the launching of Steele's *Tatler* in 1709. The *Tatler's* immediate successor, the *Spectator* (1711), founded as a joint enterprise of Steele and Addison, became the most popular journal of its day. In one of the early issues, Addison announced that his publisher had just reported a daily circulation of three thousand copies for the journal, and goes on to estimate with some assurance that each copy had twenty readers (or "hearers," as the case may be).[43] Addison used these figures as a point of departure for a statement of objectives which is not only a succinct summary of the principle of "art as a means of instruction," but a statement of faith in the capacities of his readers.

> It was said of Socrates, that he brought Philosophy down from Heaven, to inhabit among Men; and I shall be ambitious to have it said of me, that I have brought Philosophy out of Closets and Libraries, Schools and Colleges, to dwell in Clubs and Assemblies, at Tea-Tables and in Coffee-Houses.

These worlds of tea-table and coffee house were not, in Addison's view, limited to the gentry and the scholars; in his "fraternity of spectators" he sees tradesmen as well as physicians, "statesmen that are out of business" as well as Fellows of the Royal Society, and all those "blanks of society" who

[40] J. W. H. Atkins, *English Literary Criticism: 17th and 18th Centuries* (London: Methuen & Co., Ltd., 1951), p. 102.

[41] Alexander Pope, *The Dunciad* (A), ed. James Sutherland (London: Methuen & Co., Ltd., 1953), p. 165n. (Vol. V of the Twickenham Edition, general ed. John Butt).

[42] Joseph Addison, *The Spectator*, No. 10, Vol. I, ed. Richard Hurd (London: Everyman, 1950), p. 32.

[43] Since there was no eighteenth-century equivalent to a "continuing index of magazine circulation," these figures are debatable. Samuel Johnson (in *Lives of the Poets*) reckoned, on the basis of stamp tax figures, that the *Spectator* had an average sale of 1,700 daily copies. Addison's editor, Richard Hurd, and others offer average daily estimates closer to those ventured by Addison himself.

until now have been "altogether unfurnished with ideas till the business and conversation of the day has supplied them." Finally he envisages the whole "female world" among his readers, but particularly the "ordinary" woman whose most serious occupation is sewing and whose drudgery is cooking. While there are some women who live in a more "exalted Sphere of Knowledge and Virtue," they are all too few, and he hopes to increase their ranks ". . . by publishing this daily Paper, which I shall always endeavour to make an innocent if not an improving Entertainment, and by that Means at least divert the Minds of my Female Readers from greater Trifles."[44]

That most of what Addison called entertainment was really both morally and aesthetically "improving" is apparent to the modern reader who selects any issue of the *Spectator* at random. Between them, Addison and Steele covered the spectrum of their age from "Puritan Piety" (Addison) to "Miseries of Prostitution" (Steele). Addison informed his readers that he belonged to a club which served as a kind of "advisory committee" for the *Spectator;* in fact, his readers "have the satisfaction to find that there is no rank or degree among them who have not their representative in this club, and that there is always somebody present who will take care of their respective interests." He describes a recent meeting of the club during which he was congratulated by some members and taken to task by others. On occasion, members of this panel try to lobby for their special interests, but Addison hastens to assure the reader that he will remain unmoved by such pressures.

> Having thus taken my Resolutions to march on boldly in the Cause of Virtue and good Sense, and to annoy their Adversaries in whatever Degree or Rank of Men they may be found: I shall be deaf for the future to all the Remonstrances that shall be made to me on this account.[45]

Running through the series (the *Spectator* was published daily until December 6, 1712) is a strong admixture of literary criticism, mostly Addison's, clearly designed to establish a link between the "wit" of the elite classical tradition and the moral truths so in keeping with the ethos of the rising middle class.[46]

That a moral reformation was inseparable from an aesthetic one became an assumption increasingly difficult to support. If it is true that the *Spectator* eventually attained a readership of twenty or thirty thousand, perhaps there came a point in eighteenth-century England when the literary development of many persons hung in the balance, attracted to the refinements of an Addison who did not write down to his readers, and not yet seduced by the sensational or sentimental devices to be utilized by his successors. If so, it was for a relatively short period, and subsequent events have blurred the evidence. Historians of literature credit the essayists with his literary achieve-

---

[44] Addison, *Spectator*, No. 10, *loc. cit.*, pp. 31–33.
[45] Addison, *Spectator*, No. 34, *loc. cit.*, p. 104.
[46] Addison, *Spectator*, No. 63, *loc. cit.*, p. 196.

ment, but suggest that they were victims of self-delusion if they believed that the moral concerns of their readers were in any way associated with a capacity for—or interest in—aesthetic growth. What Addison and the other essayists hoped for was a rapprochement between English classicism and middle class morality; what they paved the way for was compromise.[47]

Before the middle of the century the public was beginning to make its preferences abundantly clear. Defoe's *Robinson Crusoe*, which was mainly read as an adventure story, became an instantaneous bestseller seven years after the last copy of the *Spectator* was printed, and it went through numerous editions and translations during the next thirty years. In 1750, *The Oeconomy of Human Life*[48] was published, went through twenty-one editions in the eighteenth century (several more than that in the nineteenth), and was translated into six languages. This book, distinguished for its common-placeness of thought, achieved unprecedented popularity and has been characterized as testimony to "the insatiable appetite of the eighteenth century for moral platitude."[49] In the same year in which the *Spectator* was founded, Shaftesbury had written, "Thus are the arts and virtues mutually friends,"[50] but that the mid-century audience thought differently is further attested by the fate of one of the *Spectator*'s more eminent imitators, *The Rambler*. This bi-weekly periodical was founded by Dr. Johnson in the same year in which *The Oeconomy* achieved its spectacular success. Like the *Spectator* four decades earlier, *The Rambler* aimed at intellectual and aesthetic as well as moral refinements. But except for one issue written by Samuel Richardson (Number 97) the peak circulation of *The Rambler* was five hundred, or one-sixth of the circulation claimed for the *Spectator* after its tenth day of publication.[51]

Opportunity and Opportunism

While the hundred imitations of the *Spectator* published between 1712 and 1750 were remarkably short-lived, the *Gentleman's Magazine*, some fifty pages of news and entertainment features, went into five editions at its first issue in 1731. Twenty years or so later Johnson wrote of it as one of the most lucrative publications (it then had a circulation of fifteen thousand), and its manager at the end of the century, John Nicols, reported it as still a highly successful enterprise.[52]

With the public expressing its interests by buying certain kinds of literary products and by not buying others, the publisher, bookseller, and writer

---

[47] Emile Legouis and Louis Cazamian, *A History of English Literature* (New York: The Macmillan Company, 1933), p. 738.

[48] The authorship is disputed—some historians credit Dodsley, others Chesterfield, with the work.

[49] B. Sprague Allen, *Tides in the English Taste*, Vol. II of two vols. (Cambridge, Mass.: Harvard University Press, 1937), pp. 36–37.

[50] Quoted in Allen, *op. cit.*, Vol. I, p. 87.

[51] Graham, *op. cit.*, p. 120.

[52] *Ibid.*, pp. 152ff.

with a knack for gauging public opinion could become, if not wealthy, certainly most comfortable. There were five thousand people subsisting by writing, printing, publishing, and marketing papers in the London of 1722,[53] and those who earned a living in the literary market by the middle of the century would probably have to be reckoned in the tens of thousands. It was no longer necessary to be a "man of letters" or a university graduate to be a professional writer. Housewives and bookkeepers who wanted to make a few extra pounds now wrote novels, as did country clergymen who had formerly dabbled in botany or archeology. Few of these writers felt any need to defend either their works or their profits, and few apparently were concerned about literary standards.

No longer were elegant and polished "wits" and intellectuals endeavoring to search out truth, beauty, and reason for themselves and a few readers much like themselves. Instead middle-class novelists such as Richardson and Fielding were writing for their social peers. They, and Smollett and Sterne after them, may have been concerned with truth and reason, at least insofar as these values were related to morality, but they were little concerned with beauty. Their world, as Leslie Stephen put it, had become that of "the middle-class John Bull . . . the generation which listens to Wesley must have also a secular literature, which, whether sentimental as with Richardson or representing common sense with Fielding, must at any rate correspond to solid substantial matter-of-fact motives, intelligible to the ordinary Briton of the time."[54] Fielding himself, satirist though he often was, offered a summation of this solemn atmosphere. Denouncing those writers who merely amuse or shock, he made it clear that he was even not "afraid to mention Rabelais, and Aristophanes himself," among those who have ridiculed the only means to moral health and wisdom: "sobriety, modesty, decency, virtue and religion. . . ." He then went on to state a precept which was adhered to—with varying degree of sincerity—by most writers of his age.

> In the exercise of the mind, as well as in the exercise of the body, diversion is a secondary consideration, and designed only to make that agreeable, which is at the same time useful, to such noble purposes as health and wisdom.[55]

Indeed, so ingrained were these moral precepts that the majority of mid-century writers quite uncalculatingly fulfilled the reader's need to be convinced that he was being improved while being amused, diverted, or horrified. Adults told themselves that novel reading was instructive for young people, and the upper classes were persuaded that reading or playgoing was uplifting for the lower. The actor, writer, and producer Garrick, in his *Bon Ton*, lightly ridiculed such rationalizations in a conversation between master and servant.

[53] Laprade, *op. cit.*, p. 249.
[54] Stephen, *op. cit.*, p. 219.
[55] Henry Fielding, *The Covent Garden Journal*, No. 10 in *The Works of Henry Fielding*, Vol. X of ten vols., ed. James P. Browne (London: Bickers & Sons, Ltd., 1903), p. 26.

Sir John: Why, what did I promise you?

Davy: That I should take sixpen'oth at one of the theaters tonight, and a shilling place at the other to-morrow.

Sir John: Well, well, so I did. Is it a moral piece, Davy?

Davy: Oh! Yes, and written by a clergyman; it is called the "Rival Cannanites; or the Tragedy of Braggadocia."

Sir John: Be a good lad, and I won't be worse than my word; there's money for you.[56]

A few writers, particularly lady novelists writing for the education of young girls, seem to have found it unnecessary to follow the caveat "to amuse," with apparently no great loss in sales. Parents of the innocents saw to it that they kept such books as Mrs. Chapone's *Letters on the Improvement of the Mind*—consisting of two hundred pages of solid advice on religion, the Bible, the affections, the temper, and politeness—constantly by their sides. According to the moralizing novelist Hannah More, Mrs. Chapone's work "forms the rising age," and another contemporary, Samuel Hoole, has the heroine in his *Aurelia* envisage an ideal woman as one whose dressing table features Mrs. Chapone's volume:

> On the plain toilet, with no trophies gay
> *Chapone's* instructive volume open lay.[57]

At the other extreme were the sensational novelists who loaded their works with sex and sadism, inserting, as a kind of afterthought, a warning line or two, pointing out to the reader that his, or more frequently her, fate will be a ghastly one if he or she slips from the path of virtue. Under the guise of "satiric indignation," revelations of vice and licentiousness in high and low places were exploited in novels, on the stage, and in the magazines as well as in the press—some true, some offered under the pretext of being true.[58] Almost any device "enabled authors to pass in satiric review various classes and professions in corrupt society."[59] Charles Johnstone (1719–1800) suggested—with disarming candor in view of the fact that he himself was the author of *Chrysal*, one of the more notorious of these exposés—the extent which the moralizing note was merely an excuse for feeding the appetite for prurient detail.

There cannot be a stronger argument against the charge of degeneracy in moral virtue and religion brought against the present age, than the avidity with which

[56] Quoted in Pedicord, *op. cit.*, p. 31.

[57] Quoted in Chauncey B. Tinker, *The Salon and English Letters* (New York: The Macmillan Company, 1915), pp. 177–79.

[58] An idea of the topics covered is conveyed by the titles of a few of these novels: *Love-Letters between a Nobleman and his Sister; The Unnatural Mother; or Innocent Love Persecuted*, being the history of the fatal consequences that attended the . . . passion of a gentleman . . . and a young Lady; *The Cruel Mistress*, being the genuine trial of E. B. and her daughter for the murder of Jane Buttersworth, their servantmaid, etc.; *The Fatal Connexion, Colonel Digby and Miss Stanley.*

[59] Sherburn, *op. cit.*, p. 1031.

all works exposing the breaches of them by the unerring proof of facts, are read by all people.[60]

In his preface to the first edition of the *Dunciad* (1728) Pope had made it clear through the words of a fictitious commentator on his work ("Martinus Scriblerus") that he was disturbed both by the pedants and fops of the literary world and by the sheer numbers of authors who cropped out all over the country once paper became cheap and plentiful in supply.

> He [our Poet] lived in those days, when (after providence had permitted the Invention of Printing as a scourge for the sins of the learned) Paper also became so cheap, and printers so numerous, that a deluge of authors cover'd the land: . . . our author . . . did conceive it an endeavour well worthy an honest satyrist, to dissuade the dull and punish the malicious, *the only way that was left*. In that public-spirited view he laid the plan of this Poem. . . .[61]

Thus Pope, in the early third of the century of the Enlightenment, served as the conscience of conservatism. In challenging the idea of technical progress as a good in itself, he anticipated the coming debate about the defensive position of the creative individual in a mass society. His was not an article of faith but an article of doubt, and towards the end of the first edition he issues a strong warning not to underestimate these changes and the people who were capitalizing on them.

> Do not, gentle reader, rest too secure in thy contempt of the Instruments for such a revolution in learning, or despise such weak agents as have been described in our poem, but remember what the *Dutch* stories somewhere relate, that a great part of their Provinces was once overflow'd, by a small opening made in one of their dykes by a single *Water-Rat*.

He concludes the poem with a prophecy: "Art after Art goes out, and all is Night./ . . . Thy hand great Dulness! lets the curtain fall,/ And universal Darkness covers all."[62]

Fourteen years later, in the preface to *The New Dunciad* (1742), Pope writes that he is setting out "to declare the *Completion* of the *Prophecies* mention'd at the end of the former [Book]."[63] By that time his fellow authors had begun to wonder whether the first edition, outlet for injured professional pride though it may have been, did not also have some of the character of a true prediction.

Rising Dismay

After the middle of the century the writer faced two problems which had not previously struck him as matters for concern. Was the expanding audi-

---

[60] Quoted in Tompkins, *op. cit.*, p. 47.

[61] Pope, *Dunciad, loc. cit.*, pp. 49–50.

[62] Pope, *Dunciad, loc. cit.*, p. 192n.

[63] Quoted in Ian Jack, *Augustan Satire, 1660–1750* (Oxford: The Clarendon Press, 1952), p. 119.

ence for literary products (now beginning to reach into the lower classes as well)[64] in fact capable of, or interested in, being "improved" either aesthetically *or* morally by means of the written and spoken word which it was consuming in ever-greater volume? And what was this new state of affairs —in which he depended for his livelihood upon pleasing this broad public instead of one or two aristocratic or political patrons—doing to the integrity of the artist?

The writers who became most disturbed by these problems were not members of the aristocracy who might have been expected to look with some distaste on the cultural encroachments of the nouveau-riche and the tradespeople. Nor were they embittered men who had failed to achieve recognition. They were those writers, mainly of middle-class origin, who had supported themselves by producing serious works for the very public about which they were now becoming skeptical. The *Spectator*, the *Tatler*, and most of their imitators had tried to show these new readers what constituted good taste—in morals, manners, music, architecture, furniture, and landscape gardening as well as in literature. For thirty or more years, the best had been made available to all who could read. Those who had offered it, Garrick, Goldsmith, Johnson, Fielding, and others, began to echo Pope's early and not very exalted opinion of public taste. He had worried about fashions in taste, "snob appeal," and the fickleness of the public.

> Some ne'er advance a Judgment of their own
> But catch the spreading notion of the Town.

> Some judge of authors' names, not works, and then
> Nor praise nor blame the writings, but the men.

> Some praise at morning what they blame at night;
> But always think the last opinion right.[65]

Now Fielding found the bulk of mankind "clearly void of any degree of taste" and suggested that the common denominator of the audience of this day was very low indeed.

> It is a quality in which they advance very little beyond a state of infancy. The first thing a child is fond of in a book is a picture; the second is a story; and the third is a jest. Here, then, is the true Pons Asinorum, which few readers ever get over.[66]

---

[64] It is almost impossible to pinpoint the moment when the reading public began to include a significant number of the working classes, but most literary historians put it roughly around 1760–70. Tompkins, for example, in *The Popular Novel in England: 1770–1800*, reports that novel-reading had replaced story-telling in the farmhouses, and that in town "the milliner's apprentice, who turns up in contemporary satire with the regularity of Macaulay's schoolboy, spared twopence at the library for a volume of *The Fatal Compliance* or *Anecdotes of a Convent*."

[65] Pope, *Essay on Criticism* in *The Best of Pope*, ed. George Sherburn (New York: The Ronald Press Company, 1940), pp. 64–65.

[66] Fielding, *loc. cit.*, Vol. X, p. 28.

And from a less detached viewpoint a Mr. Jackson, who wrote essays but was primarily a designer and painter of wallpaper in Battersea, berated the level of public taste in a piece on engraving and printing.

> Persons who should prefer the gaudy and unmeaning Papers (so generally met with) . . . would prefer a Fan to a picture of Raphael. . . . It seems also, as if there was a great Reason to suspect wherever one sees such preposterous Furniture, that the Taste in Literature of the Person who directed it was very deficient, and that it would prefer Tom D'Urfy [writer of scurrilous ballads and melodrama in the first quarter of the eighteenth century] to *Shakespeare, Sir Richard Blackmore* to *Milton* . . . an Anagrammatist to Virgil. . . .[67]

He concludes, of course, with a commercial "snob appeal": the reader of his essay could demonstrate his sensitive taste in literature and on all other counts by buying Mr. Jackson's "classical" wallpaper.

Doubts about the capacities of their audience forced writers in turn to face the problem of the effects of a broadening market on the writer himself. Pope, himself an author living from the sale of his works, despite his general pessimism about the quality of much contemporary writing, was convinced that the literary genius would eventually win public support, and, conversely, that the writer who did not live well must also be dull. "To prove them *poor,*" wrote an anonymous contributor to *Mist's Journal* in 1728, Pope "asserts that they are *dull;* and to prove them *dull* he asserts they are *poor.*"[68] His successors were not so sure; Johnson, Fielding, and Goldsmith were writing works that were certainly not "dull" in Pope's meaning of the word for an audience which made it increasingly clear that it was not capable of awarding the good writers with more popularity than the bad. How, they asked, does the author's conviction that his readers are both fickle and debased in their taste affect his integrity and creativity, and how does the book and periodical publishers' insistence on quantity affect the level of the writer's work?

For Oliver Goldsmith, who contributed to at least ten periodicals and was responsible for innumerable compilations and translations which he undertook in order to supplement the income derived from his other works, these were not academic questions. He debated them with all the fervor of a man who feels his professional reputation at stake. Consciously or otherwise, the writer is influenced by the preferences of his audience; it may mean, as Goldsmith said, in his early essay *Upon Taste,* that

> . . . genius, instead of growing like a vigorous tree, extending its branches on every side . . . resembles a stunted yew, tortured into some wretched form, projecting no shade, displaying no flower, diffusing no fragrance, yielding no fruit, and affording *nothing but a barren conceit* for the amusement of the idle spectator.[69] (Italics supplied.)

[67] Quoted in Allen, *op. cit.,* Vol. I, pp. 243–44.
[68] Quoted in James Sutherland, *op. cit.,* p. xlviii.
[69] Quoted in Allen, *op. cit.,* Vol. II, p. 189.

In the course of his prolific years to come, Goldsmith reflected often upon the ethical and artistic conflicts of the writer dependent on popular preferences and answered his own question whether genius must now produce only "barren conceit" alternately yes and no. His first original work, *Enquiry into the Present State of Polite Learning in Europe* (1759), explored the dilemma in which the writer for a growing market found himself. In this book, and in his *Citizen of the World* letters written during the next few years, he managed to place himself squarely on both horns of the dilemma.

For example, on the question of financial dependence on a paying audience, he wrote in Chapter VIII of the *Enquiry:*

> A long habit of writing for bread thus turns the ambition of every author at last into avarice . . . he despairs of applause and turns to profit. . . . Thus the man who, under the protection of the great, might have done honor to humanity, when only patronized by the bookseller, becomes a thing little superior to the fellow who works at the press.[70]

A few years later (in the meantime he had published his short-lived periodical *The Bee*, written a life of Voltaire as hack-work for the booksellers, and received a much-needed advance of sixty pounds, presumably with the help of Samuel Johnson, on the *Vicar of Wakefield*) he wrote a paean of thanks that the patronage of the public had replaced the "protection of the great." The writer comes into his own as the crucial shift from Patron to Public is completed:

> At present the few poets of England no longer depend on the Great for subsistence, they have now no other patrons but the public, and *the public*, collectively considered, *is a good and generous master.* . . . A writer of real merit now may easily be rich if his heart be set only on fortune: and for those who have no merit, it is but fit that such should remain in merited obscurity. (Italics supplied.)

Not only will he reap his due rewards; for the first time, he can now be self-respecting and independent:

> He may now refuse an invitation to dinner, without fearing to incur his patron's displeasure, or to starve by remaining at home. He may now venture to appear in company with just such clothes as other men generally wear, and talk even to princes, with all the conscious superiority of wisdom. Though he cannot boast of fortune here, yet he can bravely assert the dignity of independence.[71]

Or again, in the *Enquiry*, he had written that the author who turns to the bookseller because he can no longer find patronage gets paid for quantity and not for quality; that "in these circumstances the author bids adieu to fame, writes for bread . . ." with "phlegmatic apathy."[72] In the ninety-third

[70] Goldsmith, *Enquiry into the Present State*, *loc. cit.*, p. 57.
[71] Goldsmith, *Citizen of the World*, Letter LXXXIV, *op. cit.*, p. 234.
[72] Goldsmith, *Enquiry into the Present State*, *loc. cit.*

Citizen of the World letter, on the other hand, he pointed out that "almost all of the excellent productions . . . that have appeared here [in England] were purely the offspring of necessity" and went on to recommend fasting for the sharpening of genius.

> Believe me, my friend, hunger has a most amazing faculty of sharpening the genius; and he who with a full belly, can think like a hero, after a course of fasting, shall rise to the sublimity of a demi-god.[73]

Johnson, usually less torn by conflicts between writer and market, raised similar questions. Who is to judge the merit of an author, he asked at about the same time that Goldsmith voiced concern about the fate of the literary genius, and how is he to find his way to recognition in all this "miscellany"? In discussing this problem, Johnson first described some of the needs and predispositions of a "mass" audience.

> He that endeavours after fame by writing, solicits the regard of a multitude fluctuating in pleasures, or immersed in business, without time for intellectual amusements; he appeals to judges, prepossessed by passions, or corrupted by prejudices, which preclude their approbation of any new performance. Some are too indolent to read anything, till its reputation is established; others too envious to promote that fame which gives them pain by its increase.

He then went on to develop a catalogue of audience reaction.

> What is new is opposed, because most are unwilling to be taught; and what is known is rejected, because it is not sufficiently considered, that men more frequently require to be reminded than informed. The learned are afraid to declare their opinion early, lest they should put their reputation in hazard; the ignorant always imagine themselves giving some proof of delicacy, when they refuse to be pleased. . . .

If an author achieves recognition, he concludes, it will certainly not be attributable to the discernment of his readers:

> . . . and he that finds his way to reputation through all these obstructions, must acknowledge that he is indebted to other causes besides his industry, his learning, or his wit.[74]

Such an audience cannot serve as judge; the writer therefore has to examine the literary scene himself. He must look at the works which are being purchased at so great a rate, and he must try to determine why the public had not soared upward on the two wings of morality and beauty as Addison had hoped they would, and as Pope, for all his self-assurance about the recognition of his own works, had feared they would not.

---

[73] Goldsmith, *Citizen of the World*, Letter XCIII, *op. cit.*, p. 256.
[74] Johnson, *The Rambler*, No. 2, *British Essayists*, XVI, 76.

IV

INDICTMENT

In asking themselves what effect the growing market for printed goods was having on the moral, intellectual, and aesthetic development of the individual and upon the country as a whole, English literary men probably became the first group consciously to face the problem of culture in modern society. Examining the scene about him, the eighteenth-century critic was not so much concerned with the new format in which literature was being produced, such as popular magazines, newspapers, cheap editions or reprints of books; this concern was to develop later, when these new literary shapes had become firmly entrenched features of modern society. He tended, rather, to focus upon changes in content which resulted from the fact that many writers were deliberately catering to the lower levels of taste in the growing audience. The term "popular writer," in the derogatory sense, came into usage for the first time in this period. Oliver Goldsmith used it in his *Enquiry* when he expressed fear that "affectation in some popular writer" would lead "others to vicious imitation."[75] Pope did not actually use the word "popular" in his *Dunciad*, but he argued that the drive for popularity accounted for the low level to which many writers of his time had sunk.[76]

Marked changes in the content of the drama and the novel took place in the first half of the century, changes which amounted to a wholehearted endorsement of character-types of the emerging middle class. The genre which replaced Restoration drama, sentimental or "weeping" comedy, centered around the professional and domestic problems of middle-class characters. The hero of these realistic dramas was likely to be an everyday sort of person who was a model of virtue, and the villain an everyday sort of person with familiar and commonplace vices. These changes may have contributed to the respectability of the theater but, according to at least one well-qualified observer, they also made it considerably less amusing. Fielding declared that "in banishing humour from the stage, which was tantamount to banishing human nature, the dramatist made the stage as dull as the drawing-room."[77] This shift from socially elevated characters to city merchants and apprentices in private life—a shift epitomized by the domestic tragedies of George Lillo in the 1730's—brought about a notable change in the experience of the audience: it was now possible for the ordinary theater-goer to identify with the heroes and heroines on the stage. Restoration dramatists had created half-real people acting out unreal situations; in the new dramas of middle-class life, realism and believability were para-

---

[75] Goldsmith, *Enquiry into the Present State, loc. cit.*, pp. 47ff.
[76] Pope, *Dunciad* (B), *loc. cit.*, pp. 272–73.
[77] Fielding, quoted in Ernest A. Baker, *The History of the English Novel*, Vol. IV of ten vols. (London: Witherby, 1934), p. 15.

mount goals.[78] This possibility of identification through straightforward imitation was the basis for many moral (as contrasted with aesthetic) anxieties which began to harass the intellectuals of the mid-century as they attempted to assess and to come to terms with new literary trends.

It was the novel that stimulated most of the uneasiness about the consequences of identification with fictional characters. Many more novels were written in a year than there were plays produced, and for many it was surely easier to read novels than to attend the theater. A small book, to be sure, cost about three times as much as a seat in the upper gallery at one of the licensed theaters; but books could be borrowed from friends and from circulating libraries, and they could be read and re-read at the convenience of the reader. Not only was the novel a convenient form of recreation, but its length and considerably less rigorous construction made it more suitable to the limning of the details and nuances of middle-class life. In general, its contents differed from the romance of the seventeenth and early eighteenth centuries in much the same way as sentimental comedy differed from the Restoration drama. Realism of character and situation was, as Samuel Johnson pointed out in his *Rambler* essay, "The Modern Form of Romance," the distinguishing feature of the new fiction.

> The works of fiction, with which the present generation seems more particularly delighted, are such as exhibit life in its true state, diversified only by accidents that daily happen in the world, and influenced by passions and qualities which are really to be found in conversing with mankind.

Johnson goes on to explain how this stress on realism creates a new problem for the writer. He can no longer rely on his book-learning alone, secure in the knowledge that he is better informed than most of his readers. He must become an astute observer of the world of people around him. Should he make a mistake, every "common reader" will know it, because "our present writers" are "engaged in portraits, of which every one knows the original, and can detect any deviation from exactness of resemblance."[79]

Dangerous Realism

Restoration comedy had mirrored the foibles of the aristocracy with a light but cutting touch, containing no small amount of caricature. The playgoer or the reader may well have been amused by the wit and elegance of these clever plays, but he would have been hard put to identify with their highly stylized characters. Moreover, the heroic romance of the same period was no less stylized and distant from everyday life. As Johnson remarked, it had discouraged identification by resorting to machines and other conven-

[78] F. W. Bateson, *English Comic Drama: 1700–1750* (Oxford: The Clarendon Press, 1929), p. 8.

[79] Johnson, *The Rambler*, No. 4, *British Essayists*, XVI, 82–83.

ient but far-fetched expedients such as "giants to snatch a lady away from the nuptial rites" and "knights to bring her back from captivity."[80] Johnson's analysis of the problems raised by the new stress on realism is so pertinent that his essay on the modern novel warrants closer reading. He asks the question whether, in their eagerness to portray reality, contemporary novelists might not so closely interweave the reprehensible with the exemplary qualities of a character that the reader will become as favorably disposed to evil as to virtue.

> Many writers, for the sake of following nature, so mingle good and bad qualities in their principal personages, that they are both equally conspicuous; and as we accompany them through their adventures with delight, and are led by degrees to interest ourselves in their favor, we lose the abhorrence of their faults, because they do not hinder our pleasure, or, perhaps, regard them with some kindness for being united with so much merit.

In exploring this dilemma Johnson points out that there have been, in the course of history, some "splendidly wicked" men whose crimes were never viewed as "perfectly detestable" because their often agreeable personalities cast a pleasing aura about them. He protests against true-to-life portrayal of such characters because they are "the great corrupters of the world, and their resemblance ought no more to be preserved than the art of murdering without pain."

For all his scorn of the *deus ex machina*, Johnson regretted the passing of those highly unrealistic romances which he had read in his youth.

> In the romances formerly written, every transaction and sentiment was so remote from all that passes among men, that the reader was in very little danger of making any applications to himself; the virtues and crimes were equally beyond his sphere of activity; and he amused himself with heroes and with traitors, deliverers and persecutors, as with beings of another species . . . who had neither faults nor excellence in common with himself.

Johnson formulated very precisely the processes of identification and imitation encouraged by the new realistic fiction.

> But when an adventurer is levelled with the rest of the world, and acts in such scenes of the universal drama as may be the lot of any other man, young spectators fix their eyes upon him with closer attention, and hope, by observing his behavior and success, to regulate their own practices, when they shall be engaged in the like part.

While such processes could have unhappy consequences, Johnson believed that identification with fictional characters might be put to constructive use and realistic stories made a boon to the educator: "these familiar histories may perhaps be made of greater use than the solemnities of professed

[80] *Ibid.*

morality, and convey the knowledge of vice and virtue with more efficacy than axioms and definitions." Perhaps, Johnson concluded (with notably greater emphasis on effects than on artistic integrity), the author should manipulate reality a bit. Virtue should be judiciously exalted, and vice, while not to be eliminated altogether, should always be portrayed in a way which leaves the reader with a feeling of repulsion.

> In narratives, where historical veracity has no place, I cannot discover why there should not be exhibited the most perfect idea of virtue . . . the highest and surest that humanity can reach . . . which . . . may, by conquering some calamities and enduring others, teach us what we may hope and what we can perform. Vice, for vice is necessary to be shown, should always disgust.

As though he were formulating a self-regulatory code for novel-writers, he concludes with a plea for what amounts to "all-white or all-black" character portrayals:[81]

> . . . nor should the graces of gayety, or the dignity of courage, be so united with it [vice] as to reconcile it to the mind: wherever it appears, it should raise hatred by the malignity of its practices, and contempt by the meanness of its stratagems; for while it is supported by either parts or spirits, it will be seldom heartily abhorred. . . . There are thousands of readers . . . willing to be thought wicked, if they may be allowed to be wits.[82]

Johnson was not alone in his complaints about the abuses of realism. Lady Mary Wortley Montagu, a writer of charming letters though not a professional critic, touched upon the matter in a private correspondence. Referring to the realism of the character portrayals in Richardson's *Clarissa* and *Pamela*, she singled them out as the "two books that will do more general mischief than the works of Lord Rochester."[83] And Oliver Goldsmith went even further than Johnson in recommending that novels be especially adapted to youth. In an essay on education, he expressed concern about the effects of true-to-life characterizations and advocated that

> . . . there be some men of wit employed to compose books that might equally interest the passions of our youth . . . to be explicit as possible, the old story of Whittington, were his cat left out, might be more serviceable to the tender mind than either Tom Jones, Joseph Andrews or an hundred others. . . .

---

[81] Johnson's criticism of Shakespeare was based largely on the grounds that he did not do any judicious weighing of good against evil in his characterizations. In the preface to his edition of Shakespeare he writes that on the contrary Shakespeare "carries his persons indifferently through right and wrong and at the close dismisses them without further care, and leaves their examples to operate by chance. This fault the barbarity of his age cannot extenuate; for it is always a writer's duty to make the world better. . . ."

[82] Johnson, *The Rambler*, No. 4, *loc. cit.*, pp. 84–88.

[83] Mary Wortley Montagu, *Complete Works*, ed. Lord Wharncliffe, two vols. (Paris: 1837), pp. 100–105.

Instead of suggesting that professional writers adapt their works to the educational needs of youth, Goldsmith proposed that schoolmasters be put to work composing novels:

> Were our schoolmasters, if any of them have sense enough to draw up such a work, thus employed, it would be much more serviceable to their pupils, than all the grammars and dictionaries they may publish these ten years.[84]

While both Johnson and Goldsmith distinguished between mature and immature readers—their worries about the effects of realism were largely confined to youth—they did not draw hard and fast lines between various levels of fiction. Moral problems, they felt, were posed by all realistic fiction, whether the work of a great or hack writer.

Dr. Johnson, while on one occasion he had recommended that characters be thoroughly good or thoroughly evil, nevertheless endorsed realism, though it necessarily involved the picturing of wickedness. In his *Lives of the Poets*, published nearly thirty years after the *Rambler* essay on fiction, he insists that the writer, while occasionally justified in gratifying the audience by making things pleasant, is bound also to show life as it really is.[85]

True-to-life portrayals could easily become boring, and writers resorted to many devices for sustaining interest in the ordinary people and situations portrayed in their novels and plays. Two methods for insuring audience appeal were full descriptions of tender sentiments and, at the other extreme, detailed spellings-out of scenes of aggression, violence, or horror. Very often, in the manner of the Hollywood motion picture, these two sets of attractions were combined in the same production, always making sure that the sensitive hero was the victim and not the perpetrator of aggression.

These devices for offsetting boredom confronted the creative writer with a number of additional problems.

First, does not the realistic portrayal of *crime and violence*, of which the English audience was considered to be inordinately fond, both reflect and encourage sadism in the audience?

Second, when everyday characters are made less boring by a generous endowment of *sentimentality*, are not the heads of the readers filled with romantic notions which will stand them in no good stead as they go about the business of making a living (or marrying a man) in the workaday world? Worse still, may they not use identification with the unreal world of emotion as a means of escape from the exigencies of everyday life?

[84] Goldsmith, *The Bee*, No. 6 in *Citizen of the World*, *op. cit.*, p. 399.
[85] Johnson, *Lives of the English Poets*, Vol. II of two vols. (New York: Derby and Jackson, 1857), p. 135.
This does not mean a victory of realism over moralism in Dr. Johnson's approach to literature. As René Wellek points out in his *History of Modern Criticism*, the two strands—together with an element of abstractionism—were closely interwoven in all of Johnson's criticism but "more frequently the moralist is dominant to the exclusion and even detriment of the critic." Vol. I of two vols. to date (London: Jonathan Cape, Ltd., 1955), p. 83.

Third, perhaps again because of the very familiarity of these realistic characters and situations, the audience began to attach increasing importance to novelty and variety as values in themselves. How, asked the writer, can we keep this desire for sensationalism from even further debasing the taste of the public?

Fourth, with an avalanche of mass-produced material which makes few demands on the reader and not many more on the writer, is there not a very real danger that the world of letters may be entering a period of *mediocrity?*

Crime and Violence

Though the modern media have more graphic, and more ubiquitous, representational devices at their disposal than did those of the eighteenth century, descriptions of sadism and brutality did not spring full-blown from the comic book or the television set. As a matter of fact, some of the "horror" novels which enjoyed popularity in the last three decades of the century make those "comic" books of sex and sadism which are sold from under the counter today look pallid by comparison.

The genre called "Gothic" romance, foreshadowed by Walpole's *Castle of Otranto* (1764), reached its peak a quarter of a century later in M. G. Lewis' *The Monk*, a romance built almost entirely around scenes of sadism, sensuality, and fright.[86] Lewis' work rapidly went through a number of editions and set a new standard for brutality which was to be imitated in most of the English Gothic novels to come. But while these horror tales stirred up small furors at the time of publication, the peak of popular as well as intellectual reaction was not reached until after 1800.

The debate over crime and violence in the drama, however, was waged with vigor throughout the eighteenth century. Concern about the murders and tortures which had long been commonplace on the stage had formed part of the objections to the theater raised by the neo-Puritans. But in general neither they nor their successors discriminated between profanity and lewdness on the one hand and criminal or brutal behavior on the other. Furthermore, when Defoe and others referred to the stage as a "nursery of crime," they were as much distressed about the behavior of the audience and about the "corrupting" environs of the theater as they were about what took place on the stage. Among less moralistic critics, aggression and violence on the stage were the main objects of concern. Even Addison, who was rather tolerant of the excesses of the opera and stage, raised the issue:

> But among all our Methods of moving Pity or Terror, there is none so absurd and barbarous, and what more exposes us to the Contempt and Ridicule of our Neighbours, than that dreadful butchering of one another which is so very frequent upon the *English* stage.

[86] Mrs. Radcliffe's *The Mysteries of Udolpho* was perhaps the outstanding novel of suspense of the period; in contrast to M. G. Lewis, Mrs. Radcliffe explained away the supernatural by rational means and relied on curiosity rather than fear as the main appeal of her work.

He sympathizes with French critics who had pointed to the sight of "Men stabbed, poisoned, racked or impaled" on the English stage as "the Sign of a cruel Temper" in the English national character. Addison goes on to decry the favorite climax of the stage tragedies of his day, wherein every prop for murder and torture is used in a grand free-for-all of mass slaughter.

> It is indeed very odd, to see our Stage strewed with Carcases in the last Scene of a Tragedy; and to observe in the Ward-robe of the Play-house several Daggers, Poinciards, Wheels, Bowls for Poison and many other Instruments of Death.[87]

But in spite of such disdain, the English audience's love of blood and violence continued to be fed. In the mid-thirties, Henry Fielding published his skit, *Pasquin*, which ridiculed several of the dramatic excesses of the day, not least the addiction to slaughter and poison. Twenty years later, Oliver Goldsmith observed that ". . . death and tenderness are leading passions of every modern buskined hero; this moment they embrace, and the next stab, mixing daggers and kisses in every period."[88] And David Hume, in his treatise *Of Tragedy*, excoriated such realistic portrayals of horror because they interfere with the main objectives of tragedy.

> An action, represented in tragedy, may be too bloody and atrocious. . . . Such is that action represented in the *Ambitious Stepmother*, where a venerable old man, raised to the heights of fury and despair, rushes against a pillar, and striking his head upon it, besmears it all over with mingled brains and gore. The *English* theatre abounds too much with such images.[89]

Unlike present-day discussion of this topic, no eighteenth-century critic seems to have condoned fictional or dramatic portrayals of "crime and violence," and reference to the Aristotelian concept of catharsis is in this connection (though not in connection with suffering from other causes) conspicuously absent.

Sentimentality

Goldsmith, in his *Essay on the Theatre*, reports the reaction of "a friend" to the unembroidered presentation of middle-class city-types and their practical problems. The friend left the theater in the middle of a play about a money-lender, remarking, "it is indifferent to me whether he be turned out of his counting house on Fish Street Hill, since he will still have enough left to open shop in St. Giles's. . . ."[90] While the drama tried to counteract such

[87] Addison, *Spectator*, No. 44, *loc. cit.*, p. 133.
[88] Goldsmith, *Citizen of the World*, Letter XXI, *op. cit.*, p. 56.
[89] David Hume, *Of Tragedy* in *Four Dissertations* (London: Printed for A. Millar, 1757), pp. 198–99.
[90] Goldsmith, *A Comparison between Sentimental and Laughing Comedy* in *op. cit.*, Vol. III, p. 380.

boredom with violence and other "special attractions," the novelists, for their part, had their own devices. Richardson had set the tone: portrayals of the plights and successes of the middle and lower-middle classes could be invested with considerable appeal by the inclusion of detailed descriptions of their affairs of the heart. Goldsmith's *Vicar of Wakefield* is generally considered to be an outstanding work of this genre and Mackenzie's *The Man of Feeling* represents the extreme of the novel which combined the ordinary and the realistic in character and setting with detailed descriptions and exaltations of sentiment.[91]

In the novel of sentiment and the novel of sensibility (which differed from each other more in degree than in kind) the emotions were more important than behavior, and rationality in either thought or behavior was relegated to crude and insensitive souls. Forgiveness and repentance were the pinnacles of human feelings, and the reasons for actions which led to forgiveness or repentance were as irrelevant as the murder which opens the modern mystery story. It was the detailed and lengthy portrayals of emotions that gave rise to the first discussions about the dangers of escapism.

Because of the improbable nature of the seventeenth- and early eighteenth-century romance, and perhaps also because it had been read by fewer people than was the novel of sentiment, few before the middle of the century had been concerned about the effect of fiction on the reader. Addison, to be sure, had poked mild fun at a gentlewoman who consumed many of these fanciful tales and eventually undertook to while away her time by re-doing her estate to resemble a romantic grotto,[92] but was neither indignant nor alarmed about the social consequences of such indulgence.

The stress on sentimental bliss in the novels of the second half of the century gave rise to a more socially significant kind of concern. Over-indulgence in fiction has two serious consequences: it keeps the reader from useful endeavors and it fills his head with romantic dreams which it will be impossible to attain in real life. Goldsmith, despite *The Vicar of Wakefield*, often warned against the dangers of living in the transported world of sentiment. In a letter to his brother about his nephew's education, he even advised the father to prohibit novel reading altogether. Such romantic pictures of the world are snares and delusions to youth:

> They teach the young mind to sigh after beauty and happiness which never existed; to despise the little good which fortune has mixed in their cup, by expecting more than she gave. . . .[93]

[91] The prevailingly sentimental tone of the novels of this period has been attributed in part to the fact that there was a great influx of women novelists who wrote for the largely female novel-reading public. Certainly contemporary satire on such lady novelists was not lacking: Smollett, among others, went out of his way, in *Humphrey Clinker*, to point out that the failure of one of his characters as a novelist was excusable because the ladies had the field of "spirit, delicacy, and knowledge of the human heart" all to themselves.

[92] Addison, *Spectator*, No. 37, *loc. cit.*, p. 112.

[93] Quoted in Francis Gallaway, *Reason, Rule, and Revolt in English Classicism* (New York: Charles Scribner's Sons, 1940), p. 115.

The reading of sentimental novels, in short, is not practical. But the pastime is perhaps more dangerous for the young girl than for the young man, because she who is fed on sentiment and sensibility will be hard pressed to love a man whose daily life is filled with the routine demands of earning a living for wife and family. Furthermore, as Cowper noted with some indignation, the young lady is likely to become so over-stimulated by the reading of such "sentimental frippery and ream," of "sniv'ling and driv'ling folly," that no mere insertion of a warning will "quench the fire."[94]

The middle-class character had best be equipped with middle-class sentiments, for too great a concern with tender feelings ill-equips a youth for bourgeois life. Richardson's Charlotte Grandison argues that "a mild, sedate convenience is better than a stark staring mad passion. . . . Who ever hears of darts, flames, Cupids . . . and such like nonsense in matrimony? Passion is transitory. . . ."[95]

But such warnings did not stem the tide of sentimental literature which provided readers with escape from the humdrum of everyday life. The middle class may have wanted to see itself in a mirror but it wanted to see its materialistic self dressed up and made more appealing with delicate sensibilities.

Novelty and Variety

Concern about man's search for distraction did not come into being with the dawn of the eighteenth century and the development of saleable literary goods. We have noted in an earlier chapter that Montaigne, and later Pascal, had debated the issue in the sixteenth and seventeenth centuries. But it was Voltaire's *Essay on Taste*, published in 1757, which alerted writers and scholars to the implications of the problem in a society rapidly becoming inundated with all kinds of written entertainment.

Examining the general cultural scene of his times, Voltaire found that

. . . the publick, fond of novelty, applauds their intention; but this applause is soon succeeded by satiety and disgust. A new set of artists start up, invent new methods to please a capricious taste, and depart still further from nature . . . Overwhelmed with new inventions, which succeed and efface each other with incredible rapidity, they scarcely know where they are. . . .[96]

Looking at the growing market for literary products and at the manifest

[94] William Cowper, *The Progress of Error in Poetical Works of William Cowper*, ed. H. S. Milford (London: Oxford University Press, 1934), p. 24.

[95] Richardson, *The Novels of Samuel Richardson*, Vol. XIX of twenty vols. (London: Chapman and Hall, 1902), pp. 15–16.

[96] François Marie Arouet Voltaire, "Essay on Taste" in: Alexandre Gerard, *An Essay on Taste: With Three Dissertations on the Same Subject by Mr. de Voltaire, Mr. d'Alembert, and Mr. de Montesquieu* (London: A. Millar, 1759), p. 220.

inclinations of the audience which was purchasing them, the English men of letters found ample proof that Voltaire's concern was justified.

David Garrick faced the public demand for novelty in his three-fold capacity as dramatist, actor, and theater manager. In the course of his thirty-year career he found it increasingly necessary to water down his artistic standards with "propping-up" devices and double feature billings which would supply "the many various objects that amuse these busy curious times."[97] Dr. Johnson devoted one of his *Idler* essays to "terrific" diction—a mannerism of obscurity adopted by some writers to add a note of novelty to the commonplace. In explaining the motivation behind this device (which he dubs the "bugbear" style), Johnson says that the demand to see "common things in an uncommon manner" is characteristic of the times. The kinds of devices which popular writers resort to are those on the order of telling time by algebra, drinking tea by stratagem, in short

> . . . to quit the beaten track only because it is known, and to take a new path, however crooked or rough, because the straight was found out before.

In another *Idler* essay he speaks of "the multiplication of books," particularly of compilations, and notes that they serve no real purpose but merely "distract choice." He concludes, however, that such writers do little harm in the long run because they are merely symptoms of a short-lived fad.[98]

It was the magazines which most conspicuously catered to the demand for variety, but oddly enough, these popular "miscellanies," whose number increased rapidly as the century wore on, were not attacked with any consistency by the serious writers.[99] Oliver Goldsmith, however, did devote one of his essays to some good-natured raillery of the magazines. He compares his lot as an essayist who can write upon only one subject at a time with those more "fortunate" magazine writers who can write upon several and thus avoid the risk of boring their readers. The magazine which he describes resembles the *Gentleman's Magazine* or some similar eighteenth-century original of *Reader's Digest:*

> If a magazine be dull upon the Spanish war, he soon has us up again with the Ghost in Cock Lane; if the reader begins to doze upon that, he is quickly roused by an Eastern tale: tales prepare us for poetry, and poetry for the meteorological history of the weather. It is the life and soul of a magazine never to be long dull upon one subject; and the reader, like the sailor's horse, has at least the comfortable refreshment of having the spur often changed.

[97] David Garrick, "Prologue," *The Farmer's Return from London* in *Poetical Works of David Garrick*, Vol. I of two vols. (London: D. Kearsley, 1785), pp. 186–88.

[98] Johnson, *The Idler*, No. 36 and No. 85, *British Essayists*, XXVII, 124, 297–98.

[99] It is possible that the intellectuals were inclined to consider the magazine beneath their notice, just as they seem to have left criticism of the popular novels of the latter part of the century to "middlebrow" writers.

Ironically complaining that he sees no reason why the magazine writers should "carry off all the rewards of genius," Goldsmith goes on to outline a plan for changing the format of his own essays, making them a magazine in miniature in which he proposes to "hop from subject to subject." He also gives notice that, if properly encouraged, he will decorate his magazine with pictures. The journal is to be called the *Infernal Magazine* and, unlike other of the same genre, it will live up to its advertised promise to astonish society. Obeisances are then made to the prospective audience in the usual style of eighteenth-century prospectuses, and Goldsmith assures his readers-to-be that the magazine is to be run by gentlemen of distinction (and means) who will perform this public service not for personal gain but purely for their own amusement.[100]

Nuances of feeling and sentiment offered one way to add appeal to the pedestrian characters and situations which dominated the popular writings of the time. Exotic settings provided another. The opening up of the Far East to British trade had resulted in what was perhaps one of the most sweeping fads England has ever experienced. Music, fabrics, dress styles, furniture, architecture, gardening, and painting—nothing escaped the great demand for the Oriental. The "nabob" who disappeared into China for a year or two and came home with his pockets full of gold became, for a time, a hero. Writers made short shrift of turning the situation to their own advantage. Nabobs were adulated on the stage where they often proved to be a great dramatic convenience, and essays, letters, and novels took the ordinary Englishman into extraordinary surroundings, replete with elaborate trappings and a heavy veil of mystery (it need hardly be added that the adventurer usually followed tradition and remained an Englishman for all that). In these tales of Oriental adventure, the "wisdom of the East" was often exalted, as in William Whitehead's prologue to Arthur Murphy's version of Voltaire's *L'Orphelin de la Chine* (1759)—"and boldly bears Confucius' morals to Britannia's ears. Accept th' imported boon."[101]

A few chauvinistic voices were heard saying, in effect, "What does the Orient offer that England cannot match or better?" But by and large the fashion for the Oriental, which was as popular among royalty as among shopgirls, was not considered as dangerous to the reader as was indulgence in the sentimental. Furthermore, it was good for trade and perhaps, with its tales of hard-won riches, even provided additional incentives, if any were needed, for concentrating on the practical (and remunerative) aspects of life.

For the most part, the world of letters confined itself to pointing to the Chinese fad as one more proof of the public's insatiable need for novelty and variety. The jaded European, as Goldsmith remarked with considerably more detachment than he had shown in his remarks about the novel of

---

[100] Goldsmith, *Specimen of a Magazine in Miniature* in *The Miscellaneous Works of Oliver Goldsmith*, ed. David Masson (London: The Macmillan Company, 1925), p. 288.

[101] Quoted in Allen, *op. cit.*, Vol. II, pp. 25–26.

sentiment, "has, of late, had recourse even to China, in order to diversify the amusements of the day."[102] He himself, not without some apology, used the Oriental touch as a device for strengthening the appeal of his commentary on various aspects of contemporary life, as his *Citizen of the World*—"letters, from a Chinese philosopher residing in London to his friends in the East"— testifies. In his introduction to these letters, he first complains about the fickleness of the audience and the indiscriminate way in which praise is lavished on the "mob" of popular writers, and then reports a dream in which

> . . . the success of such numbers [of authors] at last began to operate on me. If these, cried I, meet with favour and safety, some luck may, perhaps, for once attend the unfortunate. I am resolved to make a new adventure.

He then comments that, while thus far the "frippery and fireworks of China" have merely served to "vitiate" the public taste, he will "try how far they can help to improve our understanding."[103]

Goldsmith and his fellow writers were less tolerant of the far reaches to which the public's desire for novelty had led in the opera and drama. The seventeenth-century theater had catered to a rather more heterogeneous audience than had the printed works of the time. To sustain the interest of people with diverse tastes it had made use of a variety of audience appeals. The "spectacular" or "sensational" devices to which eighteenth-century dramatists and theater managers resorted were, therefore, not essentially different in kind from those used in the days of Addison (or, for that matter, in the Elizabethan period). Addison had, in fact, devoted more than one issue of the *Spectator* to the abuses of the operatic stage, though his remonstrances were mild in comparison with those Pope was to write in twenty years and those of Goldsmith and Fielding forty years later. Addison found many of the popular attention-getting devices quite legitimate—his plea was merely for a more judicious application. Thunder and lightning, bells and ghosts, all have their "proper season" and, used with restraint, are to be applauded. The same is true of the much-maligned handkerchief, the "principal machine" for the "moving of pity": it should not be eliminated, but its flutterings should have some connection with the words of the actor.[104] About one minor attraction, however, he was not quite so tolerant. In another issue of the *Spectator* he writes that it is customary to impress the audience with the lofty character of the hero by the lofty height of the plumes on his head, as though "a great Man and a tall Man" were the same thing. Not only is this an affront to the audience, but most embarrassing for the actor because, "notwithstanding any Anxieties which he pretends for his Mistress, his Country or his Friends, one may see by his Actions that his

[102] *Ibid.*
[103] Goldsmith, "Editor's Preface," *Citizen of the World, op. cit.*, p. 4.
[104] Addison, *Spectator*, No. 44, *loc. cit.*, p. 133.

greatest Care and Concern is to keep the Plume of Feathers from falling off his Head."[105]

Addison's sharpest sarcasm was reserved for the indiscriminate mixing of the representational with the real. In ridiculing the release of live birds from a cage on the stage of the opera house, he objected not that they were put there in the first place but that their songs emanated all too obviously from man-blown instruments hidden behind the scenery. Apparently intending to frighten stage-managers into their senses, he concludes with a description of where such absurdities might lead.

> I found . . . that there were great Designs on Foot for the Improvement of the Opera; that it had been proposed to break down a part of the Wall, and to surprise the Audience with a Party of an hundred Horse, and that there was actually a Project of bringing the *New-River* into the House, to be employed in Jetteaus and Waterworks.[106]

Had Addison lived on to the middle of the century, he would have found that instead of giving the stage-managers pause, he may have put new ideas into their heads, for audio-visual claptrap became more than ever the order of the day as the stage and opera had more strenuously to compete with magazines and novels for public attention.

Eloquent satirizers were not lacking as the abuses multiplied. Pope certainly did not overlook the stage as he lampooned the world of letters of his time:

> The play stands still; damn action and discourse,
> Back fly the scenes, and enter foot and horse;
> Pageants on pageants, in long order drawn,
> Peers, heralds, bishops, ermine, gold, and lawn. . . .[107]

But again it remained for Goldsmith to conduct the most thorough-going analysis.

A *Citizen of the World* letter is devoted to a description of the seasonal opening of the two licensed theaters, the Drury Lane and Covent Garden. Goldsmith first remarks on the competition between the two houses in which

> . . . the generals of either army have . . . several reinforcements to lend occasional assistance. If they produce a pair of diamond buckles at one house, we have a pair of eyebrows that can match them at the other. . . . If we can bring more children on the stage, they can bring more guards in red clothes, who strut and shoulder their swords to the astonishment of every spectator.

He ridicules the idea that the audience—despite the virtuous platitudes of the times—can possibly derive any instruction from such performances, and

[105] Addison, *Spectator*, No. 42, *loc. cit.*, p. 127.
[106] Addison, *Spectator*, No. 5, *loc. cit.*, p. 18.
[107] Pope, *First Epistle to the Second Book of Horace* in *The Best of Pope, op. cit.*, pp. 236–37.

reports that, "what with trumpets, hallooing behind the stage and bawling upon it," he himself always gets dizzy long before the performance is over. Calling the situation what it largely was—a money-making proposition— Goldsmith expresses surprise that the play-writing trade has not set up an apprentice system, since there would seem to be nothing easier than to write for the English stage.

> The author, when well acquainted with the value of thunder and lightning; when versed in all the mystery of scene-shifting and trap-doors; when skilled in the proper periods to introduce a wire-walker or a waterfall; . . . he knows all that can give a modern audience pleasure.

And—as in the case of the *Infernal Magazine*—he continues his essay with some ironic advice to the author who wishes to achieve popularity. First, he should never expect the actor to adjust to the requirements of a drama; it is the author's responsibility to appraise the particular abilities of each actor, and to write his play around their respective talents for expressing fear, pain, or surprise. Such moans and groans and exclamations are the surest way to win the applause of the audience. There is, in fact, no other way to win an audience. The author will find his consolation in the knowledge that once having acquired such skills, he needs no other talents, and the playgoer can relax in the certainty that once in the theater he can "dismiss from the mind all the fatigue of thinking."[108]

To this facetious advice to the dramatist can be added a number of other examples. In his *Essay on the Theater* written two decades after the *Citizen of the World* Goldsmith formulates the problem of the "paying" audience in terms so modern that they might well be taken for a mid-twentieth-century discussion of the motion picture. He begins with a criticism of sentimental comedy and suggests that such plays are largely popular because the dramatists go out of their way to cater to the public demand for novelty. He then acts as his own antagonist, saying that after all the theater is "formed to amuse mankind, and that it matters little, if this end be answered, by what means it is obtained." Whatever pleases the audience is good, "success . . . is a mark of [its] merit." Assuming his own role once more, he then raises the question—since become very familiar, but no more answered in our time than in his—what would happen if the audience were provided with *good* drama?[109]

But the English audience continued to enjoy the various devices hit upon for its excitement and amusement. The grotesque effect of the "intermingling of daggers and kisses" is reported by a German visitor to a British play, in which the leading lady was so moved by her tragic situation that she was incapacitated for the rest of the performance.

---

[108] *Ibid.*, Letter LXXXIX, pp. 219–20.
[109] Goldsmith, *A Comparison between Sentimental and Laughing Comedy, loc. cit.*

. . . and had to be carried off the stage unconscious. And the audience, too, unable to endure the strain, departed, so that the piece had to be finished without the leading lady, before a handful of unusually hardboiled spectators.[110]

However powerful the appeal of the tragic emotions, it was for lavish displays that the eighteenth-century audience reserved its most unbounded enthusiasm. During Garrick's management of the Drury Lane, four lush pantomimes and Garrick's own "spectacular" *The Jubilee* all ran considerably longer than any serious drama produced in the same period. After a very brief initial run, most of the genuine works of art, as Garrick regretfully remarked even of his Shakespeare productions, had to be "propped up" by the addition of well-advertised and ever "new" baubles such as parades, masquerades, and dances.[111]

It was this demand for novelty from the reading and playgoing audiences which made it possible for almost any writer to have his day of popularity, provided only he could convince his public that he was giving them something they had never experienced before. Pope attempted to discourage the opportunists who catered to this propensity by deriding them with names and titles, but he had the advantage of perusing the scene fairly early in the century when one book could contain them all. His successors, unable to cope with the deluge case by case, were of necessity considerably less specific.

Mediocrity

The idea of cyclical movements in the arts and sciences is to be found in almost any age. In eighteenth-century England, this concept, together with the idea that his own period was one of decline, seems first to have been formulated by David Hume in the essay on *The Rise and Progress of the Arts and Sciences* (1742). He states that when the "arts and sciences come to perfection in any state . . . they naturally, or rather necessarily, decline . . . and seldom or never revive in that nation. . . ."[112] A few years later, somewhat less dogmatically, Voltaire echoed Hume from across the Channel: "The taste of a nation may degenerate and become extremely depraved; and it almost always happens that the period of its perfection is the forerunner of its decline."[113]

Neither Hume nor Voltaire seems to have related his ideas about a decline directly to the growing audience and the popular literature with which it was being fed, though Hume did say that the public's desire for novelty "leads men wide of simplicity and nature, and fills their writings with affec-

[110] Quoted in John A. Kelley, *German Visitors to the English Theaters in the Eighteenth Century* (Princeton, N. J.: Princeton University Press, 1936), p. 55.

[111] Pedicord, *op. cit.*, pp. 135–39.

[112] David Hume, *The Rise and Progress of the Arts and Sciences* in *Philosophical Works*, Vol. III of four vols. (London: Tait, 1826), p. 152.

[113] Voltaire, *loc. cit.*

tation and conceit."[114] But other writers of the mid-century did connect their fears with the new tyranny of public demand and the new spate of popular works. Among the first protagonists of this concept, we find Pope and Swift complaining about the lack of literary qualifications of writers in general; we find less eminent authors complaining about hack novelists and their methods of production; and we find readers as well as writers complaining about the literary unworthiness of the new crop of fictional characters emerging in eighteenth-century literature. Finally, we find a group of philosophers and writers seriously disturbed about the fact that, with the increase in literacy, anyone and everyone can become a literary critic, that incompetents are now passing judgment, and that literary standards may, as a result, be shattered altogether.[115]

Some time before the publication of the first edition of *The Dunciad* (1729), Pope wrote to Swift that it was the "little" writers of the world who made him angry, the "party writers, dull poets, and wild criticks."

> My spleen is at the little rogues of it; it would vex one more to be knocked on the head with a piss-pot than by a thunderbolt. . . . But to be squirted to death, as poor Wycherly [the eminent Restoration comic playwright had died in 1716] said to me on his death-bed, by apothecaries' apprentices, by the understrappers of under-secretaries to secretaries who were no secretaries—this would provoke as dull a dog as Phillips himself.[116]

The objective of the book was, in his own words, to "dissuade the dull and punish the malicious" authors of his day. The poem consists of direct and often highly personal attacks not only on those writers whom Pope considered to be second-rate, but on the booksellers, book-puffers, and book-reviewers who by promoting such writers were assuaging the public hunger for information and novelty. The heroine, or better, the *bête noire* of *The Dunciad* is the Goddess of Dullness, a "laborious, heavy, busy, bold and blind" deity who seems to be coming into her own in the eighteenth-century world of letters. In addition to her coterie of writers and hacks, she is surrounded by a public whom Pope categorizes as Tasteless Admirers, Flatters

[114] Hume, *Of Simplicity and Refinement in Writing* in *Philosophical Works, op. cit.*, Vol. III, p. 223.

[115] Thomas Carlyle, in reviewing English literature of the eighteenth century in his *Lectures on the History of Literature* (1838), regretted the quackery resulting from the selling of literary goods and reflected that it would bring about great confusion among "all men." ". . . an observer sees the quack established; he sees truth trodden down to the earth everywhere around him; in his own office he sees quackery at work, and that part of it which is done by quackery is done better than all the rest; till at last he, too, concludes in favor of this order of things and gets himself enrolled among this miserable set, eager after profit, and of no belief except the belief always held among such persons, that *Money will buy money's worth*, and that *Pleasure is pleasant*. But woe to that land and its people if, for what they do, they expect payment at all times! It is bitter to see. . . . All men will suffer from it with confusion in the very heart of them."

[116] Quoted in Sutherland, *op. cit.*, pp. x–xi. Presumably John Phillips, 1631–1706, was a nephew of Milton, employed largely as translator and hack-writer.

of Dunces, Indolent Persons, and Minute Philosophers. Early in the poem the Goddess requests the Dunces to instruct a group of young students who enter the scene. The consequence of their teaching is that the youths taste the cup "which causes total oblivion of all Obligations, divine, civil, moral or rational" and are thus rendered unfit to play a constructive role in life.[117] In other words, the future of civilized society has become endangered because the students, who are the hope of that society, are being corrupted by dull, stupid, uncreative reading material produced by incompetents.[118]

The second edition of *The Dunciad* (1743) was considerably less personal and at the same time broader in scope than the first, going beyond the realm of literature proper to address itself to the theater, the opera, and even to education and politics. The two editions together compose the major broadside against particular writers; and the popular "little rogues" of literature whom Pope attacked have, as one of his recent editors has pointed out, all vindicated his judgment by sinking into oblivion.[119]

The fear of a decline centered on both the novel and the drama. In the case of the novel, the peaks attained by Richardson and Fielding, and later by Sterne and Smollett, were infinitely higher than anything achieved in the subsequent two or three decades of the century. Their works, in retrospect, were seen not as a starting point of a new era in the novel, but as its culmination. It was the serious-minded journalists rather than the few great literary figures of the latter half of the century who trained their sights on the cruder novelists.[120] To take one instance, *The Sylph*, a short-lived single-essay periodical published late in the century, devoted an issue to a lively parody of the way in which the popular novels were being slapped together: the trick is to spread the words mechanically across the page, shuffle them about to form sentences, and

> . . . according to the arrangement and collection of them [they] become *narrations, speeches, sentiments, descriptions, etc.*, and when *a very great quantity of them* . . . are wedged together after a particular form and manner, they are denominated a NOVEL. . . .[121]

Another magazine writer recommended, in the manner of Swift, that engines be adopted to make the novel writing process easier, and contributors to several other respected journals of the latter half of the century made frequent quips about the plagiarisms, repetitions, and patchwork that often

---

[117] Pope, *Dunciad* (B), *loc. cit.*, pp. 337–38.

[118] Pope, *First Epistle to . . . Horace, loc. cit.*, p. 233.

[119] Sutherland, *op. cit.*, p. xlii.

[120] In twentieth-century terminology we might say that this is a typical example of the middlebrows criticizing the lowbrows. Highbrows, as we have seen, did not differentiate, at least not until the end of the century when Jane Austen's parodies of the novel of terror might be viewed as the highbrow singling out the middlebrow.

[121] *The Sylph*, No. 19, quoted in J. T. Taylor, *Early Opposition to the English Novel: The Popular Reaction from 1760 to 1830* (New York: King's Crown Press, 1943), p. 43.

went into what was released as a novel. With such a multitude turning out novels, grumbled one, all themes have been used up; the novel has had its day:

> The manufacture of novels has been so long established, that in general they have arrived at mediocrity. . . . We are indeed so sickened with this worn-out species of composition, that we have lost all relish for it.[122]

The deterioration in the English drama after 1740 has been attributed in part to the sheer accident that no great dramatist developed in this period; but the fact that audiences represented a broader social background and were at the same time artistically less interested than audiences of the first half of the century also deserves consideration.[123] Furthermore, as we have already remarked, middle-class realism tended to be more boring on the stage than in print. Another reason ventured for the decline in the drama was that the physical alterations made in order to accommodate larger audiences required adaptations by playwright and actor which militated against "good theater." The lighting was dim, the acoustics poor, and the exaggeration required to overcome these deficiencies lent a farcical note to the tragic and comic alike.

But for many artists it was the multiplication of "judges and critics" which seems to have been most portentous of a decline in the literary world. As the ability to read spread to all ranks of society, it seems that anyone could become an arbiter of standards; "in short," as one periodical essayist remarked, "fiddlers, players, singers, dancers and mechanics themselves are all sons and daughters of taste. . . ."[124] Oliver Goldsmith, in his *Enquiry*, which he prefaced with the remark that he takes the decay of genius in his age for granted, placed much of the blame squarely on the multiplying number of critics or would-be critics.[125]

What rankled most seems not to have been the professionals but the amateurs in the audience. Writers had long had the field of literary standards to themselves, and the only threat to their self-imposed criteria was the necessity of now and then composing a paean of praise to a wealthy patron, when they were fortunate enough to have one. In the final analysis, this concern about the voices of the people amounted to a rallying behind Goldsmith in his pessimistic mood—"when only patronized by the bookseller the writer becomes a thing little superior to the fellow who works at the press"—rather than behind his optimistic formulation: "the public, collectively considered, is a good and generous master." Not only was "everyone" becoming articulate in the expression of literary judgments; worse still, there were so many

[122] Quoted in Tompkins, *op. cit.*, p. 5.
[123] Bateson, *op. cit.*, p. 145.
[124] Quoted in Allen, *op. cit.*, Vol. I, p. 110.
[125] Goldsmith, *Enquiry into the Present State, loc. cit.*, p. 58.

levels of audience opinion that it seemed to the artists that their tastes were irreconcilable.

From all sides came the complaint. Fielding wrote: "How is it possible at once to please/ Tastes so directly opposite as these?"[126] and Garrick addressed the several levels of his audience as follows:

> What shall we do your different tastes to hit?
> You relish satire (to the pit) you ragouts of wit (to the boxes)
> Your taste is humour and high-season's joke. (First Gallery)
> You call for hornpipe and for hearts of oak. (Second Gallery)[127]

The critic Warburton sympathized with the fate of the dramatists who

> . . . are often used like ladies of pleasure: they are received with rapture and enthusiasm by the public on their first appearance, but on farther acquaintance are received very coolly, though they have indeed by this time greatly improved themselves in the *art of pleasing*.[128]

Cibber, speaking in his role of stage manager, was first to point out a new way of looking at the audience, one which was eventually to effect a compromise between the standards of the artist and the divers tastes of the new public. In one of his *Two Dissertations on the Theatres*, he speaks of the phrase "The Town" which was commonly used to designate the audience. Ask an author or an actor (individually) whom he has in mind when he uses this phrase, predicts Cibber, and he will tell you that he means the "judging few" —but if you ask him to specify these judging few you will see that each will point to his respective friends, to "those who approve, and cry up their several Performances." Ask a theatrical manager and he will also refer to those opinions of the Town which are most agreeable to him and which echo what he wants most to hear. Actually, Cibber continues, the matter is not so simple. It is necessary to distinguish several levels of influence within the audience. Regardless of walk of life, it is those people who are interested in and who, in their respective circles, give encouragement to the theater who constitute the true "opinion leaders."

> I think, the Town may be supposed to include all Degrees of Persons, from the highest Nobleman, to the lowly Artisan, etc., who, in their different Stations, are Encouragers of dramatic performances: Thus all persons, who pay for their places, whether Noble, Gentle, or Simple, who fill the Boxes, Pit and Galleries in a theatrical Sence, form the Town.[129]

[126] Fielding, "Prologue," *The Universal Gallant* in *op. cit.*, Vol III, p. 165.
[127] Garrick, "Epilogue to Arthur Murray's *All in the Wrong*," in *op. cit.*, Vol. I, pp. 173–74.
[128] Quoted in Pedicord, *op. cit.*, p. 119.
[129] Theophilus Cibber, *Two Dissertations on the Theatres* (London: Printed for the Author, 1756), p. 5.

In a way, Cibber's remarks might be construed as a plea for democracy in art. Many more gifted artists, in the face of the dilemma posed by the growing middle- and lower-class audience, were to attempt to find theoretical grounds for supporting this pluralistic viewpoint. But the task was difficult, and there were class as well as aesthetic barriers to be faced.

In the early half of the century, the middle class struggled successfully to assert its values and interests against those prevailing among the aristocracy. The increasing industrialization and the new importance attaching to the role of the worker in the latter half of the century, however, brought about a shift in focus: the middle class now began to suspect that its most dangerous enemies were below instead of above it. And while class lines in the world of letters were not sharply etched, neither were they altogether obscured.

As the charity schools and the Sunday schools went about fulfilling their missions of increasing the literacy rate among the workers and farmers, the problem of who should read soon became even more controversial than the problem of whom should be written about. In this case the anxiety seems not to have originated with the literati.[130] Insofar as it can be located at all, it seems, rather, to have originated with the non-intellectuals of the middle class. The issues they raised were not aesthetic; they did not fear that literature might become debased in order to meet the tastes and capacities of a working-class audience. The problem was one of economic self-interest: if workers developed a strong predilection for reading, might they not acquire a distaste for manual work along with it?

The gist of the argument against workers reading was that the poor will remain tractable and useful only so long as they are kept in "some degree of ignorance." The Bible, perhaps, might be permitted, but any other type of reading is more than likely to make workers dissatisfied with the "manual labor" which is "destined to occupy their lives."[131] Correctives proposed ranged from putting a complete stop to the teaching of reading to children of the lower classes to censoring their reading so that only religious works would be accessible to them. A letter-to-the-editor in the *Gentleman's Magazine* proposed a rather modern-sounding method of censorship: a citizens' book-reviewing board should be established which would draw up approved reading lists for youth, workers, and other "lower orders." This committee, made up of "worthy persons," would peruse the novel output annually, print their lists in "a monthly publication," and point out "such as were of an improper tendency with candour, and recommending those of merit."[132]

It was in this atmosphere of aesthetic and class concerns that the debate about "taste" took place—what is it, who has it, how can it be acquired?

---

[130] Samuel Johnson, for one, asked by an affluent acquaintance whether his workers would become less industrious if they were to attend school and learn how to read, answered with an unequivocal "No, Sir."

[131] Taylor, *op. cit.*, p. 101ff.

[132] *Ibid.*, p. 97.

V

THE DEFENSE

In the seventeenth and early eighteenth centuries the slowly expanding upper-middle class, composed of men of business and men of property, had tended to identify with the aesthetic tastes and aspirations of the aristocracy. There was no need for writers to adjust to the professed interests of this new audience because it was indistinguishable from the reading public which had existed before. The problems of the literati had not so much to do with who was to judge literature as with the role of literature in relation to other intellectual pursuits, the limits of the genres, and the place of the poet in the wide scheme of things. Questions might be raised whether the poet excelled the philosopher in his function as teacher (this in the sixteenth century); or about the comparative status of writer and scientist (this in the seventeenth century); or whether the classical rules were the only yardsticks to be legitimately applied in judging a work of literature (this in the early eighteenth).

By the middle of the century a middle class, not only consisting of wealthy businessmen and landowners, but of shopkeepers, clerks, apprentices, and farmers was becoming increasingly affluent, literate, and ambitious. Its literary interests were not necessarily identical with those of the upper classes, its educational background was certainly more primitive and, at the same time, its cultural pretensions were distinctly noticeable.

The new audience did not have a solid classical education, and it cared more for displays of feeling than arguments from reason. Furthermore, middle-class realism did not allow for pleasure in purely intellectual pursuits. The problem was to get ahead, to improve oneself with practical information—a bent that was to reach a climax in the nineteenth-century craze for the statistical and instantly utilitarian, for the kind of guides and manuals on every activity under the sun which Matthew Arnold found so distressing and which he was to dismiss with the lofty phrase "culture works differently." In such a situation the lines between art and life, between literature and persuasion, between the aesthetic and the emotional experience became easily blurred and often indistinguishable.[133] After the middle of the century the position of the critic is therefore by no means unequivocal. He may speak about the qualities of a book, the intellectual and emotional processes involved in producing it, the critical process of evaluating it—but whatever approach he takes, concern with the experience of the reader or of different types of readers is rarely absent.[134] In short, once the profession of letters depended for support entirely upon the interest, goodwill and purchasing

[133] René Wellek, *A History of Modern Criticism,* Vol. I of two vols. to date (London: Jonathan Cape, Ltd., 1955), p. 26.
[134] Sherburn, *op. cit.,* p. 997.

habits of a broad public, it began to pay serious attention to the way in which this public experienced literary products and to raise questions about its role in the formulation of literary standards. The task was to distinguish, for the writer and for the public on which he was dependent, between the wheat of art and the chaff of trash.

Most mid-eighteenth-century writers were themselves part of the middle class which came into its own in the course of industrial revolution. Its empiricist spirit informed their approach to literary problems; and the ways in which they coped with the demands of an increasingly diversified public were as varied as the tastes of that public itself—ranging from Oliver Goldsmith's belief that the "universal presumption" to taste would have a "debauching" effect to Edmund Burke's faith in the idea of democracy in literary standards. By the middle of the century almost every writer of note could point to at least one essay—and often a volume—on the subject of taste.

Goldsmith questioned whether "natural" good taste was not being corrupted by the numerous examples of "false" taste which prove singularly attractive to the "unwary mind and young imagination."[135] But despite his disparaging remarks about the actual competence of the theater audience, Goldsmith credited contemporary audiences with having some "innate" standards of judgment which, if they could be corrupted, could also be improved. Fielding, while he agreed that "natural taste" could be corrupted, expressed even more aptly than Goldsmith that faith in progress characteristic of eighteenth-century writers when he described how the "small seeds of taste" which are present in practically all men can be fructified by training and education. Fielding goes on to say that he will "probably . . . in a future paper endeavour to lay down some rules by which all men may acquire some degree of taste."[136] That this paper was not written serves as one commentary on the obstacles met in attempting to seek out and describe those bases of judgment which all men were presumed to hold in common.

One conspicuous feature of mid-eighteenth-century thought was a faith in the perfectibility of human nature which seemed to go hand in hand with faith in material progress. Is it not possible, several writers began to ask, that it is merely lack of proper education which keeps the audience from developing into true connoisseurs?

The Search for Common Standards

Three paths were followed in the search for common principles: (1) recourse to a feeling of "inner conviction" that there must be such principles; (2) attempts to prove their existence by deriving them from certain tests; and (3) efforts to deduce them by determining how they work. At no point,

---

[135] Goldsmith, *Taste, loc. cit.,* pp. 314–15.
[136] Fielding, *Covent Garden Journal,* No. 10, *loc. cit.,* p. 29.

however, did any analyst of taste get so far as to describe or define what those principles might in fact be.

The first of the three approaches—the argument of inner conviction—started early in the century and sought validation by pointing to "simple" people who manifested clear judgment and true taste. Anticipating the admiration later to be accorded the "natural" man, the "noble savage," and the "unspoilt child," the *Tatler*, for example, had presented a young woman "who had that natural sense which makes her a better judge than a thousand critics," and the *Guardian* pointed to a foot soldier as the "politest man in a British audience, from the force of nature, untainted with the singularities of an ill-applied education."[137] Later, Hume and Edmund Burke (the latter in his early work on aesthetics) based their concepts of taste common to all men on their own inner conviction that universal standards of judgment exist. Burke, in his *Essay on Taste*, first defined his subject as "that faculty or those faculties of the mind, which are effected with, or which form a judgment of, the works of imagination and the elegant arts." The objective of his inquiry is

> to find whether there are any principles, on which the imagination is affected, so common to all, so grounded and certain, as to supply the means of reasoning satisfactorily about them. And such principles of taste I fancy there are. . . .[138]

And we shall presently see, however, though Burke continued his essay by discussing the human faculties involved in the acquisition of taste, he neither isolated any particular principles, nor did he demonstrate that "common" human faculties underlie them. Hume similarly postulated the universality of taste. All people whose "organs" are sound have a "considerable uniformity of sentiment" and from this uniformity "we may thence derive an idea of the perfect and universal beauty."[139] But Hume, too, failed to specify common aesthetic principles.

Even those who clung strongly to the idea of uniformity in taste in the abstract could not avoid the evidence of considerable disagreement when it came to judging a given work. Failing to define the common principles they sought, they could at least describe, and attempt to explain away, those tastes which were so deviant that they could not be considered manifestations of the assumed principles. Burke, who was echoed almost word for word by the Scottish literary critic Hugh Blair a few years later, resorted to the analogy of sensory taste in discussing these deviants. He pointed out that a man might be found who could not distinguish between milk and vinegar or who called both tobacco and vinegar sweet, milk bitter, and sugar sour. Such a man, said Burke, cannot be considered a person of taste, nor can he even be called a man of wrong taste. He is, quite simply, "absolutely mad":

[137] Addison, *Tatler*, No. 165; *Guardian*, No. 19. *British Essayists*, III, 319; xiii, 162.

[138] Edmund Burke, *Essay on Taste* in Vol. XXIV of Harvard Classics, fifty vols. (New York: P. F. Collier & Son, 1909), p. 13.

[139] Hume, *On Taste* in *Four Dissertations*, *op. cit.*, p. 215.

. . . when it is said, taste cannot be disputed, it can only mean that no one can strictly answer what pleasure or pain some particular man may find from the taste of some particular thing . . . but we may dispute, and with sufficient clearness too, concerning the things which are naturally pleasing or disagreeable to the sense.[140]

It remained for Lord Kames to draw most unequivocally upon inner conviction as "proof" of the existence of a common set of artistic standards. When he attempted to demonstrate his belief, however, he moved far from the concept of universality.

Like most critics and philosophers who tried to reduce the multiplicity of tastes in the eighteenth-century audience to some common denominator, Kames began by asserting that there is a "universal conviction" in the sphere of morality and went on to state that "This conviction of common nature or standard . . . accounts not less clearly for the conception we have of a right and a wrong taste in the fine arts." Kames disposes of the extreme exceptions in the same way as Burke: "The individual who dislikes objects which most people like or who conversely likes objects which most other people dislike" is "a monster." His principal argument for the existence of uniform taste is the fact that works of art are acknowledged as such:

We are formed . . . with an uniformity of taste . . . if uniformity of taste did not prevail, the fine arts could never have made any figure.

A "conviction of a common standard," he concludes, is therefore "part of our nature."[141]

Further validation of the inner conviction theory was sometimes sought by the application of certain "tests." Cultural products exist; those which have a universal appeal and which have stood the test of time can be accepted as proof of the existence of common standards. Addison had anticipated the universality test: the fact that he, a cultivated English gentleman, could enjoy the folk songs of all countries in which he traveled demonstrated that whatever is enjoyed by "a multitude" must have been judged by a universal standard:

Human Nature is the same in all reasonable Creatures; and whatever falls in with it, will meet with Admirers amongst Readers of all Qualities and Conditions.[142]

[140] Burke, *op. cit.*, pp. 14–15. Blair, in his *Lectures on Rhetoric*, writes: "If any one should maintain that sugar was bitter and tobacco was sweet, no reasoning could avail to prove it. The taste of such a person would infallibly be held to be diseased merely because it differed so widely from the taste of the species to which he belongs." Vol. I of three vols. (Basle: J. Decker, 1801), p. 35.

[141] Henry Home, Lord Kames, *Elements of Criticism*, Vol. III of three vols. (Edinburgh: Kincaid and Bell, 1762), pp. 358–65.

[142] Addison, *Spectator*, No. 70, *loc. cit.*, Vol. I, p. 215.

Joshua Reynolds in his *Discourses* picked up this argument—all questions of taste can be settled by an appeal to the "sense" which all mankind has in common. He, too, avoided the question of what standards, principles, or criteria compose this common sense. What he does say is that the better acquainted a writer is with the works of various periods and of various countries, the more likely is it that he will be able to derive these unspecified —but uniform—standards. To the test of universality, Reynolds then added the test of permanence.

> What has pleased, and continues to please, is likely to please again: hence are derived the rules of art.[143]

If one accepts these two proofs of the existence of common artistic standards, as most mid-century writers evidently did accept them, it follows, as Hugh Blair put it in his *Lectures on Rhetoric*, that it is to the concurrence of the majority that one must look for standards of taste.

> That which men concur the most in admiring must be held to be beautiful. His taste must be esteemed just and true, which coincides with the general sentiments of men. In this standard we must rest . . . the common feelings of men carry the same authority, and have a title to regulate the taste of every individual.[144]

Thus did the writers of the mid-eighteenth century pay their respects to their new patrons, the great audience. But the discussion did not end on a note of faith in a common denominator.

The works of Lord Kames, particularly his *Elements of Criticism*, illustrate the entanglement in which those who attempted to describe the workings of common principles found themselves.[145] He begins by equating the now familiar terms—common nature, common sense, common standards—with good taste. By and large, Kames observes, every man is aware that such common standards exist. Like Burke and Blair, he condemns the taste of the individual whose judgment deviates: "We justly condemn every taste that swerves from what is thus ascertained by the common standard." At the same time he postulates the mysterious "we" (which also appears in Burke's remarks on taste) endowed with the right to condemn.

The critical question becomes, then, who constitutes this "we," and here, despite his use of the term "common" standards, Kames begins to differentiate. In the sphere of moral judgment he feels that one may rely on "everyone's" standards. When it comes to judgment in literature and the arts it will hardly do to "collect votes indifferently." In the aesthetic domain "a wary choice" must be made. His preliminary assumption of a "universal conviction" notwithstanding, Kames goes on specifically to exclude the

---

[143] Quoted in Gallaway, *op. cit.*, p. 53.
[144] Hugh Blair, *Lectures on Rhetoric*, Vol. I of three vols. (Basle: J. Decker, 1801), pp. 34–35.
[145] Kames, *op. cit.*, *passim.*

greater part of mankind from the right to contribute to the "common" standard. "Particularly"—and here Kames establishes rigid class lines in what seems to have started as a democratic premise—"particularly all those who depend for food on bodily labor are totally devoid of taste." They can share in the formulation of moral principles and they must comply with them, but they can have no voice in the worlds of art and literature.[146] But Kames is not content to stop with the elimination of workers; there are others to be disenfranchised in cultural matters. At the other extreme are the rich and opulent who delight in conspicuous consumption, who are "voluptuous" both morally and aesthetically, and these, too, are disqualified. Since the manifest objective of this upper crust is simply to "amaze and humble all beholders," they can have no understanding of the "faint and delicate emotions of the fine arts." All that remains are those individuals who maintain a strict separation from the lower orders but who at the same time are free from envy or imitation of the members of the aristocratic remnants of the Restoration period and their obsolete style of life. Furthermore, within this group, which by now is defined as the middle class, only those can become judges who have "good natural taste . . . improved by education, reflection and experience." In other words, only the intellectual elite are qualified to evaluate cultural products—a clear instance of the intellectual defining his social role as the mentor and cultural leader of the new middle-class order.

Having narrowed those capable of aesthetic judgment to a chosen few, Kames then doubles on his tracks and once more assures his reader that the "good" and "bad" qualities in cultural products are clearly discernible and that "mankind" is able to distinguish between them. His elite theory becomes democratic once more by means of postponement: you have only to wait until the standards now formulated and applied by the select few will be recognized as universal by all mankind. And that time, Kames is confident, is bound to come.

It remained for David Hume to summarize most succinctly the contradictory position which was maintained by those who sought universal criteria for the judging of art. The principles of taste, Hume observed, are universal "and nearly if not entirely the same in all men"; but he concluded this very sentence with the observation that "few are qualified to give judgment on any work of art, or establish their own sentiment as the standard of beauty."[147]

Kames, Hume, and Blair are foremost among the critics who, beginning

---

[146] This is a far cry from the unqualified remarks of Addison earlier in the century, before the middle classes were making their tastes clearly felt through purchases of literary products. Prior to his statement that "Human Nature is the same in all reasonable Creatures," Addison had said: ". . . it is impossible that any thing should be universally tasted or approved by a Multitude, tho' they are only the Rabble of a Nation, which hath not in it some peculiar aptness to please and gratifie the Mind of Man." (*Spectator*, No. 70, *loc. cit.*).

[147] Hume, *On Taste, loc. cit.*, p. 228.

with the idea—or the hope—that standards for the judging of literary and other cultural products are held in common by all men, arrived at a conclusion almost the very opposite: the "all" spelled out to read a select few. Other writers and critics who looked for a common, egalitarian principle with as little success escaped from the dilemma by formulating concepts which may be subsumed under the rubric "the idea of diversity."

From Universality to Diversity

To recapitulate briefly, we have traced three phases in the discussion about the new public and the literary goods produced for it. First, a period of hope during which the men of letters waited for the aesthetic proclivities of this public to catch up with their moral inclinations. Second, a period of "opportunity and opportunism," when new writers and new products developed at a rapid rate, and the literati adopted a policy of watchful waiting. Third, a period of dismay among the intellectuals during which both audience and media were severely strictured. The controversy over "taste" might be said to constitute a fourth period. This discussion, as we have seen, was conducted as though the participants hoped that the manifold differences in taste, and the obviously low level of taste in some segments of the audience, were more apparent than real, and that they would eventually find underlying standards on which both artist and audience could agree. But the exploration came to nothing more than to a more or less general agreement: those literary and artistic accomplishments which hold up through space and time are "good," be they folk ballads or Greek sculpture, and the fact that some such achievements do so hold up indicates that common standards of judgment do exist. These assertions were of little use in resolving the conflict between the integrity of the artist and the inclinations of the public which paid the piper. What did emerge from the exploration, however, was a widespread conviction that the experience of this public had to be taken into account in any discussions of literary standards.

As the search for common standards waned, such psychological and descriptive concepts as perception, individual differences, national differences and "comparative" or "historical" views became increasingly conspicuous in the works of the critics, who paid increasing attention to the need for enjoyment, pleasure, amusement, and recreation. The emphasis, in short, was placed more and more on the analysis of the audience experience, as though in the hope that a study of reader gratifications would lead inductively to new knowledge about the nature of "common" standards.

To what extent this shift in emphasis resulted from the writer's dependence on his audience and to what extent it reflected the absence of powerful literary figures is a moot question. Fielding expounded a "great man" theory in an almost sociological vein. In a *Covent Garden Journal* article on the "Commonwealth of Literature," he traced the general state of literature through a variety of phases: first, an "ecclesiastical" democracy; then a period of absolutism co-existent with the political absolutism in the age of Henry VIII; next, an era of literary aristocracy, headed first by Shakespeare, Ben Jonson, and Beaumont and Fletcher, next by Dryden, and finally by Pope, whom Fielding always sees as literary autocrat. But in his own period, Fielding sees a decline in literary leadership; "after the demise of King Alexandre the literary state relapsed again into a democracy, or rather into downright anarchy. . . ."[148]

While the stress on the effects of literary works on their readers became dominant, not all of the writers, philosophers, and literary critics involved in the discussion of standards were in agreement as to whether the experience of the audience should be looked upon as the only valid basis for literary criteria.

In general, three early approaches to the problem of effects can be distinguished. The first we might call relative; the second psychological; the third descriptive. Needless to say, then as now, these categories overlapped conspicuously.

Relative concepts had some history in the world of letters before the participants in the taste controversy got hold of them. The *Tatler*, as early as 1710, had suggested that the way of life and the peculiarities of a writer or a reader serve to some extent to condition their respective tastes.[149] This concept of relativity (which is in reality a qualified endorsement of diversity in taste) finds a good deal of application in the works of Addison and the later writers who explored such questions as the relationship between exposure and taste. The idea of relativity also became manifest in a new approach to the study of literature itself. Pope, for example, in the preface to his controversial edition of Shakespeare, had stressed the importance of historical, climatic, and national factors in the conditioning of ideas as to what constitutes good or bad literature.[150] But it was Johnson who, in his *Lives*, set the stage for the comparative historical study of literature as well as, incidentally, for exact textual study.[151] The comparative study of literature, in short, went hand in hand with the comparative approach to the study of the *impact* of literary works.

There was a strong relationship between such comparative or relative approaches and the psychological theories and hypotheses which were being aired at the same time. The expression "association of ideas" seems to have become a favorite one in the analysis of audience experience, and there was general agreement that a great variety of such associations could be expected when a widely assorted group of people were exposed to the same work. Pleasure in literary experience thus was more and more conceived as a matter of individual sentiment, not necessarily connected with objective standards of beauty or reason. Whatever a given individual with his own

---

[148] Fielding, *Covent Garden Journal*, No. 23, *loc. cit.*, pp. 41–47.
[149] Richard Steele, *Tatler*, No. 173, *British Essayists*, III, 356–60.
[150] Needham, *op. cit.*, p. 36.
[151] *Ibid.*, p. 52.

perceptive mechanisms found agreeable was also acceptable.[152] Even Johnson, despite his firmer adherence to rational principles, insisted that these were subordinate to individual response. If such principles are to be applied, he felt, they must be applied with caution, and he goes on to speak of "the cant of those who judge by principles rather than perception."[153]

At the other extreme of the descriptive approach we find those who brushed rules aside altogether, and justified their doing so on the grounds that the audience reacts impulsively in the process of reading and does not have time, even though it might have the capacity, to apply them. *The Monthly Review*, for one, supported Lord Kames' attack on the rules on these very grounds, and paraphrased him with approval:

> For when the mind is affected or disgusted, the affection or aversion takes place, as it were, by impulse and gives no time for the formal application of given principles to influence the judgment.[154]

The long-range effect of this new attention to audience experience was to legitimize emotional gratifications. While it is clear that an endorsement of emotion has persisted to the present time, it is by no means apparent to what extent the shift from the application of rational standards to the analysis of emotional response was the result of the need to take into account a new mass audience and a new group of literary products. What is clear, as a recent historian has put it, is that "examination of the mechanism of the mind by more philosophical thinkers like Hume resulted in the analysis of reason into imagination and belief, of common sense into intuition. The basis of classical art was shattered by these blows . . . and uncertainty paved the way for the emphasis on emotion as the most important factor in life and art."[155]

Recognition of this kind of gratification was comparatively unknown in the early decades of the century, when any literary or other cultural product had to subordinate (or pretend to subordinate) pleasure to moral uplift. For the first time in the century we find terms such as "relaxation" and "amusement" used without apology.

> Such is the nature of man, that his powers and faculties are soon blunted by exercise. . . . During his waking hours, amusement by intervals is requisite to unbend his mind from serious occupation. The imagination . . . contributes more than any other cause to recruit the mind and restore its vigor, by amusing us with gay and ludicrous images; and when relaxation is necessary, such amusement is much relished.[156]

---

[152] Gallaway, *op. cit.*, p. 347.
[153] Quoted in Sherburn, *op. cit.*, p. 1001.
[154] Edward Niles Hooker, "The Reviewers and the New Criticism, 1754–70," *Philological Quarterly*, Vol. XIII (1934), 197.
[155] Gallaway, *op. cit.*, p. 345.
[156] Kames, *op. cit.*, Vol. I, p. 337.

This acknowledgment has no didactic overtones. It was as if a sense of defeat in the search for a common aesthetic perception in the audience were accompanied by a sense of release from the obligation to assist in its moral reformation. Hume, for example, discusses how man seeks to escape from the pressures which weary him when he is alone with his thoughts.

> To get rid of this painful situation, it [the mind] seeks every amusement and pursuit; business, gaming, shows, executions; whatever will rouse the passions, and take its attention from itself.

He proceeds to list the kinds of passion that may be roused by such means and remarks that whether they be agreeable or disagreeable, happy or sad, confused or orderly, they are still preferable to "the insipid languor" of a man thrown back upon his own inner resources. He points to the gambling room to validate his thesis; wherever the most exciting play is going on, most members of the company may be found, even though that table may not have the best players. To identify with people who are experiencing the passions of loss or gain is to relieve oppression.

> It makes the time pass the easier with them, and is some relief to that oppression, under which men commonly labour, when left entirely to their own thoughts and meditations.[157]

Archibald Alison, a critic writing later in the century, analyzed the various "qualities of mind" which can be evoked by reading. He even distinguished between passive and active gratifications.

> The qualities of mind which are capable of producing emotion, are either its active or its passive qualities; either its *powers* and capacities, as beneficence, wisdom, fortitude, invention, fancy, etc., or its *feelings and affections*, as love, joy, hope, gratitude, purity, fidelity, innocence, etc.[158]

As in many analyses of audience experience undertaken after the middle of the century, one is struck by Alison's pragmatism, which is in such strong contrast to the moralizing tone uppermost in the middle of the century. It was this almost scientific approach to the experience of the audience which paved the way for a new conception of the critic's role.

The Critic as Mediator

Dissatisfaction with the kinds of rigid and pedantic literary criticism which had prevailed in the early part of the century had been brewing for some time. Swift already had attacked such pedantry; his *Battle of the Books* overflows with denunciations of the "malignant deity, called Criticism." The

---

[157] Hume, *Of Tragedy, loc. cit.*, pp. 186–87.
[158] Archibald Alison, *On Taste* (1790), quoted in Needham, *op. cit.*, p. 181.

mixture of bookishness and glibness in these critics was of no benefit other than to give "the coffee house wits some basis for literary pretensions."[159] Pope, who did not need the inspiration he apparently got from Swift on the subject, similarly attacked the destructiveness, or at best the futility, of those who lived by petty and often meaningless attacks on the writing of others. Nothing is sacred to these critics; on any subject "they'll talk you dead/ For Fools rush in where Angels fear to tread."[160] Later Goldsmith, in discussing German writings, echoed the disdain of his eminent predecessors for this type of critical hairsplitting.

> Their assiduity is unparalleled; . . . they write through volumes while they do not think through a page. Never fatigued themselves, they think the reader can never be weary; so they drone on, saying all that can be said on the subject, not selecting what may be advanced to the purpose.[161]

Again it was Addison who presaged a new concept, this time of the critic's role. He was to be creative and constructive: in a phrase, a "revealer of beauties." Beginning with Addison's influential pieces on *Paradise Lost* in the *Spectator*, almost every important author had at least one book-length criticism written about his work entitled *The Beauties of . . . .*[162] This concept of a revelatory function for the critic implied that he was to assume a role of responsibility in relation to the general public as well as to his fellow writers and intellectuals, and most of the writers and critics of the mid-century followed suit. It was the critic's function, as Johnson put it, to help men "to enjoy life or to endure it."[163] At the same time, it was characteristic of the mid-century writers—in their optimistic mood—to view the critic's contribution as a means of raising the aesthetic level of the public. In this light, the critic has an educational role. Goldsmith sees him—and he is speaking of the "man of taste" as contrasted with the scholar or compiler—as "placed in a middle station, between the world and the cell, between learning and common sense."

But perhaps the most far-reaching change which took place in the concept of the critic was that a two-way function was premised for him. Not only was he to reveal the beauties of literary works to the general public by means of which, in Goldsmith's terms, "even the philosopher may acquire popular applause"; he must also interpret the public back to the writer. In brief, the critic not only "teaches the vulgar on what part of a character to lay the emphasis of praise," he must also show "the scholar where to point his application so as to deserve it." Goldsmith believed that the absence of such critical mediators explained why wealth rather than true literary fame

---

[159] Quoted in Atkins, *op. cit.*, pp. 173–75.
[160] Pope, *Essay on Criticism*, *loc. cit.*, p. 71.
[161] Goldsmith, *Enquiry into the Present State*, *loc. cit.*, p. 31.
[162] Sherburn, *op. cit.*, pp. 841–42.
[163] Quoted in Atkins, *op. cit.*, p. 312.

was the goal of so many writers. The result, he feared, might be that nothing would be remembered of the literary works of his time.[164]

We have observed that Goldsmith, in his endeavor to come to grips with the dilemma of the writer, represented a variety of sometimes conflicting views. We have seen, however, that it was likely to be Goldsmith in his optimistic rather than in his pessimistic vein who set the tone for what was to come. So, too, his view of the "ideal" critic, of his function as one of mediation between the audience and the writer, was to prevail. Critics, writers, and philosophers—Johnson, Burke, Hume, Reynolds, Kames, and the Wartons—all adopted Goldsmith's premise as they began to analyze the experience of the reader.

A critic must try to understand what goes on in the minds of the readers. In Johnson's words he must ". . . improve opinion into knowledge, and . . . distinguish those means of pleasing which depend upon known causes." Johnson then outlines what we might today look upon as a scientific, descriptive approach to the study of media experience, pointing out that

> ". . . literary criticism, which has . . . hitherto known only the anarchy of ignorance, the caprices of fancy and the tyranny of prescription . . . can now be placed under the dominion of science."[165]

Joseph Wood Krutch points to him as the formulator of the concept that the critic "derives his right from the rights of the general public of which he is a part—not from the fact that he *is* a critic. He will generally agree with the public's considered judgment because literature is to be judged, not in the light of learning . . . but in accordance with the same common sense which guides us as we go about the business of life."[166] It was this orientation to audience experience which opened up an entirely new dimension in the debate over art and popular culture. In spite of their conflicts and contradictions, the mid-eighteenth-century English writers paved the way for the nineteenth-century critics and philosophers who were to formulate the metaphysics of cultural democracy. They were the first to recognize the importance, in an increasingly industrialized and mobile society, of relaxation, amusement, and escape from the pressures of work, whether the individual be a tired businessman or manual worker, and in so doing were far more detached than were their counterparts across the Channel. While Hume, for one, analyzed the psychological factors involved in "distraction" or amusement, Schiller and Goethe were to take a moral position: the public may need distraction, but unless they find a less passive way to achieve it, culture will surely degenerate.[167]

---

[164] Goldsmith, *Enquiry into the Present State, loc. cit.*, p. 47.
[165] Johnson, *The Rambler*, No. 92, *British Essayists*, XVII, 182.
[166] Krutch, *op. cit.*, p. 497.
[167] See "The Artist and His Public" in Chapter 2, pp. 18-28.

CHAPTER 4

The Triumph of Mass Idols

The following study is concerned with the content analysis of biographies. This literary topic had inundated the book market for the three decades previous to the writing of this article in 1943, and had for some time been a regular feature of popular magazines. Surprisingly enough, not very much attention had been paid to this phenomenon, none whatever to biographies appearing in magazines, and little to those published in book form.[1]

It started before the first World War, but the main onrush came shortly afterwards. The popular biography was one of the most conspicuous newcomers in the realm of print since the introduction of the short story. The circulation of books by Emil Ludwig,[2] André Maurois, Lytton Strachey, and Stefan Zweig, reached a figure in the millions, and with each new publication, the number of languages into which they were translated grew. Even if it were only a passing literary fad, one would still have to explain why this

The first published version of this chapter appeared as "Biographies in Popular Magazines" in *Radio Research: 1942-1943*, edited by Paul F. Lazarsfeld and Frank Stanton (New York: Duell, Sloan and Pearce, 1944).

[1] Cf. Edward H. O'Neill, *A History of American Biography* (Philadelphia: University of Pennsylvania Press, 1935). His remarks on pp. 179ff. on the period since 1919 as the "most prolific one in American history for biographical writing," are quoted by Helen McGill Hughes, *News and the Human Interest Story* (Chicago: University of Chicago Press, 1940), p. 285f, copyright 1940 by the University of Chicago. The book by William S. Gray and Ruth Munroe, *The Reading Interests and Habits of Adults* (New York: The Macmillan Company, 1930), which analyzes readers' figures for books and magazines, does not even introduce the category of biographies in its tables on the contents of magazines, and applies it only once for books in a sample analysis of readers in Hyde Park, Chicago. The only comment the authors have to offer is: "There is some tendency to prefer biographies and poetry, especially in moderate doses to other types of reading except fiction" (p. 154). Finally, I want to quote as a witness in this case of scientific negligence, Donald A. Stouffer, *The Art of Biography in Eighteenth Century England* (Princeton, N. J.: Princeton University Press, 1941), who in his excellent and very thorough study says: "Biography as a branch of literature has been too long neglected" (p. 3).

[2] Up to the spring of 1939, 3.1 million copies of his books were sold: 1.2 million in Germany, 1.1 million in the U.S., 0.8 million elsewhere. Cf. Emil Ludwig, *Traduction des oeuvres* (Moscia, 1939), p. 2.

fashion has had such longevity and is more and more becoming a regular feature in the most diversified media of publications.

Who's Who, once known as a title of a specialized dictionary for editors and advertisers, has nowadays become the outspoken or implied question in innumerable popular contexts. The interest in individuals has become a kind of mass gossip. The majority of weeklies and monthlies, and many dailies too, publish at least one life story or a fragment of one in each issue; theater programs present abridged biographies of all the actors; the more sophisticated periodicals, such as *The New Republic* or *Harper's*, offer short accounts of the main intellectual achievements of their contributors; and a glance into the popular corners of the book trade, including drug store counters, will invariably fall on biographies. All this forces the conclusion that there must be a social need seeking gratification by this type of literature.

One way to find out would be to study the readers' reactions, to explore by means of various interviewing techniques what they are looking for, what they think about the biographical jungle. But it seems to be rather premature to collect and to evaluate such solicited response until more is known about the content structure itself.

As an experiment in content analysis, a year's publication of *The Saturday Evening Post* (*SEP*) and of *Collier's* for the period from April 1940 to March 1941 was covered. It should not be inferred that the results as presented here are without much change applicable to all other magazines which present general and diversified topics. From a few selections taken from less widely circulated and more expensive magazines, ranging from *The New Yorker* to the dollar-a-copy *Fortune*, it seems very likely that the biographies presented there differ in their average content structure and therefore in their social and psychological implications from the lower-priced popular periodicals. The difference in contents corresponds to a difference in readership.

It is regrettable that a complete investigation could not be made for the most recent material, but samples taken at random from magazines under investigation showed that no basic change in the selection or content structure has occurred since this country's entry into World War II.

I

BIOGRAPHERS' IDOLS

Before entering into a discussion of our material we shall briefly look into the fate of the biographical feature during the past decades.

Production—Yesterday

Biographical sections have not always been a standing feature in these periodicals. If we turn back the pages we find distinct differences in the number of articles as well as in the selection of people treated.

Table 4-1 gives a survey of the professional distribution of the "heroes" in biographies between 1901 and 1941.[3]

TABLE 4-1.

DISTRIBUTION OF BIOGRAPHIES ACCORDING TO PROFESSIONS IN *THE SATURDAY EVENING POST* AND *COLLIER'S* FOR SELECTED YEARS BETWEEN 1901–1941

	1901–1914 (5 sample yrs.)		1922–1930 (6 sample yrs.)		1930–1934 (4 years)		1940–1941 (1 year)	
	No.	%	No.	%	No.	%	No.	%
Political life	81	46	112	28	95	31	31	25
Business and Professional	49	28	72	18	42	14	25	20
Entertainment	47	26	211	54	169	55	69	55
Total Number	177	100	395	100	306	100	125	100
Yearly average of biographies	36		66		77		125	

This table indicates clearly a tremendous increase in biographies as time goes on. The average figure of biographies in 1941 is almost four times as high as at the beginning of the century. The biography has nowadays become a regular weekly feature. Just to illustrate how relatively small the number of biographies was forty years ago: in fifty-two issues of the *SEP* of 1901–02 we find altogether twenty-one biographies as compared with not less than fifty-seven in 1940–41. The smallness of the earlier figure in comparison to the present day is emphasized by the fact that nonfictional contributions at that time far outnumbered the fictional material. A fair average of distribution in the past would be about three fictional and eight nonfictional contributions; today we never find more than twice as many nonfictional contributions and in the majority of cases even fewer.

We put the subjects of the biographies in three groups: the spheres of political life, of business and professions, and of entertainment (the latter in the broadest sense of the word). Looking at our table we find for the time before World War I very high interest in political figures and an almost equal distribution of business and professional men, on the one hand, and of entertainers on the other. This picture changes completely after the war. The figures from political life have been cut by 40 per cent. This numerical relation seems to be rather constant from 1922 up to the present day. If we re-formulate our professional distribution by leaving out the figures from political life we see even more clearly the considerable decrease of people from the serious and important professions and a corresponding increase of entertainers. The social impact of this change comes to the fore strikingly if we analyze the composition of the entertainers. This can be seen from Table 4-2.

While at the beginning of the century three quarters of the entertainers were serious artists and writers, we find that this class of people is reduced by

[3] For the collection of data prior to 1940 the writer is indebted to Miss Mariam Wexner.

TABLE 4-2

PROPORTION OF BIOGRAPHIES OF ENTERTAINERS FROM THE REALM
OF SERIOUS ARTS[a] IN *SEP* AND *COLLIER'S* FOR SELECTED YEARS
BETWEEN 1901–1941

(In per cent of total biographies of entertainers in each period)

Period	Proportion entertainers from serious arts	Total no. entertainers
1901–1914 (5 sample yrs.)	77	47
1922–1930 (6 sample yrs.)	38	211
1930–1934 (4 yrs.)	29	169
1940–1941 (1 yr.)	9	69

[a] This group includes literature, fine arts, music, dance, theater.

half twenty years later and tends to disappear almost completely at present.

As an instance of the selection of biographies typical of the first decade of the century, it is notable that out of the twenty-one biographies of the *SEP* 1901–02, eleven came from the political sphere, seven from the business and professions, and three from entertainment and sport. The people in the political group are numerically prominent until before Election Day in the various years: candidates for high office, i.e., the president or senators; the secretary of the treasury; an eminent state governor. In the business world, we are introduced to J. P. Morgan, the banker; his partner, George W. Perkins; James J. Hill, the railroad president. In the professions, we find one of the pioneers in aviation; the inventor of the torpedo; a famous Negro educator; an immigrant scientist. Among the entertainers there is an opera singer, Emma Clavé; a poet, Eugene Field; a popular fiction writer, F. Marion Crawford.

If we look at such a selection of people we find that it represents a fair cross-section of socially important occupations. Still, in 1922 the picture is more similar to the professional distribution quoted above than to the one which is characteristic of the present day magazines. If we take, for example, *Collier's* of 1922, we find in a total of twenty biographies only two entertainers, but eight business and professional men and ten politicians. Leaving out the latter ones, we find among others: Clarence C. Little, the progressive President of the University of Maine; Leonard P. Ayres, the very outspoken Vice-President of the Cleveland Trust Company; Director-General of the United States Railroad Administration, James C. Davis; President of the New York Central Railroad, A. H. Smith; and the City Planner, John Nolen. From the entertainment field, we have a short résumé of the stage comedian, Joe Cook (incidentally, by Franklin P. Adams), and an auto-biographical sketch by Charlie Chaplin.

We might say that a large proportion of the heroes in both samples are idols of production, that they stem from the productive life, from industry, business, and natural sciences. There is not a single hero from the world of sports and the few artists and entertainers either do not belong to the sphere of cheap or mass entertainment or represent a serious attitude toward their art as in the case of Chaplin. (We have omitted from our discussion and our figures a number of very short biographical features which amounted to little more than anecdotes. These were published fairly regularly by the *SEP* until the late twenties under the headings "Unknown Captains of Industry," "Wall Street Men," sometimes called "Bulls and Bears," "Who's Who and Why," "Workingman's Wife," "Literary Folk.") The first quarter of the century cherishes biography in terms of an open-minded liberal society which really wants to know something about its own leading figures on the decisive social, commercial, and cultural fronts. Even in the late twenties, when jazz composers and the sports people are admitted to the inner circle of biographical heroes, their biographies are written almost exclusively to supplement the reader's knowledge of the technical requirements and accomplishments of their respective fields.[4] These people, then, are treated as an embellishment of the national scene, not yet as something that in itself represents a special phenomenon which demands almost undivided attention.

We should like to quote from two stories which seem to be characteristic of this past epoch. In a sketch of Theodore Roosevelt, the following comment is made in connection with the assassination of McKinley:

> We, who give such chances of success to all that it is possible for a young man to go as a laborer into the steel business and before he has reached his mature prime become, through his own industry and talent, the president of a vast steel association—we, who make this possible as no country has ever made it possible, have been stabbed in the back by anarchy.[5]

This unbroken confidence in the opportunities open to every individual serves as the *leitmotiv* of the biographies. To a very great extent they are to be looked upon as examples of success which can be imitated. These life stories are really intended to be educational models. They are written—at least ideologically—for someone who the next day may try to emulate the man whom he has just envied.

A biography seems to be the means by which an average person is able to reconcile his interest in the important trends of history and in the personal lives of other people. In the past, and especially before the first World War,

[4] See, for instance, the *SEP*, September 19, 1925, where the auto-racer, Barney Oldfield, tells a reporter details of his racing experiences and of the mechanics of racing and automobiles; September 26, 1925, in which the vaudeville actress, Elsie Janis, comments on her imitation acts and also gives details of her techniques. The same holds true for the biography of the band leader, Sousa, in the *SEP*, October 31, 1925, and of the radio announcer, Graham McNamee, May 1, 1926; after a few remarks about his own life and career, McNamee goes on to discuss the technical aspects of radio and his experiences in radio with famous people.

[5] *The Saturday Evening Post*, October 12, 1901.

popular biography lived in an optimistic atmosphere where understanding of historical processes and interest in successful people seemed to integrate pleasantly into one harmonious endeavor.

> We know now that the men of trade and commerce and finance are the real builders of freedom, science, and art—and we watch them and study them accordingly. . . . Of course, Mr. Perkins is a "self-made man." Who that has ever made a career was not?[6]

This may be taken as a classical formulation for a period of "rugged individualism" in which there is neither the time nor the desire to stimulate a closer interest in the organizers and organization of leisure time, but which is characterized by eagerness and confidence that the social ladder may be scaled on a mass basis.

Here and there we find a casual remark on the function of biographies as models for individual imitation. "In 1890 a book appeared entitled *Acres of Diamonds*, by Russell H. Conwell. This book dealt especially with the problems of attaining success in life. The author attempted to encourage the reader by giving examples of the struggles and triumphs of noted successful men and women. This pattern of encouraging the reader by citing examples of great men has continued, and in recent years a number of books have appeared in which most of the content dealt with case histories of noted individuals. Some psychologists have suggested that interest in autobiographies and biographies has arisen in part from the attempts of the readers to compare their own lives with those about whom they read, and thus to seek encouragement from the evidence of the struggles of successful people."[7]

Helen M. Hughes in her suggestive study has not avoided the tendency to settle the problem of biographies by rather simplified psychological formulae. By quoting generously O'Neill, Bernard MacFadden, and André Maurois, she points to the differences of the more commemorative and eulogistic elements in earlier biographies and the "anxious groping for certainty of people who live in times of rapid change," which is supposed to be connected with the present interest in biography.

Consumption—Today

When we turn to our present-day sample we face an assortment of people which is both qualitatively and quantitatively removed from the standards of the past.

Only two decades ago people from the realm of entertainment played a very negligible role in the biographical material. They form now, numeri-

---

[6] *The Saturday Evening Post*, June 28, 1902.

[7] Mandel Sherman, "Book Selection and Self Therapy" in *The Practice of Book Selection*, ed. Louis R. Wilson (Chicago: University of Chicago Press, 1939), p. 172. Copyright 1939 by the University of Chicago.

THE TRIUMPH OF MASS IDOLS

cally, the first group. While we have not found a single figure from the world of sports in our earlier samples given above, we find them now close to the top of favorite selections. The proportion of people from political life and from business and professions, both representing the "serious side," has declined from 74 to 45 per cent of the total.

Let us examine the group of people representing non-political aspects of life. Sixty-nine are from the world of entertainment and sport; twenty-five from that which we called before the "serious side." Almost half of the twenty-five belong to some kind of communications professions: there are ten newspapermen and radio commentators. Of the remaining fifteen business and professional people, there are a pair of munitions traders, Athanasiades (118)[8] and Juan March (134); Dr. Brinkley (3), a quack doctor; and Mr. Angas (20), judged by many as a dubious financial expert; Pittsburgh Phil (23), a horse race gambler in the "grand style"; Mrs. D'Arcy Grant (25), a woman sailor, and Jo Carstairs (54), the owner of an island resort; the Varian brothers (52), inventors of gadgets, and Mr. Taylor (167), an inventor of fool-proof sports devices; Howard Johnson (37), a roadside restaurant genius; Jinx Falkenburg (137), at that time a professional model; and finally, Dr. Peabody (29), a retired rector of a swanky society prep school.

The "serious" people are not so serious after all. In fact there are only nine who might be looked upon as rather important or characteristic figures of the industrial, commercial, or professional activities, and six of these are newspapermen or radio commentators.

We called the heroes of the past "idols of production": we feel entitled to call the present-day magazine heroes "idols of consumption." Indeed, almost every one of them is directly, or indirectly, related to the sphere of leisure time: either he does not belong to vocations which serve society's basic needs (e.g., the heroes of the world of entertainment and sport), or he amounts, more or less, to a caricature of a socially productive agent. If we add to the group of the sixty-nine people from the entertainment and sports world the ten newspaper and radio men, the professional model, the inventor of sports devices, the quack doctor, the horse race gambler, the inventors of gadgets, the owner of the island resort, and the restaurant chain owner, we see eighty-seven of all ninety-four non-political heroes directly active in the consumers' world.

Of the eight figures who cannot exactly be classified as connected with consumption, not more than three—namely, the automobile producer, Sloan; the engineer and industrialist, Stout; and the air line czar, Smith— are important or characteristic functionaries in the world of production. The two armament magnates, the female freight boat skipper, the prep school head, and the doubtful market prophet remind us of the standardized pro-

[8] The figures in parentheses refer to the bibliography of stories studied; see Appendix to this chapter. Figures 1 to 57 refer to the *SEP* and figures 101 to 168 refer to *Collier's*. On the difference between the *SEP* and *Collier's*, see Appendix, Tables 4-4 and 4-5.

tagonists in mystery novels and related fictional merchandise: people with a more or less normal and typical personal and vocational background who would bore us to death if we did not discover that behind the "average" front lurks a "human interest" situation.

By substituting such a classification according to spheres of activity for the cruder one according to professions, we are now prepared to present the vocational stratifications of our heroes in a new form. It is shown in Table 4-3 for the *SEP* and *Collier's* of 1940–1941.

TABLE 4-3

THE HEROES AND THEIR SPHERES

	Number of stories	Per cent
Sphere of production	3	2
Sphere of consumption	91	73
Entertainers and sports figures	69	55
Newspaper and radio figures	10	8
Agents of consumers' goods	5	4
Topics of light fiction	7	6
Sphere of politics	31	25
Total	125	100

If a student in some very distant future should use popular magazines of 1941 as a source of information as to what figures the American public looked to in the first stages of the greatest crisis since the birth of the Union, he would come to a grotesque result. While the industrial and professional endeavors are geared to a maximum of speed and efficiency, the idols of the masses are not, as they were in the past, the leading names in the battle of production, but the headliners of the movies, the ball parks, and the night clubs. While we found that around 1900 and even around 1920 the vocational distribution of magazine heroes was a rather accurate reflection of the nation's living trends, we observe that today the hero-selection corresponds to needs quite different from those of genuine information. They seem to lead to a dream world of the masses who no longer are capable or willing to conceive of biographies primarily as a means of orientation and education. They receive information not about the agents and methods of social production but about the agents and methods of social and individual consumption. During the leisure in which they read, they read almost exclusively about people who are directly, or indirectly, providing for the reader's leisure time. The vocational set-up of the dramatis personae is organized as if the social production process were either completely exterminated or tacitly understood, and needed no further interpretation. Instead, the leisure time period seems to be the new social riddle on which extensive reading and studying has to be done.

The human incorporation of all the social agencies taking care of society as a unity of consumers represents a literary type which is turned out as a standardized article, marketed by a tremendous business, and consumed by another mass institution, the nation's magazine reading public. Thus biography lives as a mass element among the other elements of mass literature.

It will be very important to check how far the war situation confirmed, changed, or even reversed the trend. A few casual observations may be mentioned.

The *New York Times* "Magazine" on July 12, 1942, published an article "Wallace Warns Against 'New Isolationism.'" The Vice-President of the United States is photographed playing tennis. The caption for the picture reads "Mr. Wallace's Serve." This picture and its caption are a very revealing symbol. The word "serve" does not refer to social usefulness, but to a feature in the vice-president's private life.

This remark can be supplemented by quoting a few issues of the *SEP* and *Collier's*, picked at random from their publications during the summer of 1942. While everywhere else in this study we have limited ourselves to the analysis of strictly biographical contributions, we should like, by quoting some of the topics of the entire issues which we have chosen for this year, to emphasize the over-all importance of the spheres of consumption. Not only has the selection of heroes for biographies not changed since America's active participation in the war, but many other of the non-fictional articles are also still concerned with consumers' interests.

Of the ten non-fictional articles in the *SEP*, August 8, 1942, five are connected with the consumers' world: a serial on Hollywood agents; a report on a hometown circus; a report on roadside restaurants; an analysis of women as book readers; and an essay on the horse and buggy. In an issue one week later, August 15, 1942, there is a report on the International Correspondence School; the continuation of the serial on the Hollywood agents; and a biography on the radio idol, Kate Smith. Or let us look at *Collier's*, which as a whole, devotes a much higher percentage of articles to war topics than the *SEP*. Out of nine articles in the issue of July 4, 1942, five belong to the consumers' world. There is again one on the horse and buggy, another one on a baseball hero, a third one on an Army comedian, a fourth one on a Broadway producer, and finally, one on budget buffets. Three weeks later, on July 25, out of ten articles, again five belong to the same category.

In other words, out of thirty-seven articles found in four issues of two leading popular magazines during the present crisis, not less than seventeen treat the gustatory and entertainment features of the average citizen. Much of the fare presented to the reading public during the times immediately preceding the war and during the war itself was almost completely divorced from important social issues.

Our discovery of a common professional physiognomy in all of these portraits encouraged us to guess that what is true of the selection of people will also be true of the selection of what is said about these people. This hypothesis has been quite justified, as we propose to demonstrate in the following pages. Our content analysis not only revealed impressive regularities in the occurrence, omission, and treatment of certain topics, but also showed that these regularities may be interpreted in terms of the very same category of consumption which was the key to the selection of the biographical subjects. Consumption is a thread running through every aspect of these stories. The characteristics which we have observed in the literary style of the author, in his presentation of personal relations, of professions and personalities, can all be integrated around the concept of the consumer.

For classification of the stories' contents, we decided on a four-fold scheme. First there are what one might call the sociological aspects of the man: his relations to other people, the pattern of his daily life, his relation to the world in which he lives. Second, his psychology: what the nature of his development has been and the structure of his personality. Third, his history: what his encounter with the world has been like—the object world which he has mastered or failed to master. Fourth, the evaluation of these data which the author more or less consciously conveys by his choice of language. Granted that this scheme is somewhat arbitrary, we think that our division of subject matter has resulted in a fairly efficient worksheet, especially when we consider the backward state of content analysis of this type.

We proceeded to collect all the passages in the 125 stories pertaining to our four categories. It is not intended here to analyze the 2,400 quotations exhaustively, but merely to present a few observations or hypotheses which their study suggested to us and which we hope may be stimulating to further research in content analysis. As we studied our stories, we looked almost in vain for such vital subjects as the man's relations to politics or to social problems in general. Our category of sociology reduces itself to the *private lives* of the heroes. Similarly, our category of psychology was found to contain mainly a static image of a human being to whom a number of things happen, culminating in a success which seems to be none of his doing. This whole section becomes merged with our category of history which is primarily concerned with success data, too, and then takes on the character of a catalogue of "*just facts*." When we survey the material on how authors evaluate their subjects, what stands out most clearly is the biographers' preoccupation with justifying their hero by means of undiscriminating *superlatives* while still interpreting him in terms which bring him as close as possible to the level of the average man.

II

Private Lives

The reader may have noticed in public conveyances a poster called "Private Lives" depicting the peculiarities of more or less famous people in the world of science, sports, business, and politics. The title of this feature is a fitting symbol for all our biographies. It would be an overstatement, but not too far from the truth, to say that these stories are exclusively reports on the heroes' private lives. While it once was rather contemptible to give much room to the private affairs and habits of public figures this topic is now the focus of interest. The reason for viewing this as an overstatement is in a way surprising: we learn something, although not very much, about the man's professional career and its requirements, but we are kept very uninformed about important segments of his private life.

Inheritance and Parents—Friends and Teachers

The personal relations of our heroes, on which we are enlightened, are, as a whole, limited to two groups, the parents and the friends. Both groups are taken in a specific sense: the parents comprising other older relations or forebears of former generations, the friends being more or less limited to people who were valuable in the hero's career. In more than half of the stories the father or the mother or the general family background is at least mentioned. Clark Gable's "stubborn determination" seems derived from his "Pennsylvania Dutch ancestors" (6); the very efficient State Department official, Mrs. Shipley, is the "daughter of a Methodist minister" (8); Senator Taft is a "middle-of-the-roader like his father" besides being "an aristocrat by birth and training" (101). We are let in a little bit on the family situation of Brenda Joyce because "somewhere there was a break-up between mamma and papa" (110). The general pattern of the parental home, however, is more on the Joan Carroll side, where we find the "young, quietly dignified mother . . . the successful engineer father . . . a star scout brother six years her senior" (143); we hear in a very sympathetic way about the old Fadimans, "the father a struggling Russian immigrant and pharmacist, the mother a nurse" (47); we learn a good deal about ancestors as in the case of Clark Gable cited above. Of the Secretary of Labor, Frances Perkins, we are told that her "forebears had settled all over New England between 1630–1680" (22); the female freighter skipper, D'Arcy Grant, has "an ancestral mixture of strong-headed swashbuckling Irish and pioneer Americans" (25); Raymond Gram Swing is the "heir of a severe New England tradition" (42); the Varian brothers have "Celtic blood" (52); in the woman matador, Conchita Cintron, we find "Spanish, Connecticut Irish, and Chilean elements" (116).

The curious fact here is not that the authors mention parentage, but that they have so much to say about it and so little to say about other human relations. It is a good deal as if the author wants to impress on the reader that his hero, to a very considerable extent, must be understood in terms of his biological and regional inheritance. It is a kind of primitive Darwinian concept of social facts: the tendency to place the burden of explanation and of responsibility on the shoulders of the past generations. The individual himself appears as a mere product of his past.

The element of passivity is also found in the second most frequently mentioned group of personal relationships: friends and teachers. Let us look again into some of the material. We hear that the woman diplomat, Mrs. Harriman, was made "Minister to Norway because of her many powerful and loyal friends" (14); of the friendship between the hard-hit restaurateur, Johnson, and his wealthy doctor-friend (37); the movie actress, Brenda Marshall, was somehow saved in her career "by the friendship of a script girl" (161); Senator Byrnes got a good start because "a disillusioned old Charlestonian . . . showed him the ropes" (18) while Miss Perkins is " 'protected' by her personal secretary . . . (who) worships her" (22).

There is very rarely an episode which shows our heroes as active partners of friendship. In most cases their friends are their helpers. Very often they are teachers who later on become friends. Perhaps it is stretching a point to say that a vulgarian Darwinism is supplemented at this point by a vulgarian distortion of the "milieu" theory; the hero is a product of ancestry and friendship. But even if this may be somewhat exaggerated, it nevertheless helps to clarify the point, namely, that the hero appears in his human relationships as the one who takes, not as the one who gives.

We can supplement this statement by going back to our remark that decisive human relationships, and even those which are decisive for private lives, are missing. The whole sphere of the relations with the opposite sex is almost entirely missing. This is indeed a very strange phenomenon. We should assume that the predilection for such people as actors and actresses from stage and screen, night club entertainers, and so forth, would be tied up with a special curiosity in such people's love affairs, but this is not the case at all. The realm of love, passion, even marriage, seem worth mentioning only in terms of vital statistics. It is quite a lot to be informed that Dorothy Thompson "got tangled up in love"; very soon Lewis "asked point blank whether she would marry him" (9); Senator Byrnes "married the charming wife who still watches over him" (18); the industrial tycoon, Sloan, remarks, "Mrs. Sloan and I were married that summer . . . she was of Roxbury, Mass." (24); Mrs. Peabody married the rector "at the close of the school's first year" (29). We are told about Raymond Gram Swing only that he was married twice (42); as far as Lyons', the baseball player's, bachelor situation goes we hear that he "almost married his campus sweetheart" (53); while his colleague, Rizzuto, is "not even going steady" (57). In the high life of politics we are glad to know that Ambassador Lothian "gets on well with women" (115); and that Thomas Dewey is "a man's man, but women go for him" (117); we are briefly informed that Chris Martin "married, raised a family" (121); and that "one girl was sufficiently impressed to marry" Michael Todd, the producer, at the tender age of seventeen (131).

These statements of fact, in a matter of fact way, as, for instance, the mention of a marriage or a divorce, is all that we hear of that side of human relations which we were used to look upon as the most important ones. If we again imagine that these popular biographies should at a very distant historical moment serve as the sole source of information, the historian of the future would almost be forced to the conclusion that in our times the institution of marriage, and most certainly the phenomena of sexual passions, had become a very negligible factor. It seems that the fifth-rate role to which these phenomena are relegated fits very well with the emphasis on parentage and friendship. Love and passion require generosity, a display of productive mental and emotional forces which are neither primarily explained nor restrained by inheritance and advice.

A rather amusing observation: we found that the eyes of the hero were mentioned in almost one-third of the stories. It is quite surprising that of all possible physiognomic and bodily features just this one should be so very popular. We take delight in the baseball umpire Bill Klem's "bright blue eyes," in his "even supernaturally good eyes" (104); or in the "modest brown eyes" of General Weygand (107). Miss Cintron, the matador, is "blue-eyed" (116); the night club singer, Moffett, has "very bright blue eyes" (119).

We are not quite certain how to explain our biographers' bodily preferences. The eyes are commonly spoken of as "the windows of the soul." Perhaps it gratified the more inarticulate reader if the authors let him try to understand the heroes in the same language in which he believes he understands his neighbor's soul. It is just another example of a cliché served up in lieu of a genuine attempt at psychological insight.

Home and Social Life—Hobbies and Food Preferences

The heroes, as we have seen, stem predominantly from the sphere of consumption and organized leisure time. It is fascinating to see how in the course of the presentation the producers and agents of consumer goods change into their own customers. Personal habits, from smoking to poker playing, from stamp collecting to cocktail parties, are faithfully noted in between 30 and 40 per cent of all stories under investigation. In fact, as soon as it comes to habits, pleasures, and distractions after and outside of working hours, the magazine biographer turns out to be just a snoopy reporter.

The politicians seem to be an especially ascetic lot—Taft "doesn't smoke" (101); neither does General Weygand (107); the former British Ambassador, Lothian, "hasn't taken a drink in twenty-five years" (115). There is also the movie actor, Chris Martin, who "doesn't smoke cigars or cigarettes" (121); the German Field Marshal Milch whose "big black Brazilian cigars are his favored addiction" (146). To quote some of the favorite habits or dishes of the crowd: Dorothy Thompson is all out for "making Viennese dishes" while her "pet hates . . . are bungled broth and clumsily buttered tea bread" (9). We are invited to rejoice in Art Fletcher's "excellent digestion" (7). We hope that Major Angas is equally fortunate, for: "Eating well is his secondary career"; he is "perpetually hungry" (20). The circus magnate, North, also seems to have a highly developed sense for food and what goes with it: "His cud-cutters for a three-pound steak are a Martini, a Manhattan, and a beer, in that invariable order, tamped down with a hatful of radishes" (26).

As for the innocent hobbies of our heroes: Art Fletcher likes "the early evening movies" and also "to drive about the country" (7); Senator Byrnes finds recreation in "telling of the long saltily humorous anecdotes which all Southerners love" (18). The pitcher, Paige, is "an expert dancer and singer" (19); Westbrook Pegler "plays poker" (28); and his special pet foe, Mayor Hague, also "likes gambling" (36); his colleague, the London *Times* correspondent, Sir Willmott Lewis, also "plays poker" (49), while Swing takes to badminton (42). More on the serious side is Greer Garson who "reads a great deal and studies the theater every minute she is free" (113). The hobby of golf unites Senator Taft (101), the fascist, Muti (114), the "Blondie" cartoonist, Chic Young (165), the baseball player, Lyons (53), and Ambassador Lothian (115).

We are furthermore told who likes to be "the life of the party," and who does not; and also how the daily routine in the apartment or private house is fixed. The Fletchers, for instance, "retire early and rise early" (7); while Hank Greenberg "lives modestly with his parents" but also "likes night clubs, bright lights, and pretty girls" (56). We hear of the actress Stickney's charming "town house" (145), of the "fifteen rooms and five baths and the private elevator to the street" of political Boss Flynn (138); of the way in which the ballet director Balanchine is "snugly installed in an elaborate Long Island home, and a sleek New York apartment" (152).

As to social gatherings: Nancy Hamilton's parties "aren't glittering at all, but they are fun" (103). The newspaperman, Silliman Evans, "has introduced the Texas-size of large scale outdoor entertainment" (39); while his colleague, Clifton Fadiman, has "very little social life, seldom goes to dinner parties" (47). His habits seem related to those of the private island queen, Jo Carstairs: ". . . A few friends of long standing make up one of the world's shortest guest lists" (54).

And so it goes, through over two hundred quotations, changing a study in social relations into consumers' research. It is neither a world of "doers" nor a world of "doing" for which the biographical curiosity of a mass public is evoked. The whole trend goes toward acceptance: the biological and educational heritage; the helpful friends and teachers; the physical protection of the house, and the physiological one of eating and drinking; the security of social standing and prestige, through social entertaining; the complete resting of mind and work-wise energy through the gamut of hobbies. Here we come very close to decisive trends to which the modern individual seems subjected. He appears no longer as a center of outwardly bound energies and actions; as an inexhaustible reservoir of initiative and enterprise; no longer as an integral unity on whose work and efficiency might depend not only his kin's future and happiness, but at the same time, mankind's progress in general. Instead of the "givers" we are faced with the "takers." These new heroes represent a craving for having and taking things for granted. They seem to stand for a phantasmagoria of world-wide social security; for an attitude which asks for no more than to be served with the things needed for reproduction and recreation; for an attitude which has lost any primary interest in how to invent, shape, or apply the tools leading to such purposes of mass satisfaction.

We cannot avoid getting something of a distorted picture of society if we look at it exclusively through the personal lives of a few individuals. But in the past an effort was made to show the link between the hero and the nation's recent history. As one of those earlier biographers, D. G. Phillips, put it:

> Each era, conscious of the mighty works that could be wrought, conscious that we are all under sentence of speedy death, eagerly seeks out the younger man, the obscure man. It has need of all powers and all talents. Especially of the talents for creating, organizing, and directing.[9]

Today the emphasis is on the routine functions of nourishment and leisure time and not on "the talents for creating, organizing, and directing." The real battlefield of history recedes from view or becomes a stock backdrop while society disintegrates into an amorphous crowd of consumers. Greer Garson and Mahatma Gandhi meet on common ground: the one "likes potatoes and stew and never tires of a breakfast of porridge and haddock" (113); the other's "evening meal is simple—a few dates, a little rice, goat's milk" (124); Hitler and Chris Martin "don't smoke . . ." (121).

III

JUST FACTS

Phillips comments made on Pierpont Morgan's "Right Hand" about sixty years ago may serve as a transition from the sociology of our heroes to their psychology. With its emphasis on the independence and leadership awaiting the exercise of personal initiative, it expresses the ideal character type of private capitalism.

[9] D. G. Phillips, "The Right Hand to Pierpont Morgan," *The Saturday Evening Post,* June 28, 1902.

There are at least two elements in this quotation, the presence of which characterizes the psychological concept of former biographies, and the absence of which is very meaningful for the present situation: development and solitude.

"The young, obscure man" has something of the heritage, however trivial in this case, of the personality as it was conceived during the rise of the middle-class culture: the individual as a totality of potentialities, mental, moral, and emotional, which have to be developed in a given social framework. Development, as the essence of human life, was connected with the idea that the individual has to find himself in the soliloquy of the mind. Human existence seemed to be made up of the loneliness of the creature and his emergence into the outer world by displaying his own gifts. Our quotation is one of the late forms of this concept: the self-developing and fighting individual with all the chances in the world for creation and conquest.

Souls Without History

In an essay on present-day man, Max Horkheimer states: "Development has ceased to exist."[10] His remarks on the immediate transition from childhood to adult life, his observation that "the child is grown up as soon as he can walk, and the grown-up in principle always remains the same,"[11] sound as if they were a comment on our biographical heroes. Among our quotations we have a collection of passages which try to tie up the childhood of the hero with his later life. Almost every second story brings some report on the road from childhood to maturity. Does this not seem to contradict our general remark, is this not a variation of the classical concept of the emerging personality? Before answering, let us examine a few representative passages: At the age of twelve "wrestling . . . was the answer to my problem," says the wrestler, Allman (13). The king of horse race betting, Pittsburgh Phil, "began betting when he was fourteen—on his own game chickens" (23). Of the inventor, Stout, it is remarked: "Wherever his family lived, he would rig up a crude shop and try to make things" (41). At twelve, the future actor, Ezra Stone, ran a kid's radio program "directing the actors and paying them off at the end of the week" (108). For the Ringling-Barnum head, J. R. North: "a real circus was his toy" (26). The future film star, Greer Garson, "wanted to be an acress from the time she could walk" (113). The night club singer Hildegarde's parents "weren't surprised when Hildegarde . . . aged eighteen months, hummed a whole aria of an opera they had carried her to" (135).

Childhood appears neither as prehistory and key to the character of an individual nor as a stage of transition to the growth and formation of the

[10] Max Horkheimer, "The End of Reason" in *Studies in Philosophy and Social Science*, Vol. IX (1941), No. 3, p. 381.
[11] *Ibid.*

abundant diversity of an adult. Childhood is nothing but a midget edition, a predated publication of a man's profession and career. A man is an actor, a doctor, a dancer, an entrepreneur, and he always was. He was not born the tender and unknown potentiality of a human life, of an intellectual, mental emotional creativeness, effective for himself and for society, rather he came into the world and stayed in it, rubber stamped with and for a certain function. The individual has become a trademark.

In more than a third of the stories an attempt at a "theory of success" seems to be made but no magic formula is offered which an average individual might follow for his own good. The bulk of the answers consists of more or less trivial suggestions that the key may be found in "instinct" of other vague qualities. The golf player, Bobby Jones, "must have been born with the deep love for the game" (11). As to the Senator: "Leadership is Byrnes' real genius" (18). Pittsburgh Phil was "a good horse player by instinct" (23). The businessman, Durand N. Briscoe, seemed to have an instinct for promotion and speculation" (24). The achievements of the football coach, Kendrigan, are a mystery even to him: "how he did it he never figured" (50). The airline tycoon, Cyrus R. Smith, may count on "an unerring gambler's instinct" (51). This key formula of instinct is supplemented by a collection of almost tautological truisms: The fascist, Muti, "loves his danger highly spiced" (114). The sociable ambassador, Lothian, "likes newspapermen" (115). Howard Johnson knows what makes a restaurant successful: "A man that is properly supervised never goes haywire" (37). And as far as Clark Gable's success is concerned (and this could be applied to all the 125), "The answer . . . is personality" (6).

We venture to interpret this pseudo-psychology of success as another aspect of the timeless and passive image of modern man. Just as childhood is an abbreviation of the adult's professional career, so is the explanation of this career nothing but an abstract, rather inarticulate, reiteration that a career is a career and a success is a success.

The psychological atmosphere breathes behaviorism on a very primitive level. Childhood as well as that vague realm of instincts represents, so to speak, the biological background from which a variety of human qualities emerge. It is a psychology which shows no need of asking why and, precisely in the same sense in which we tried to show it for sociology, testifies to the transformation from the worship of a spontaneous personality to the adoration of an existence shaped and molded by outside forces. These people live in a limbo of children and victims. The way leads to what we are inclined to call "a command psychology" because people are not conceived as the responsible agents of their fate in all phases of their lives, but as the bearers of certain useful or not so useful character traits which are pasted on them like decorations or stigmas of shame.

There are a few traits which seem to have some bearing on a man's ability to manipulate his environment. We mean the columnist who is a "spotlight stealer" (9); the playwright and actress who never overlooks "good spots for herself" (103); the producer who is "his own ballyhoo artist" (131). We mean the baseball manager who is "chemically opposed to being on the sucker end of a ball game" (2); the smart night club star who sees "no point in disclosing that King Gustave's favorite singer had been born over her father's delicatessen store" (135); the actress who has real "talent for meeting people" (103); the person who shows up "at the right place at the right time" (109); who is a "great man in flying, handshaking and backslapping trips" (21).

The majority of such attitudes are likely to evoke a slyly understanding smile on the part of the observer and reader. These are the "sure-fire" tricks on the road to success, a little doubtful, but not too bad; these are the equipment of the shrewd man and the smart woman. But these psychological gadgets exhaust the list of qualities pertaining to creative and productive abilities. They generate an atmosphere of pseudo-creativeness in an attempt to convince us that a man has contributed his personal, individual share to the general cause of progress. "Something new has been added," insists the advertisement, but beware of inquiring too closely into the nature of the novelty. Thus, the good-natured statements of a certain lack of meticulous innocence on the road to success, become for the sociological interpreter a sad revelation of a lack of originality in productive strength.

This is brought out even more clearly when we turn to the presentation of the actual history of success. Here success is not even attributed to some happy instinct—it merely happens. Success has lost the seductive charm which once seemed to be a promise and a prize for everybody who was strong, clever, flexible, sober enough to try. It has become a rigid matter on which we look with awe or envy as we look at the priceless pictures in our galleries or the fabulous palaces of the rich. The success of our heroes of consumption is in itself goods of consumption. It does not serve as an instigator for more activity, it is introduced as something we have to accept just like the food and drink and the parties; it is nourishment for curiosity and entertainment.

The mythology of success in the biographies consists of two elements, hardship and breaks. The troubles and difficulties with which the road to success is paved are discussed in the form of stereotypes. Over and over again we hear that the going is rough and hard. The baseball umpire goes "the long, rough road up to that night of triumph" (104); the lightweight champion "came up the hard way" (123); a Senator knew in his youth the "long hours of hard work" (149); and the ballet director "worked hard" (152). In identical words we hear that the baseball manager (2) and the great film star (6) "came up the hard way." The "hard way" it was for Dorothy Thompson (9) and for Billy Rose (43). We are reminded of official military communiques, reporting a defeat or stalemate in a matter-of-fact tone, rather than descriptions of life processes.

The same applies to the reverse side of hardship: to the so-called breaks.

All our stories refer to successes and it is fair enough that somehow we must be informed when and how the failures stopped. Here the tendency to commute life data into facts to be accepted rather than understood becomes intensified. Usually, the beginning of the peak is merely stated as an event: A high civil servant was "fortunate in her first assignment" (8); a cartoonist merely gets a "telegram offering him a job on the paper" which later leads to his fame (34); a columnist "bursts into certain popularity" (42); an actor "got a break" (112); another "got the job and it turned out well" (121); for a middleweight champion "the turning point of his career had arrived" (142). If any explanation is offered at all, we are told that the turn occurred in some freakish way: the night club singer gets started by "a king's whim" (135); Clark Gable's appointment as a timekeeper with a telephone company appears as the turning point in his career (6); a baseball player goes on a fishing trip, loses his old job and thereby gets another one which leads to his success (133a).

These episodes of repetition and freakishness seem to demonstrate that there is no longer a social pattern for the way up. Success has become an accidental and irrational event. The dangers of competition were tied up with the idea of definite chances and there was a sound balance between ambition and possibilities. Appropriately enough, our heroes are almost without ambition, a tacit admission that those dangers of the past have been replaced by the cruelties of the present. It is cruel, indeed, that the ridiculous game of chance should open the doors to success for a handful, while all the others who were not present when it happened are failures. The "facts" of a career are a reflection of the lack of spontaneity. Behind the amusing, fortuitous episode lurks a terrible truth.

The spectacle of success, hardships, and accidents is attended in the biographies by an assortment of numbers and figures which purport to bestow glamour and exactness to the narration. The ideal language of modern biographies seems to belong to the scientific mentality which sees its ideal in the transformation from quality into quantity. Life's riddle is solved if caught in a numeric constellation. The majority of figures refer to income, to which may be added relatively few data on capital. Other figures pertain to the spectators of a ball game, to the budget of a city, or to the votes of an election.

Hardships and breaks are standard articles for the reader. They are just a better brand of what everyone uses. The outstanding has become the proved specimen of the average. By impressing on the reading masses the idols of our civilization, any criticism or even reasoning about the validity of such standards is suppressed. As a social scientist the biographer represents a pitiless, almost sadistic trend in science, for he demonstrates the recurring nature of such phenomena as hardships and breaks, but he does not attempt to reveal the laws of such recurrence. For him knowledge is not the source of power but merely the key to adjustment.

Catalogue of Adjustment

When we turn to a study of the approval and disapproval which our authors attach to the various character traits they describe, we find a striking and simple pattern.

In tone the catalogue of these traits, like the mythology of success, resembles a digest of military orders of the day: brusque laudations and reprimands. There is no room for nuances or ambiguity. In content it is on a very simple level and the criterion of approval or disapproval is also very simple. The yardstick is social adjustment. Once we realize the subconscious and conscious opinions of present-day society on what an adjusted person should and should not be, we are thoroughly familiar with the evaluation of character traits and their owners. The yardstick has three scales: behavior toward material tasks; behavior toward fellow men; and behavior in relation to one's own emotions. The one who is efficient scores in the first sphere; the one who is sociable, in the second; and the one who is always restrained, in the third.

In a separate study of all passages mentioning character traits, we found that of a total of seventy-six quotations referring to a hero's commendable behavior toward "things to be done," not fewer than seventy, or over 90 per cent, mentioned competence, efficiency, and energy; the remaining six referred to ambition. The majority read: "very capable" (154); "no sacrifice of time, effort, or my own convenience was too great" (24); "an inordinately hard worker" (48); "was never fired for inefficiency" (167); "thorough and accurate" (16); "being idle is her idea of complete torture" (140).

Out of a total of forty-eight quotations mentioning commendable behavior in relation to people, all forty-eight quote "co-operation," "sociability," and "good sportsmanship." There is a constant repetition of such adjectives as "co-operative," "generous," and "sociable." A baseball manager is "easy to meet, sociable, unsparing in his time with interviewers" (27). The "sociable" Chief of the Passport Division (8); the Secretary of Labor, "a delightful hostess" (22); the Republican candidate for the presidency with his "liking for and interest in people" (133); the matador, "genial, friendly, hospitable" (116); a smart actress, "amiable and friendly" (140) —they all belong to one big happy family which knows no limits in being pleasant and agreeable to each other. Like Don James, the barker for sideshows, they all seem to have "hearts so huge and overflowing" (127).

The number of quotations pertaining to disapproved character traits is very small, but conspicuous among them are criticisms of the unrestrained expression of emotion. It is virtually horrible that one of our baseball heroes "is no man for a jest when losing a game" (53); that a movie actress "cannot bear to be teased" (105); or that our Secretary of Labor's "public relations are unfortunate" (22). Unrestrained behavior traits like being "irritable and harsh" (32), "swift, often furious testiness" (117), being "unbalanced" (56), or even possessing a "somewhat difficult personality" (117) are really most unpleasant. Such faults can be tolerated only if they are exceptional —like the man who "for once got his feelings beyond control" (23).

The catalogue of normalcy leaves no room for individuality. This catalogue levels human behavior by the rejection of emotional eruptions; the bad marks given to the poor "joiners" and the temperamental people; the complete lack of creative and passionate behavior among the commendable qualities. The absence of love and passion in our catalogue of human relations finds its counterpart in this catalogue of human qualities. It is a world of dependency. The social implications of such atmosphere seem to be considerable because in their social status the majority of our heroes are either their "own boss" or they have climbed to such a high step in the social ladder that whole worlds separate them from the average employee. Yet the few "big ones" do not differ basically from the many little ones. They demonstrate, taken as a group, not the exception, but the typical cross-section of the socio-psychological condition of modern society.

The foregoing examples from our catalogue of character traits should make clear why we emphasize the double feature of the absence of development and solitude. The average man is never alone and never wants to be alone. His social and his psychological birth is the community, the masses. His human destiny seems to be a life of continuous adjustment: adjustment to the world through efficiency and industriousness; and adjustment to people by exhibiting amiable and sociable qualities and by repressing all other traits. There is no religious or philosophical framework according to which the character traits are classified and evaluated. The concepts of good and bad, of kindness and sin, of truth and falsehood, or sacrifice and selfishness, of love and hate are not the beacons which illuminate our human landscape. The character image on which an affirmative judgment is passed in the biographies is that of a well-trained employee from a well-disciplined lower middle-class family. Our people could occupy an imaginary world of technocracy; everybody seems to reflect a rigid code of flexible qualities: the rigid and mechanized set-up of a variety of useful mechanical institutions. Behind the polished mask of training and adjustment lurks the concept of a human robot who, without having done anything himself, moves just such parts and in just such directions as the makers wished him to do.

Formerly it was only the sick who needed handling because it was known that their symptoms were similar to many others. Now everyone is reduced to the same dependency. The pride of being an individual with his own very personal ways and interests becomes the stigma of abnormality. Interest in the consumption of others is an expression of lack of interest in genuine consumption. The detailed character description is dominated by the same acceptance and passivity which came to the foreground in the concept of souls without development.

IV

LANGUAGE

Superlatives

Our analysis would not be complete without some discussion of our stories' language which has several characteristic features. The most obvious one is the superlative.[12] Once we are made aware of this stylistic device, it cannot be overlooked. The heroes themselves, their accomplishments and experiences, their friends and acquaintances, are characterized as unique beings and events. The superlative gives a good conscience to the biographer—by applying a rhetorical gadget, he achieves the transformation of the average into the extraordinary. Mr. Muti is "the toughest Fascist of them all" (114); Dr. Brinkley is the "best advertised doctor in the United States" (3); our hero is the "luckiest man in the movies today" (121); another is "not only the greatest, but the first real showman in the Ringling family" (26). There is a general who is "one of the best mathematicians this side of Einstein" (107). There is a columnist with "one of the strangest of courtships" (9); another statesman with "the world's most exciting job" (144). There are also the downward-pointed superlatives. Some sportsman was once "the loudest and by all odds the most abusive of the lot" (2); a newspaper man is "one of the most consistently resentful men in the country" (28); another person is "one of the unhappiest women that ever lived" (154).

As if the biographer had to convince himself and his public that he is really selling an excellent human specimen, he sometimes is not satisfied with the ratio of one superlative per sentence but has to pack a lot of them into a single passage. Pittsburgh Phil is "the most famous and the most feared horse player in America" (23). The German Labor Front is "the best led, most enlightened and most powerful labor organization in Europe" (21). The producer, Lorentz, "demands the best writing, the best music and the best technical equipment available" (126). The baseball manager, Clark Griffith, "was the most colorful star on the most colorful team in baseball" (2). Tilden is ". . . the greatest tennis player in the world and the greatest guy in the world" (111).

This wholesale distribution of highest ratings defeats its own purpose. Everything is presented as something unique, unheard of, outstanding. Thus

[12] A study by this writer on popular German biographies in book form shows that they also are characterized by the use of superlatives. These books by Emil Ludwig, Stefan Zweig, and others are on a different intellectual level, yet it seems probable that similar sociological implications hold for them as for magazine biographies. See, Leo Lowenthal, "Die biographische Mode" in *Sociologica*, Frankfurt a.M.: Europäische Verlagsanstalt, 1955, pp. 363–86.

nothing is unique, unheard of, outstanding. Totality of the superlative means totality of the mediocre. It levels the presentation of human life to the presentation of merchandise. The most vivacious girl corresponds to the best tooth paste, the highest endurance in sportsmanship corresponds to the most efficient vitamins; the unique performance of the politician corresponds to the unsurpassed efficiency of the automobile. There is a pre-established harmony between the objects of mass production in the advertising columns and the objects of biography in the editorial comment. The language of promotion has replaced the language of evaluation. Only the price tag is missing.

The superlative pushes the reader between two extremes. He is graciously attempting to become conversant with people who are paragons of human accomplishment. He may be proud that to a great extent these wonderful people do nothing but entertain him. He has, at least in his leisure time, the best crowd at his fingertips. But there is no road left to him for an identification with the great, or for an attempt to emulate their success. Thus the superlative, like the story of success itself, brings out the absence of those educational features and other optimistic implications which were characteristic of biographies during the era of liberalism. What on first sight seems to be the rather harmless atmosphere of entertainment and consumption is, on closer examination, revealed as a reign of psychic terror, where the masses have to realize the pettiness and insignificance of their everyday life. The already weakened consciousness of being an individual is struck another heavy blow by the pseudo-individualizing forces of the superlative. Advertisement and terror, invitation to entertainment, and summons to humility form their unity in the world of superlatives. The biographer performs the functions of a side show barker for living attractions and of a preacher of human insignificance.

High and Low Language

The use of the superlative is reinforced by frequent references to an assortment of mythical and historical associations, in order, it would seem, to confer pseudo-sanctity and pseudo-safety to the futile affairs of modern mass culture. Clark Gable does not just make a career—he lives the "Gable saga" (6), and the movie actress, Joyce, experiences at least a "little saga" (110). "Historic" is the word for Ilka Chase (140) as well as for Hildegarde (135). What happens to the softball player Novikoff is "fabulous" (158); the fate of the actress Morison is "history" (162); of the movie producer Wallis (166) as well as of the baseball player Allen (45) "a miracle"; the baseball manager Griffith experiences "baseball destiny," he accomplishes "a historic piece of strategy" (2). Greek mythology is a favorite; Clark Gable lives in "Olympian regions" (6); the passport administrator Shipley (8) as well as the gadget

inventor Taylor (167) have an "Herculean task"; the producer Todd is
called an "Archon" (131) and our Taylor "Orpheus" (167). Of course
Christianity and the middle ages have to help Dorothy Thompson "like a
knight with a righteous sword" (9); the Nazi Ley is the "Jacob of German
labor" with "labor itself the Esau" (21). Vice-President Wallace is "Joseph, a
dreamer of dreams" (38); Casals is a "good Samaritan" (106). There are
no limits. Ruth Hussey sometimes "looked a bit like a Buddha" (151); the
showman Rose like a "priest of Osiris" (43). And so it goes on with myths,
legends, sagas, destinies, miracles.[13] And yet, in the same breath which be-
stows the blessings of venerable symbols on our heroes, they and we are brought
together on the easy level of slang and colloquial speech. McCutcheon, the
cartoonist, might be called the "king" of his island possession, but we hear
that "kingship is a safe investment" (1); Fletcher, who made history, is also
"the soul—or the heel—of honesty" (7); Swing, called "an apostle," has
also "radio's best bedside manner" (42). When Taft's father was president,
the "crown of Roosevelt I fitted him like a five and ten toupee" (101). There
is a boxer who finds it "good business to be brave" (12); there is "gossip—a
dime a gross" (23); there is talk of a "personal blitzkrieg" (29); of "votes
enough to elect a bee to a beehive" (109); of the "moguls of celluloid" (137);
of "that genius business" (152). The historizing hymns of praise and trans-
figuration correspond to movie "palaces" and the sport "stadiums." It is a
colossal façade, a "make-believe ballroom," as one radio station announces
its swing program. Behind the façade of language there rules, just as behind
the architectural outside make-up, a versatility of techniques, gadgets, and
trucks, for which nothing is too expensive or too cheap that may serve the
purpose of entertaining or being entertained.

These substitutes and successors of creative production require a language
which substitutes for elucidating, revealing, stimulating words a linguistic
confusion that strives to produce the illusion of rooted tradition and all-
around alertness. Thus this new literary phenomenon complies with the
highest artistic criteria: inner, necessary, inseparable connection between
form and content, between expression and the expressed—in short, a
linguistic creation which will not permit an anatomic clear-cut separation
between words and their intentions! These biographies as a literary species
are "true."

[13] Helen McGill Hughes, *op. cit.*, p. 183, is aware of the fact that the association of
"classical" names has a stimulating effect on what she calls "the city demos": "Stated in
terms of his popular literature, the mind of modern man lives in the present. And as the
present changes, so his news is voluminous and rapidly succeeded by more news. But
what fascinates him is the news story—the true story—even though it may duplicate
Bluebeard or *Romeo and Juliet* so exactly that the headline tells the news just by mentioning
the familiar names. The human interest of the common man in the modern world will,
and does, ensnare him into reading folktales or even the classics, dull and unreal as he
finds them in themselves, if they are paraphrased as the careers of twentieth century
Electras, Macbeths and Moll Flanders, for he is pre-occupied with the things that depart
from the expected and make news."

Especially for You

The pseudo-individualization of the heroes corresponds to the pseudo-individualization of the readers. Although the selection of heroes and what is reported about them are as thoroughly standardized as the language of these reports, there is the superlative functioning as the specifying agent for the chosen hero and there is also, as crown and conclusion, the direct speech as the bearer of a personal message to the reader. Affably or condescendingly, everyone is personally invited to attend the spectacle of an outstanding life. Individual meets individual; the biographer takes care of the introduction.

Coach Fletcher and his wife "can be reached only by telegram provided you know the address" (7). Should you happen to be a Brenda Joyce fan: "If you come at the right time, you will see her second-hand car" (110). Watching our election campaign: "If Hull and Mr. Taft are the candidates, your emotion will not be fired, nor will your sleep be disturbed by them" (109). For those interested in film stars: "Let's sit down with Bill Powell and listen to his story" (112); "perhaps, girls, you would like to know how Clark Gable got that way" (6). Reporting McCutcheon's acquisition of an island, the author teases the reader: "so, you want to be a king" (1). For the car owner: "You can't help seeing Johnson's restaurants if you drive along main highways" (37). There is the London *Times* representative Sir Wilmott Lewis: "Meet him on Pennsylvania Avenue. He will stop and talk to you as if you were a five hundred audience" (49). Umpire Klem "knows the multitudinous rules of baseball better than you know the alphabet" (104). Let there be no mistake: the night club singer Moffett "went to the very best schools, my dear" (119). But let's not neglect her colleague Hildegarde: "If you haven't heard her or seen her, don't stand there—go, do something about it" (135). Casals' biographer is a little less imperative: "Meet the blond bowman from Spain" (106). Dependability is the word for Miss Fitzgerald: ". . . you can bank on her for the truth" (105).

The direct apostrophe is similar in function to the superlative: it creates elation and humiliation. The reader, besides being admitted to the intimate details of the hero's habits in eating, spending, playing, has the pleasure of personal contact. There is nothing of the measured distance and veneration which a reader in the classics in biography had to observe before the statesman of the past, or the poet or the scientist. The aristocracy of a gallery of isolated bearers of unusual achievements seems to be replaced by a democratic meeting which requires no special honors and genuflection before the great.

But the ease of admission is not devoid of menacing features. The "You" means not only the friendly gesture of introduction but also the admonishing, calling voice of a superior agency, proclaiming that one has to observe, has to comply. The language of directness betrays the total coverage planned by all modern institutions of mass communication. "Especially for You" means all of you.

V

THE READER

Magazine biographies have undergone a process of expansion as well as of atrophy. They have become a standard institution in magazines which count their audience by the millions. It is significant that in the middle of World War II *The Saturday Evening Post* and *Collier's* were able to double their sales price without incurring any serious setback in circulation. But the scope of this expanding world of biographies narrowed down to the highly specialized field of entertainment. If we ask again what social need they serve, we might find the answer in this combination of quantitative increase and qualitative deterioration.

An hypothesis on the pseudo-educational and pseudo-scientific function of the popular biography can be formulated as follows: the task of the social scientist is, in very broad terms, the clarification of the hidden processes and inter-connections of social phenomena. The average reader who, like an earnest and independent student, is not satisfied with a mere conglomeration of facts or concepts, but wants to know what it is all about, seems to gain insight from these biographies, and an understanding of the human or social secret of the historical process. But this is only a trick, because these individuals whose lives he studies are neither characteristic of this process, nor are they presented in such a way that they appear in the full light of it. A rather satisfactory understanding of the reader is possible if we look upon the biography as an agent of make-believe adult education. A certain social prestige, the roots of which are planted during one's school days, constantly drives one toward higher values in life, and specifically, toward more complete knowledge. But these biographies corrupt the educational conscience by delivering goods which bear an educational trademark but which are not the genuine article.

The important role of familiarity in all phenomena of mass culture cannot be sufficiently emphasized. People derive a great deal of satisfaction from the continual repetition of familiar patterns. There are but a very limited number of plots and problems which are repeated over and over again in successful movies and short stories; even the so-called exciting moments in sports events are to a great extent very much alike. Everyone knows that he will hear more or less the same type of story and the same type of music as soon as he turns on the radio. But there has never been any rebellion against this fact; there has never been a psychologist who could have said that boredom characterized the faces of the masses when they participate in the routine pleasures. Perhaps, since the average working day follows a routine which often does not show any change during a life-time, the routine and repetition characteristics of leisure-time activities serve as a kind of justification and glorification of the working day. They appear in the guise of beauty and pleasure when they rule not only during the average day, but also in the average late afternoon and evening. In our biographies, the horizon is not extended to the realm of the unknown, but is instead painted with the figures of the known. We have already seen the movie actor performing on the screen and we have seen the cartoons of the competent newspaperman; we have heard what the radio commentator has to say and have noted the talents of boxers and baseball players. The biographies repeat what we have always known.

André Maurois has made a wrong prophecy:

> We shall come once more into periods of social and religious certainty in which few intimate biographies will be written and *panegyrics* will take their place. Subsequently we shall again reach a period of doubt and despair in which biographies will reappear as a source of confidence and reassurance.[14]

The reader who obviously cherishes the duplication of being entertained with the life stories of his entertainers must have an irrepressible urge to get something in his mind which he can really hold fast and fully understand. It has been said of reading interests that: "In general, so long as the things of fundamental importance are not presenting one with problems, one scarcely attends to them in any way."[15] This remark has an ironical connotation for our biographies, for it can hardly be said that "things of importance" are not presenting us with problems today. Yet they are scarcely attended to unless we would admit that our heroes' parents, their likes and dislikes in eating and playing and, in the majority of cases, even their professions were important data during the initial stages of the second World War. But the distance between what an average individual may do and the forces and powers that determine his life and death has become so unbridgeable that identification with normalcy, even with Philistine boredom becomes a readily grasped empire of refuge and escape. It is some comfort for the little man who has become expelled from the Horatio Alger dream, who despairs of penetrating the thicket of grand strategy in politics and business, to see his heroes as a lot of guys who like or dislike highballs, cigarettes, tomato juice, golf, and social gatherings—just like himself. He knows how to converse in the sphere of consumption and here he can make no mistakes. By narrowing his focus of attention, he can experience the gratification of being confirmed in his own pleasures and discomforts by participating in

---

[14] André Maurois, *Aspects of Biography* (New York: Appleton-Century-Crofts, Inc., 1939), p. 203. Copyright 1929, D. Appleton & Co.

[15] Franklin Bobbitt, "Major Fields of Human Concern," quoted in Gray and Munroe, *op. cit.*, p. 47.

the pleasures and discomforts of the great. The large confusing issues in the political and economic realm and the antagonisms and controversies in the social realm—all these are submerged in the experience of being at one with the lofty and great in the sphere of consumption.

Differences Between *The Saturday Evening Post* and *Collier's*

If we study the professional distribution for the two magazines separately we find the following result.

TABLE 4-4

DISTRIBUTION OF BIOGRAPHICAL SUBJECTS BY OCCUPATION IN
THE SATURDAY EVENING POST AND *COLLIER'S* FROM
APRIL 1940–APRIL 1941

Occupation of subjects	Saturday Evening Post		Collier's	
	No.	%	No.	%
Politics	16	28	15	22
Business and professions	20	35	5	7
Entertainment, sports	20	37	49	71
Total	56	100	69	100

This table shows a considerable difference between *The Saturday Evening Post* and *Collier's* in the occupational distribution of heroes. There are far more "serious" people and far fewer entertainers in *The Saturday Evening Post*. This corresponds to a difference in the audiences of the two magazines.[16] Surveys have shown that the average *Saturday Evening Post* reader is older, wealthier, and more attached to his home and more interested in social and economic problems than the average reader of *Collier's*.

However, the difference between the two magazines becomes negligible (see Table 4-5) when we re-classify the heroes according to the spheres of politics, production, and consumption. For our purpose this is a more meaningful classification. As the two magazines are rather alike under this classification we felt justified in treating them together in the main text.

We give below the list of the biographies from *The Saturday Evening Post* and *Collier's* appearing in the issues between April 1940 and 1941.

[16] *A Qualitative Study of Magazines: Who Reads Them and Why*. McCall Corporation, October, 1939.

TABLE 4-5

COMPARISON OF *THE SATURDAY EVENING POST* AND *COLLIER'S*
HEROES ACCORDING TO GENERAL SPHERES OF ACTIVITY

Spheres	Saturday Evening Post 1940–1941		Collier's 1940–1941	
	No.	%	No.	%
Politics	16	28	15	22
Production	3	5	..	..
Consumption	37	67	54	78
Total	56	100	69	100

LIST OF BIOGRAPHIES USED

The Saturday Evening Post

Date	"Hero"	Profession	No.
4-6-40	John T. McCutcheon	Cartoonist	1
4-13, 20-40	Clark Griffith	Baseball manager	2
4-20-40	John R. Brinkley	Physician	3
5-4-40	Robert Taft	Senator	4
5-4-40	Jack Johnson	Boxer	5
5-4-40	Clark Gable	Movie actor	6
5-11-40	Art Fletcher	Baseball coach	7
5-11-40	Mrs. Shipley	Chief, Passport Division, State Department	8
5-18, 25-40	Dorothy Thompson	Columnist	9
5-25-40	Richard A. Ballinger	Former Secretary of Interior	10
6-8-40	Bobby Jones	Golfer	11
6-22-40	Bob Donovan et al.	Boxers	12
6-22-40	Bob Allman	Wrestler	13
6-22-40	Daisy Harriman	Ambassador	14
7-6-40	Oche Tone	Slovenian immigrant	15
7-13-40	Ullstein Corp.	Publishing house	16
7-20-40	Hitler	Fuehrer of Third Reich	17
7-20-40	Jimmy Byrnes	Senator	18
7-27-40	Satchel Paige	Baseball pitcher	19
7-27-40	Angas	Investment counselor	20
7-27-40	Dr. Robert Ley	Head of the German Labor Front	21
7-27-40	Frances Perkins	Secretary of Labor	22
8-3, 10, 17-40 8-17, 24-40 9-14, 21, 28-40	Pittsburgh Phil	Professional gambler (horses)	23
	Alfred P. Sloan, Jr.	Businessman	24
8-17-40	D'Arcy Grant	Woman sailor	25
8-24-40	John Ringling North	President of Ringling-Barnum & Bailey shows	26
9-14-40	Bill McKechnie	Baseball manager	27
9-14-40	Westbrook Pegler	Columnist	28
9-14-40 10-5, 12, 19, 26-40, 11-9, 16,	Endicott Peabody	Rector of Groton	29

The Saturday Evening Post

Date	"Hero"	Profession	No.
30-40	William Rogers	Actor	31
10-12-40	James C. Petrillo	Pres. Am. Fed. Musicians	32
10-12-40	Louis McHenry Howe	Presidential secretary	33
10-19-40	Jay Norwood Darling	Cartoonist	34
10-19-40	Sidney Hillman	Labor leader	35
10-26-40	Frank Hague	Mayor of Jersey City	36
11-2-40	Howard Johnson	Owner of a restaurant chain	37
11-2-40	Henry Wallace	Vice-President	38
11-23-40	Silliman Evans	Newspaperman	39
11-30-40	Jesse H. Jones	Secretary of Commerce	40
12-7-40	William B. Stout	Inventor	41
12-13-40	Raymond Gram Swing	Radio Commentator	42
12-21-40	Billy Rose	Showman	43
12-28-40	Charles A. Lindbergh	Aviator, etc.	44
12-28-40	Bobby Allen	Basketball player	45
1-4-41	Mrs. E. K. Hoyt and Toto	Gorilla owner and ward	46
1-11-41	Clifton Fadiman	Book and radio critic	47
1-18-41	Sam Rayburn	Speaker, House of Representatives	48
1-15-41	Sir Willmott Lewis	London *Times* Emissary to United States	49
2-1-41	J. H. Kendrigan	Football coach	50
2-1-41	Cyrus R. Smith	Pres. Amer. Airlines	51
2-8-41	Varian Brothers	Inventors	52
2-15-41	Theodore A. Lyons	Baseball player	53
2-22-41	Jo Carstairs	Island proprietress	54
3-8, 15-41	Preston Sturges	Movie director and writer	55
3-15-41	Hank Greenberg	Baseball player	56
3-22-41	Phil Rizzuto	Baseball player	57

Collier's

Date	"Hero"	Profession	No.
4-6-40	Robert A. Taft	Senator	101
4-13-40	Mme. Chao Wu-Tang	Chinese Partisan Chief	102
4-13-40	Nancy Hamilton	Playwright, actress	103
4-13-40	Bill Klem	Baseball umpire	104
4-20-40	Geraldine Fitzgerald	Movie actress	105
4-20-40	Pablo Casals	Cellist	106
4-27-40	General Weygand	General	107
4-27-40	Ezra Stone	Stage, radio and screen actor	108
5-4-40	Cordell Hull	Secretary of State	109
5-4-40	Brenda Joyce	Movie actress	110
5-4-40	Bill Tilden	Tennis champion	111
5-11-40	William Powell	Movie actor	112
5-18-40	Greer Garson	Movie actress	113
5-25-40	Ettore Muti	Fascist politician	114
5-25-40	Philip Kerr, Marquess of Lothian	British Ambassador	115
5-25-40	Conchita Cintron	Woman matador	116
6-8-40	Thomas Dewey	Politician	117
6-8-40	Athanasiades	Munitions merchant	118
6-15-40	Adelaide Moffett	Night club entertainer	119

Date	"Hero"	Profession	No.
6-22-40	Dutch Leonard	Baseball player	120
6-11-40	Chris Martin	Movie actor	121
6-29-40	Gene Tierney	Movie actress	122
7-20-40	Lew Jenkins	Lightweight champion	123
7-20-40	Mahatma Gandhi	Indian political leader	124
7-27-40	Jean Arthur	Movie actress	125
8-3-40	Pare Lorentz	Movie producer	126
8-10-40	Don James	Sideshow barker	127
8-24-40	Larry Adler	Harmonica player	128
8-31-40	Ernest Bevin	British Minister of Labor	129
9-7-40	Helen Bernhard	Tennis player	130
9-7-40	Mike Todd	Producer—show business	131
9-14-40	Ingrid Bergman	Movie actress	132
9-21-40	Wendell Willkie	Politician	133
9-28-40	Walters and Derringer	Baseball players	133a
10-5-40	Juan March	Industrialist	134
10-5-40	Hildegarde	Night club singer	135
10-12-40	Jack Grain	Football player	136
10-12-40	Jinx Falkenburg	Advertising model	137
10-12-40	Eddie Flynn	Democratic Nat'l Chairman	138
10-19-40	John Latouche	Writer	139
10-26-40	Ilka Chase	Actress: movie, radio, film	140
11-2-40	Winston Churchill	British Prime Minister	141
11-2-40	Ken Overlin	Middleweight champion	142
11-9-40	Joan Carroll	Child movie actress	143
11-9-40	Lord Woolton	Britain's Minister of Food	144
11-16-40	Dorothy Stickney	Actress—theater	145
11-30-40	Field Marshal Erhard Milch	Organizer of German air force	146
11-30-40	Barbara Ham	Musical writer—college girl	147
12-7-40	Martha Scott	Movie actress	148
12-7-40	Joseph H. Ball	Senator	149
12-14-40	"Schnitz"	Producer—jitterbug leader	150
12-21-40	Ruth Hussey	Movie actress	151
12-28-40	George Balanchine	Ballet director	152
1-4-41	Billy Soose	Boxing champion	153
1-4-41	Carol and Magda Lupescu	Ex-King of Roumania and paramour	154
1-4-41	Annie Laurie Williams	Hollywood literary agent	155
1-11-41	Katherine Dunham	Dancer	156
1-18-41	Dorothy Comingore	Actress: theater and films	157
1-25-41	Lou Novikoff	Softball player	158
2-1-41	Zivic Brothers	Boxers	159
2-8-41	Three young actresses in "Charley's Aunt"	Actresses	160
2-15-41	Brenda Marshall	Movie actress	161
2-24-41	Patricia Morison	Movie actress	162
3-1-41	Marilyn Shaw	National ski champion	163
3-15-41	Cliff Thompson	Hockey coach	164
3-15-41	Chic Young	Comic strip cartoonist	165
3-15-41	Hal Wallis	Movie producer	166
3-29-41	James Taylor	Inventor of gadgets	167
3-29-41	Bob Riskin	Scenario writer	168

CHAPTER 5

Literature and Society

The sociological interpretation of literature—artistic or popular—is not a favorite son of organized social science. Since the emancipation of the study of literature from the rigid research dicta and historically cogent laws of philology, almost everybody with a fair access to reading and writing feels entitled to offer historical, esthetic, and sociological criticism and generalization. The academic disciplines which have been traditionally charged with the history and analysis of literature have been caught unaware by the impact of mass literature, the best seller, the popular magazine, the comics and the like, and they have maintained an attitude of haughty indifference to the lower depths of imagination in print. A field and a challenge have thus been left open and the sociologist will have to do something about them.[1]

The following remarks, making no claim to systematization or comprehensiveness, are intended as an attempt to survey work done and to be done.

I

LITERATURE AND THE SOCIAL SYSTEM

The problems envisaged under this heading are twofold. The primary aspect is to place literature in a functional frame within each society and again within the various levels of stratification of that society. In certain primitive as well as in some culturally highly developed societies, literature is integrated into other social manifestations and is not clearly differentiated as an independent entity apart from ceremonials of cult and religion. It is rather an outlet of these institutions as, for example, tribal chants, early

The first published version of this chapter appeared as "The Sociology of Literature" in *Communications in Modern Society*, ed. Wilbur Schramm (Urbana, Ill.: University of Illinois Press, 1948).

[1] It is symptomatic that no updated comprehensive bibliography is available in the field of the sociology of literature and the arts. The most valuable resource was published nearly ten years ago. See "General Bibliography" in Hugh Dalziel Duncan, *Language and Literature in Society* (Chicago: University of Chicago Press, 1953), pp. 143–214.

Greek tragedy, or the medieval passion play. In contra-distinction, literature in the middle-class world leads an existence clearly separated from other cultural activities, with many functional differentiations. It may become the escapist refuge of politically frustrated groups, as in early romanticism, or of social frustration on a mass scale, as in the current phenomenon of literary mass entertainment. Then again, literature may function as an ideological instrument in the proper sense of that word, by exalting a specific system of domination and contributing to its educational goals, as was the case with the Spanish and French dramatists in the era of absolutism.

A secondary aspect, perhaps less fertile in terms of research materials but no less rewarding in social perspectives, lies in the study of literary forms. The epic as well as lyric poetry, the drama like the novel, have affinities of their own to a particular social destiny. The solitude of the individual or the feeling of collective security, social optimism or despair, interest of psychological self-reflection or adherence to an objective scale of values, may be mentioned as starting points of associations that lend themselves to a re-examination of literary forms in terms of social situations.[2] The preceding chapter is an example for studies in this area.[3]

II

THE POSITION OF THE WRITER IN SOCIETY

The creative writer is the intellectual per se, for whom objective source materials are merely an arbitrary arsenal of reference of which he makes use, if at all, according to his particular esthetic aims. He thus represents the prototype of intellectual behavior and the lively discussion among sociologists about the role of the intelligentsia could perhaps be extended to a more concrete level if it were supported by a historically documented analysis of both the socially relevant self-portrait and the specific functions of one of the oldest groups among the intellectual professions.

It must suffice here to enumerate a few points of departure and to mention under the heading of subjectivity the phenomena of the prophetic, the missionary, the entertaining, the strictly handicraft and professional, the political or money making self-conceptions of literary producers. On the objective level we shall have to inquire into the sources of prestige and income, the pressure of institutionalized agencies of social control, visible or anonymous, the influence of technology and the market mechanisms, all with regard to the stimulation and dissemination of artistic writing and to the social,

---

[2] The most suggestive study of this aspect is unfortunately inaccessible in English: Georg Lukacz, *Die Theorie des Romans* (Berlin: Cassirer, 1920). Thematically the problem has also been posed by Kenneth Burke, *The Philosophy of Literary Form* (Baton Rouge: Louisiana State University Press, 1941).

[3] See Chapter 4.

economic and cultural situation within which writers find themselves at various historical stages. The relationships of the princely courts, the academies and salons, the book clubs and the movie industry to the literary craft exemplify the relevant topics for systematic discussion.[4] Then there are problems which cross the subjective and objective aspects, such as, whether under conditions of modern book and magazine production the writer is still an independent entrepreneur or in fact an employee of his publisher and advertiser.

III

SOCIETY AND SOCIAL PROBLEMS AS LITERARY MATERIALS

Here we enter the traditional area of sociological research in literature. There are innumerable books and papers on the treatment of the state or society or the economy or this and the other articulate social phenomenon by any number of writers in any number of countries and languages. These more or less reliable repositories of factual information, though written for the most part by literary people and therefore more or less haphazardous in matters of social theory, cannot be dismissed lightly. They evaluate literature as secondary source material for historical analysis and become all the more valuable the scarcer the primary sources for any specific period. Furthermore, they contribute to our knowledge of the kind of perception which a specific social group—writers—has of specific social phenomena, and they belong therefore to propaedeutic studies of a history and sociology of social consciousness.

Nevertheless, a sociologist with literary interest and analytical experience in the field of *belles-lettres* must not be satisfied merely to interpret literary materials which are sociological by definition; his task is also to study the social implications of literary themes and motives which are remote from public or publicly relevant affairs. The specific treatment which a creative writer gives to nature or to love, to gestures and moods, to situations of gregariousness or solitude, the weight given to reflections, descriptions or conversations, are all phenomena which on first sight may seem sterile from a sociological point of view but which are in fact genuinely primary sources for a study of the penetration of the most private and intimate spheres of individual life by the social climate, on which, in the last analysis, this life thrives. For times that have passed, literature often becomes the only available source of information about private modes and mores.

The shortcomings of fashionable biographies of today stem in part from their increasing attempt to explain literary figures (and for good measure the entire social situation in which they were created) by short-circuited con-

---

[4] Valuable suggestions for the study of the objective aspects of this area may be found in Albert Guerard, *Literature and Society* (Boston: Lathrop, Lee and Shepard, 1935).

clusions made up of analogies with the psychology of present-day man. But women like Madame Bovary, Anna Karenina, or Faust's Gretchen cannot be interpreted by mere analogy: their problems simply cannot be experienced today because the atmosphere out of which their conflicts grew has passed. The social data of the period in which they were created and the social analysis of the characters themselves are the very material from which the meaning and the function of the works of art can be understood. If our would-be psychologists in the literary field were to be completely sincere, they would have to confess that every one of these women, if alive today, would be considered stupid, frustrated neurotics who ought to take a job or undergo psychiatric treatment to rid themselves of their obsessions and inhibitions.

It is the task of the sociologist of literature to relate the experience of the imaginary characters to the specific historical climate from which they stem and, thus, to make literary hermeneutics a part of the sociology of knowledge. He has, so to say, to transform the private equation of themes and stylistic means into social equations.[5]

While sociological discussions of literature tend to be broad and general, an intensive analysis of the storm and shipwreck that introduce Shakespeare's *The Tempest* serves as an example of close textual criticism which can yield background material helpful to an understanding of sociological implications in the rest of the play. In this brief scene, Shakespeare confronts us with persons from widely separated social classes and places them in an extreme situation which enables him to study their essential characters.

What may have appeared to Shakespeare's people as a matter-of-fact set of relationships is for us problematic. In interpreting them at all, there is the risk, of course, of making Shakespeare appear unduly aware sociologically. The purpose here, however, differs from textual literary criticism; the intent is not to burden Shakespeare's words with many meanings on different levels, but simply to listen carefully to the evidence implicit in the lines of the scene. In a sense, it is the evidence of that which was taken for granted in Shakespeare's day that is the objective of our search. Such an approach need not distort or overburden his meanings—at worst, it examines his characters, their roles, and their relationships in the light of a larger picture of social change than he himself could possibly have known.

The shipwreck scene introduces us to the villainous and worthless characters of the play. Shakespeare is concerned, naturally enough, with furthering his plot, but he must first define the villains, and in this scene he carefully sets them off against the figures of Gonzalo and the boatswain. The princely usurpers and idlers are useless in the emergency at hand and behave stupidly, whereas Gonzalo acts and speaks in a reasonable way, and the boatswain works competently and industriously. If we bring to the scene what we learn

---

[5] I should say that the work of Eric Bentley, *The Playwright as Thinker* (New York: Reynal and Hitchcock, 1946), is a highly successful attempt to translate private into social scenes and then to interpret them in sociologically meaningful terms.

from the rest of the play, it is apparent that Shakespeare uses the progressive ideas and moral concepts of his day to define his heroes, and leaves his villains in a reactionary, or at least non-progressive, torpor. In this light, we see in the villains the representatives of the declining noble class who are concerned only with enjoying the feudal prerogatives they have inherited. They have nothing in common with Prospero, Gonzalo, or simple workmen, whose actions and ideas anticipate the qualities of middle-class individualism and industriousness.

The first persons we encounter in the play are working people, acting out their professional roles in a responsible way. The master calls "Boatswain," and the boatswain answers: "Here, master; what cheer?" The master continues:

> Good, speak to the mariners: fall to't yarely, or we run ourselves aground: bestir, bestir.

We are quickly introduced to a situation structured by the needs of expedient work under conditions of utmost stress. The speakers address each other by means of their functional names. The way in which they speak to each other is that of workers getting on about their business; it could also be the way of a senior and a junior engineer. The chief gives an order, the boatswain responds, and the whole mood is relaxed, friendly, and factual despite their predicament. We can imagine that two skilled pilots might behave in the same way if their plane were in trouble.

The master expresses clearly and simply the need for speed. His words invite comparison with those of Alonso, King of Naples, when, a few seconds later, he enters the scene and commands the boatswain to "play the men." The attitude of the king is that of the feudal lord to the lowest of his subjects. He does not understand the situation and his relationship to the crew members is that of imperium and domination, not of reason.

The words of the shipmaster, however, are strictly geared to the understanding that exists among the crewmen of the purposes of the work at hand. It is interesting to note that he never again appears on the scene. He has given the plan of over-all strategy and his general directions to the boatswain, who will from now on know what to do. Authority is not something continuously visible as it was in feudal times; it is ingrained in the productive processes themselves, and the captain can, therefore, disappear. As a matter of fact, the sailors and the boatswain have a hard time trying to get the feudal lords out of their way, so convinced are the latter that their visible authority is needed, and so useless is it, actually, to the workmen. The working men are on the job, doing efficiently what has to be done without undue fear or impatience.

As the scene progresses, the crew members come on deck and the boatswain speaks to them as follows:

Heigh, my hearts! Cheerly, cheerly, my hearts! Yare, yare! Take in the topsail!
Tend to the master's whistle! Blow, till thou burst thy wind if room enough.

The boatswain reproduces the friendliness and simple efficiency of the
master, although the tone is now somewhat more paternalistic. The distance between boatswain and sailors is patently greater than that between
master and boatswain. Whereas the master has given general instructions
about the main goal to the boatswain, the latter is more specific in his dealings with the less-skilled and less-educated group at his command. Nobody,
however, uses harsh words except when the boatswain, in an ironical way,
curses the elements. Here, as generally in modern literature, the irony
expresses a feeling of limitation and constitutes an insight into the frailty of
men; it is humility in non-theological clothing. What the boatswain is
really saying is: We are doing all we can in our exchange with nature. We
shall try to use nature for our purposes, but a wind can be stronger than a
man's intelligence.

The feudal lords enter the scene at the very moment the boatswain has
acknowledged the limitations of human power by shouting at the storm.
Now it is no longer merely man against nature, but man against man.
Shakespeare pits the industrious professional and the workman against men
who are in power. Among those who appear are Alonso, King of Naples,
Antonio, usurper of the Dukedom of Milan, and Gonzalo, a minister of the
state of Naples. (Ferdinand, the innocent young prince, who later will
speak in a most human way, remains silent.) The king says,

Good Boatswain, have care. Where's the Master? Play the men.

The remarks are not unfriendly, but they are condescending. The king
wants the master, nobody else will do. He can think only in terms of hierarchy. As we have seen, however, it is a hierarchy with which the master
himself is little concerned; the entire crew from the master on down are
interested merely in the matter at hand. The boatswain does not respond
to the words of the king; he continues to behave rationally, and the only
rationality possible at the moment is to keep the deck cleared of passengers
so that the work of combating the storm is not impeded.

Antonio interrupts brusquely:

Where's the master, bos'n?

Shakespeare introduces this character by showing in his speech and, we may
assume, in his gestures the relations between social usefulness and individual
character. Antonio is a criminal and a socially useless, irrational person.
Interestingly enough, the boatswain, who had nothing to say to the king,
answers Antonio: "Do you not hear him?" He means, of course, the master.
He then adds:

You mar our labor; keep your cabins; you do assist the storm.

What Antonio is supposed to hear from the master is his whistle. We are given here an interesting juxtaposition of the old and the new societies. The master is invisible. He is the unseen supreme authority whose presence is mediated by the whistle, symbol of the rational ordering and structuring of reality. In the light of the new, the old order with its tradition, possession, and power—as these were built up in the Middle Ages—now appears ridiculous. The boatswain uses the key word that separates the two worlds when he speaks of "labor." Labor, along with its organization, is the leading principle of the new society; he who does not work, who has no useful function, is superfluous; he should disappear, he should go to the cabins. Antonio is, like the storm, a hindrance that must be overcome, made innocuous.

Gonzalo, the counsellor, takes no issue with the boatswain's orders and is only concerned to pour soothing oil on the human tempest that is brewing. "Nay, good," he says, "be patient." The boatswain's answer is in the same tone and appeals again to common sense: there can only be patience if the situation permits the crew to work patiently; because of "these roarers" there is unfortunately no time for lengthy explanation. But the boatswain goes a step further, and appeals, as it were, to the higher knowledge of the counsellor by saying:

What cares these roarers for the name of king?

The boatswain now for the first time puts the issue quite straight. Nature is stronger than men of any kind and, by implication, he who knows how to master nature is superior to a man who does not, regardless of social titles. Again, as so often in Shakespeare, we encounter the stature and the inner dignity of the man of the new society coming into being in Elizabethan England; man is justified by his work, and his character is formed by his function in society. The feudal lords, impatient and useless, have nothing to do but act out their impatience in complete separation from the real situation.

Gonzalo agrees with the boatswain, but with a defensive note:

Good, yet remember whom thou hast aboard.

The answer of the boatswain,

None that I more love than myself,

is one familiar enough in later statements of the egalitarian ethos: in our nature we are equal and are egotistic and altruistic at one and the same time; we all love ourselves but we overcome this self-love or raise it to a higher moral standing by useful work.

The boatswain then expresses the wisdom of the simple but experienced workman about the division of labor in society. He delineates the spheres of power and skill of those who work with their hands and those who work with their brains. "You are a counsellor," he says,

> If you can command these elements to silence and work the peace of the present, we will not hand a rope more; use your authority: if you cannot, give thanks you have lived so long, and make yourself ready in your cabin for the mischance of the hour, if it so hap.—Cheerly, good hearts!—Out of our way, I say.

The boatswain obviously takes Gonzalo seriously; as the scene develops it will become quite clear, in fact, that the two conceive of each other as colleagues of a sort. Neither is the source of authority; both are middlemen. They represent that middle station which the progressive forces of the new society are beginning to occupy. Not only professionally, but also in their basic character traits, they are removed from extremes. This motif of a middle station in life and in character is a theme that will come to the fore in subsequent literature and will come increasingly to mirror the image that middle-class man has of himself.

It is interesting to note that in the boatswain's speech death appears in a completely non-theological meaning. The speech is related to the sentiments of Shakespeare's sonnet LXVI; both deal with love and death and in both death is viewed not as a fulfillment but as a terminal point. The entire scene is, indeed, secular, except for the recourse to prayer at the very end. During the emergency, no one claims to be in the hands of God; safety and security are viewed within the framework of the developing modernism of the Renaissance, and the generally shared belief is that we have security only to the extent that we have reason and experience. The boatswain, we may say, speaks as if he had read Montaigne, and Gonzalo answers as if he were Montaigne.

For a moment the boatswain leaves the scene to check up, we assume, on the work of the mariners. Gonzalo then delivers the following monologue:

> I have great comfort from this fellow: methinks he hath no drowning mark upon him; his complexion is perfect gallows. Stand fast, good Fate, to his hanging! Make the rope of his destiny our cable, for our own doth little advantage! If he be not born to be hanged, our case is miserable.

Gonzalo slanders the boatswain *in absentia;* his curses are ironical—he is simply using his urbane wit and language to give himself comfort.

The boatswain enters the now empty deck and after having given instructions to the mariners, says, upon hearing a cry from the cabin:

> A plague upon this howling! They are louder than weather, or our office.

We assume that he, like Gonzalo, is giving himself comfort with his words; he curses when those he insults are not present to hear him. The curses of

both Gonzalo and the boatswain are in marked contrast to those of the re-
appearing feudal lords, who now include in their group Sebastian, the
brother of the king of Naples. (King Alonso and his son Ferdinand do not
reappear; they obviously heed the instructions of the boatswain.) Sebastian
brings the swearing to new heights:

A pox o' your throat, you bawling, blasphemous, incharitable dog!

We can infer that this powerless individual, who envies his brother in power,
must live out in words his phantasies of domination (which later jell into a
plan to murder his brother). In response to his cursing the boatswain says
simply, "Work you, then." By his answer, the boatswain codifies the basic
difference between the legitimate, well-organized rationale of ordered work
and the parasitical, impotent, and decaying rationale of unprincipled domination. As if to prove the point, Antonio now joins in to call the boatswain
a "cur," a "whoreson," an "insolent noisemaker," and in absurd fury
indicts him as being more cowardly than themselves.

At this point, the lords abandon the scene, which the middlemen, Gonzalo
and the boatswain, dominate. Gonzalo again acts as moderator, as a medi-
ator who uses psychological methods to soften the shock for the despairing
feudal lords and his king. The boatswain continues to give orders to the
crew in accord with the changing situation of the ship, until the seamen
enter shouting:

All lost! To prayers, to prayers! All lost!

In a way, the mariners are still living on a cultural level different from that
of the boatswain and Gonzalo; the latter no longer find solace in religion,
but only in themselves.

At the end of the scene, Gonzalo says:

Now would I give a thousand furlongs of sea for an acre of barren ground; long
heath, brown furze, anything. The wills above be done! But I would fain die a
dry death.

His speech is again urbane; even his invocation to the wills above seems
ironic.

Throughout the scene it is apparent that the feudal lords are unaware
of what is going on; they can only resort to vulgar behavior and direct
personal abuse. Neither Sebastian nor Antonio realizes that the real issue
is the relationship between skilled men and nature. Of course, the audience
learns that the storm has been created by Prospero, but this does not alter
their knowledge that the gentlemen lie and that the boatswain and his crew
are neither incompetent nor drunk. The feudal lords emerge as stupid;
they do not know what the relations of science, work, technology, and human
skill really are. While the boat, so to speak, sails to the new world, the old

lords are suffocating in an outmoded and completely senseless state of mind.

One example of an intensive analysis of a modern writer is a study I made some twenty years ago of Knut Hamsun which incidentally turned out to be a case of successful sociological prediction in the field of literature.[6] The particular task consisted of analyzing themes and motives having no direct connection with public issues, for they were domiciled in the private sphere. The study showed that Hamsun was intrinsically a fascist. Events have proved that, this once at least, prediction is possible for a sociologist of literature. To the surprise of most of our contemporaries, Hamsun turned out to be a close collaborator of the Nazis.

Here only a few rather disjointed examples of this type of analysis can be given. Of special interest seems to be Hamsun's treatment of nature. In the authoritarian state, the individual is taught to seek the meaning of his life in "natural" factors like race and soil. Over and over again he is told that he is nothing more than nature, specifically, than race and "natural" community. The pantheistic infatuation with nature which Hamsun demonstrates and accepts leads to this dictated identity between the individual and "natural" forces. The route is circuitous in appearance only.

The shift from the dream world of naturalness to the social reality of fascism is inherent in the forms in which the uproar of the elements, brutal nature, is experienced. Hamsun writes (and the following is merely a sample repeated in endless variations):

> A wind comes up, and suddenly it rumbles far and wide. . . . Then lightning flashes, and . . . the thunder rolls like a dreadful avalanche far beyond, between the mountains. . . . Lightning again, and the thunder is closer at hand; it also begins to rain, a driving rain, the echo is very powerful, all nature is in an uproar. . . . More lightning, and thunder and more driving rain. . . .[7]

Immanuel Kant had defined his conception of the sublimity of nature in a storm in such a way that man, in experiencing his own helplessness (as a being of nature) in the face of the superior might of natural phenomena, simultaneously experiences the inferiority of the latter in the face of his own humanity, which is greater than nature. Man can indeed succumb to nature, but this is only incidental and external to the power of his soul and mind.[8]

Kant's social consciousness bids nature be silent, as it were, about what it experiences from man and what it can do for man. But for Hamsun the storm can hardly shout loudly enough to drown out individual and social

---

[6] See Leo Lowenthal, *Literature and the Image of Man* (Boston: Beacon Press, 1957), Chapter VII.

[7] *The Last Joy* (*Die letzte Freude*) in *Gesammelte Werke*, Vol. V of twelve vols., German translation edited by J. Sandmeier (München: Albert Langen, n.d.), p. 310.

[8] See Kant, *Critique of Aesthetic Judgment*, trans. J. C. Meredith (London: Oxford University Press, 1911), pp. 110–11.

impotence. The storm is the occasion for experiencing and formulating the insignificance of the individual—the exact opposite of Kant's conception:

> When a moment of sadness and realization of my own worthlessness in the face of all the surrounding powers comes over me, I lament and think: Which man am I, or am I perhaps lost, am I perhaps no longer existent! And I speak aloud and call my name, in order to hear whether he is still present.[9]

Anxiety appears to be a sort of secret emotion bound up with this late pantheism. Kant's pride in human autonomy has no place for the sentimental uneasiness which is announced in every fear of a thunderstorm and which appears in Hamsun as a promiscuous jumble of mawkish sympathies for both natural objects and spiritual difficulties.[10] Hamsun's storm world foreshadows the affinity between the elements of brutality and sentimentality, which are united in fascist behavior.

The law of rhythm is of particular significance for Hamsun's concept of nature. The rhythmic cycle of the seasons is noted in the novels incessantly, as if in imitation of the phenomenon itself. "Then came the autumn, then came the winter."[11] ". . . but the road leads on, summer follows spring in the world. . . ."[12] In the end, the rhythmic principle takes on a normative character. What is wrong with certain people is that "they won't keep pace with life . . . but there's none should rage against life."[13] Even sexual relationships are oriented to the regularity of nature. The shepherdess will walk past the hunter's cabin in the autumn just as infallibly as she comes to him in the spring. "The autumn, the winter, had laid hold of her too; her senses drowsed."[14]

We have attained the extreme opposite of human self-consciousness before nature if man can and must never disturb the natural cycle at any point. In this new ideology, which seeks to transfigure helplessness and subjection, the individual lays down his arms before a higher power in seemingly free

[9] *The Last Joy*, p. 311.

[10] See, for example, *Pan*, trans. W. W. Worster (New York: Alfred A. Knopf, Inc., 1921), pp. 23–24. "I pick up a little dry twig and hold it in my hand and sit looking at it, and think my own thoughts; the twig is almost rotten, its poor bark touches me, pity fills my heart. And when I get up again, I do not throw the twig far away, but lay it down, and stand liking it; at last, I look at it once more with wet eyes before I go away and leave it there."

[11] *The Road Leads On*, trans. Eugene Gay-Tifft (New York: Coward-McCann, Inc., 1934), p. 46.

[12] *The Ring Is Closed*, trans. Eugene Gay-Tifft (New York: Coward-McCann, Inc., 1930), p. 152.

[13] *Growth of the Soil*, trans. W. W. Worster, Vol. II of two vols. (New York: Alfred A. Knopf, Inc., 1921), p. 246; also cf. *Rosa*, trans. A. G. Chater (New York: Alfred A. Knopf, Inc., 1926), p. 18: " 'What are you sitting here for?' 'Ah, young man!' he said, holding up the palm of his hand. 'What am I sitting here for? I sit here keeping pace with my existence. Ay, that's what I'm doing.' "

[14] *Pan*, p. 164.

volition. Man must expect the terrors of a meaningless life unless he obedi-
ently accepts as his own what may be called the alien of nature. The social
solution to the puzzle of natural rhythm is blind discipline, the rhythm of
marches and parades.

Concerning love and womanhood one might say of Hamsun's attitude
that woman attains her proper character and happiness when she unites the
home with the naturalness of true existence in her functions as housewife
and mother. We find in Hamsun unmistakable traces of the tendency to
reduce the role of woman to merely biological functions, the duty to bear
many children. This trend is part of his ideal counterpart to liberal society
—the fascist reality. "A real girl will marry, shall become the wife of a man,
shall become a mother, shall become fertility itself."[15] The apotheosis of
biological functions inevitably leads to bitter hatred of all reforms, emancipation, or spirituality which woman might desire,[16] to contempt for "the
modern woman." Real individual satisfaction seems possible only in the
sexual sphere, but not because sensual pleasure has a specific connection
with the development of the personality. It is rather hatred and malice,
associated with great disdain for woman, which are operative in this relationship.

> "Come and show me where there's cloudberries," said Gustaf. . . . And how
> could a woman say no? . . . Who would not have done the same? Oh, woman
> cannot tell one man from another; not always—not often.[17]

Hamsun dressed the role of promiscuous sexuality in all kinds of natural
myths. There is a complete lack of interest in one's partner's happiness.
Sexual relations are ruled by complete passivity, a sort of service which man
obeys:

> . . . he broke through all rules of propriety and was very friendly, picked the
> hay from her bosom, brushed it from her knees, stroked, petted, threw his arms
> around her. Some call it free will—[18]

Even when man is occupied with love, Hamsun maliciously reminds him of
his mere naturalness, a true disciple of fascism's moral relativism.

When we turn to his treatment of marginal figures, we soon discover that,
next to the peasant, Hamsun has particular sympathy for the vagabond. In
the prehistory of fascism in Germany, yeoman work was done by a conceited,
individualistic group of uprooted literati who played with the cult of the
hero. In the anticipation of fascism which we find in Hamsun's novels, the
vagabond is a forerunner of the brutal man who weeps over a dry twig and

---

[15] *The Last Joy*, p. 344.
[16] Cf. *Chapter the Last*, trans. A. G. Chater (New York: Alfred A. Knopf, Inc., 1929),
pp. 105–07.
[17] *Growth of the Soil*, Vol. II, p. 92.
[18] *Chapter the Last*, p. 102.

bares his fist to his wife. Flirtation with the anarchistic vagabond is a coquettish and spiritualized expression of the veneration of heroic forces. There is abundant evidence from every period of Hamsun's career, as in a late novel in which the vagabond August longs "to shoot the knife out of the hand of a man who was trying to make off with his wallet" because that would be a thrill for the "children of the age" in their dreary existence;[19] or in his prewar writings where he plays the same romantic game without introducing heroic crime,[20] and where he ridicules the notion of bourgeois efficiency as poverty-stricken ("no thunderbolt ever falls");[21] or even in his earliest work, where he cries for "gigantic demi-gods" and blunders into a political program for which the way has been cleared by this very heroic ideology: "The great terrorist is greatest, the dimension, the immense lever which can raise worlds."[22] It is but a short step from here to the glorification of the Leader.

Finally a word about Hamsun's relationship to mankind as a whole. It is most ironic that the biological comparison with the anthill, so popular in liberal reformist literature as a symbol of higher social aims and organization, is completely reversed by Hamsun and made into the image of the planlessness of all human existence.

Oh, that little anthill! All its inhabitants are occupied with their own affairs, they cross each other's paths, push each other aside, sometimes they trample each other under feet. It cannot be otherwise, sometimes they trample each other under feet.[23]

This picture of life and of man's aimless crawling closes the ring of antiliberal ideology. We have returned to the starting point, the myth of nature.

IV

SOCIAL DETERMINANTS OF SUCCESS

By and large the legitimate business which the sociologist of literature may have in the field of communications research consists in formulating hypotheses for research on "what reading does to people."[24] But he cannot simply pass the buck to his colleague, the empirical researcher, after having done his historical, biographical, and analytical work. There are certain

[19] *The Road Leads On*, p. 409.
[20] See *The Last Joy*, p. 298.
[21] *Children of the Age*, trans. J. S. Scott (New York: Alfred A. Knopf, Inc., 1928), p. 82.
[22] *Mysteries*, trans. A. G. Chater (New York: Alfred A. Knopf, Inc., 1927), p. 51.
[23] *The Women at the Pump*, trans. A. G. Chater (New York: Alfred A. Knopf, Inc., 1928), p. 5.
[24] See the spadework study under that title by Douglas Waples, Bernard Berelson, and Franklyn R. Bradshaw (Chicago: University of Chicago Press, 1940).

factors of social relevance which, though very decisive for the measurement of effects, will have to undergo sociological exploration on the level of theory and documentary study.

There is, first of all, the problem of finding out what we know about the influence of all-embracing social constellations on writing and the reading public. Are times of war or peace, of economic boom or depression more or less conducive to literary production? Are specific types of the literary level, literary form, and subject matter more or less preponderant? What about the outlet of distribution, the publishing house, the circulation figures, the competition between books and magazines in these various periods? What do we know about readership figures in public and university libraries, in the Army and the hospitals—again broken down according to changing social conditions? What do we know, qualitatively and quantitatively, about the ratio between literature distributed and consumed and other media of mass communication, or even non-verbalized forms of organized entertainment?[25]

A second auxiliary source lies in the area of social controls. What do we know about the influence of formal controls of production and reading? We must deal with the world-wide phenomenon of the use of tax money for public libraries, with the European practice of governmental subventions for theatres, with the American experience of supporting creative writers out of public funds during the New Deal administration, to cite a few examples. We have to study the impact of selective and cherished symbols of public rewards, from the Nobel Prize for literature to the contests arranged by publishing houses, from the Pulitzer Prize to the honors bestowed by local or regional communities on successful authors whose cradles were fortunately situated in particular localities. We should study "manipulated controls": publishers' advertising campaigns, the expectations of profit tied up with book clubs and film production, the far-flung market of magazine serializations, the reprint houses, and so on. We must not forget the area of censorship, of institutionalized restrictions from the index of the Catholic Church to local ordinances prohibiting the sale of certain books and periodicals. And, finally, we would have to analyze and systematize what we know about the impact of informal controls, of book reviews and broadcasts, of popular write-ups of authors, of opinion leadership, of literary gossip and private conversations.

A third, and certainly not the least, social determinant of success is connected with technological change and its economic and social consequences.[26] The phenomenal development of the publishing business, putting out literary

---

[25] See Paul F. Lazarsfeld, *Radio and the Printed Page* (New York: Duell, Sloan & Pearce, Inc., 1940).

[26] Theoretical groundwork for the study of modern technological change and its social consequences in the artistic field has been laid in the article by Max Horkheimer, "Art and Mass Culture," in *Studies in Philosophy and Social Science*, Vol. IX (1941), to whom the author is indebted in many ways for his thinking in the sociology of literature.

products on all levels in the low price field is surpassed only by the still more spectacular modes of production in other media of mass communication. Thus, it would be worth studying whether the financial returns received by writers in the last few decades can be attributed in large measure to improved technical facilities, including the author's working instruments, and whether this change in technique has changed the social status of writers as a group. Relatively little is known about the cumulative effects of technological improvements from one medium to the other. Do more people read more books because they see more pictures or listen to more broadcasts or is it the other way around? Or is there no such interdependence?[27] Is there a relationship between the high degree of accessibility of printed material and the methods by which educational institutions avail themselves of this material at all age levels?

As an illustration for social determinants of success, the broad, diversified, and articulated response in Germany to Dostoevski may be cited. An examination of available material in books, magazines and newspapers showed that certain psychological patterns in the German middle classes were apparently highly gratified in reading Dostoevski.[28] Unlike the study of Hamsun, here we are not concerned with the work of the writer, but with the social character of his reception.

The peculiar fate of the German middle classes, which had never experienced any sustained periods of liberal political and cultural life, kept them wavering between the mechanisms of identification with an aggressive, imperialistic, domineering set of ruling groups and a mechanism of defeatism and passivity, which, despite all the traditions of philosophical idealism, constantly induced them to attitudes of willing submission to what they sensed to be superior leadership. The ensuing sado-masochistic reactions found pliable material for acts of identification in the self-torturing and torturing protagonists of Dostoevski's novels.

The active life process of human society, all its progressive forces, indeed, the whole compass of the productive forces in general, hit a blind spot in the vision of these German masses. This is apparent, for example, in their failure to notice a gap in Dostoevski's themes, namely, earthly happiness. Happiness, measured socially, presupposes an active transformation of reality, that is to say, the removal of its gross contradictions. That would require not only a

[27] The impact of technological change on production and reproduction in the sphere of visible and audible artistic production has been exposed in a masterly fashion by T. W. Adorno in the field of music and by Walter Benjamin in the field of motion pictures. See, e.g., the former's article "On Popular Music," in *Studies in Philosophy and Social Science*, Vol. IX, No. 1 (1941) and the latter's "L'oeuvre d'art a l'époque de sa reproduction mécanisée," in *Zeitschrift für Sozialforschung*, Vol. V, No. 1 (1936). Valuable information on the interchange between films and literary production may be found in S. Kracauer's *From Caligari to Hitler: A Psychological History of the German Film* (Princeton, N. J.: Princeton University Press, 1947).

[28] See Leo Lowenthal, "Die Auffasung Dostojewskis im Vorkriegsdeutschland," in *Zeitschrift für Sozialforschung*, Vol. III, No. 3 (1934).

complete transformation of existing power relations but also a reconstruction of social consciousness. Really to direct one's impulses toward the realization of social happiness is to enter sometimes into direct opposition to the existing power apparatus. The insignificant role which the category of happiness played in the social consciousness of the German middle classes can be understood only from the totality of their social relationships. A satisfying social organization was closed to them as a declining class and, therefore, it must also be shut out from consciousness in its true meaning as happiness.

It might be argued against this conception, which uses Dostoevski as evidence of a non-activist ideology devoid of moral deed and social solidarity, that one must not expect such an approach from him the apostle of love and compassion for mankind. Nearly all the literary critiques of Dostoevski do, in fact, revolve around the theme of love and compassion, whether in elegant formulations, like the "surpassing calm, through which only a sort of deeply secret sorrow vibrates, an endless compassion . . ."[29] or in painfully popular statements, like his "heart trembles with sympathy, compassion."[30] A very naïve passage will serve to indicate the social significance:

> His predilection for the oppressed and the depraved gradually assumes the morbid form of . . . 'Russian compassion,' that compassion which excludes all upright, honest working men, and extends only to prostitutes, murderers, drunkards, and similar blossoms on the tree of mankind.[31]

This statement may be crude, but it points to something very true. The reception of Dostoevski was not bothered by the fact that in his works love remains a weak disposition of the soul, which can be understood only by presupposing a frantic defense against all social change and a fundamental passivity in the face of every truly moral act. The demand for love and compassion could mean a realization of the existence of social contradictions and the need for change; it could be the effective approach to the activity of men in their thoughts and actions. Instead, it remains a matter of mere sentiment, a permission, not a demand. That is perhaps the clearest sign of the ideological role of such a concept of love. Demand and the power to act cannot enter into the social consciousness of relatively impotent social strata any more than they can accept a principle of justice which must destroy their solidarity with the rulers and point to their common interests with the ruled.[32]

[29] Hermann Conradi, "Dostojewski," in *Die Gesellschaft*, Vol. 6 (1889), p. 528.

[30] L. Brehm, "Dostojewskis 'Dämonen,' " in *Der Deutsche*, Vol. 5 (1906), p. 346.

[31] C. Busse, *Geschichte der Weltliteratur*, Vol. II (Bielefeld and Leipsig, 1913), p. 595.

[32] Books and articles on Dostoevski which have appeared in this country since the end of the war offer a good opportunity for comparison with European experiences. My impression is that several of these publications show an atmosphere of malaise and frustration which, for the sociologist, reveals trends of spiritual needs and confusion not unrelated to the European experience with Dostoevski a generation ago.

V

SOME CHALLENGING TASKS

If a sociologist of literature wants to hold his claim to be heard in the field of modern communications research, the least he can do is to discuss a program of research that can be located within the areas proper to his field and at the same time joins up with the scientific experiences already accumulated for the other mass media. Four possible fields of research paralleling the four areas of analysis will be outlined here.

Functional Content

Obvious as it may be, the point must be made that the basic requirement for finding out what kind of gratification people expect from mass literature in a given social framework, or better, at a specific historical moment, is to have exact knowledge of the content of these works. What we need are qualitative and quantitative inventories of the contents of popular works on a comparative scale, beginning not later than the early nineteenth century. Studies made so far are scanty,[33] though speculative ideas about the assumed content are over-abundant.

Take the commonly accepted notion that the main function of mass literature is to provide an outlet for the escapist drives of frustrated people. How do we know that this was ever true or is still true today? Perhaps the functional content of the novel today is much less escapist than informative: literature has become a cheap and easily accessible tool for orientation in a bewildering outside and inside world. The reader is looking for prescriptions for inner manipulation, an abridged and understandable psychoanalytical cure, as it were, which will permit him by way of identification and imitation to grope his way out of his bewilderment. Escape involves an attitude of self-reliance and is much more likely to be found in times of individual stability than in our present period, characterized by ego-weakness needing alien crutches for survival. Whether this hypothesis is justified or not, it might fruitfully be pursued in studying the patterns of identification and imitation offered by mass literature. One might find that, in contrast to earlier literary products, the contemporary novel has a much higher density and velocity of action and an accelerating recession of reflection and description.

It would be interesting, for example, to compare the popular historical novel of today and a generation ago. We would perhaps discover that the older works tried to transmit a panorama-like picture of a period in which

---

[33] I am indebted to Ralph H. Ojemann of the State University of Iowa for bringing to my attention the excellent master thesis, written under his supervision, by Evelyn Peters: "A Study of the Types of Behavior toward Children Approved in Fiction Materials," 1946.

the reader could sit restfully next to the historical protagonist around whom the panorama developed. Today, however, this picture dissolves into a multitude of figures, situations, and actions which leave the reader without the enjoyment of sitting invisibly with one selected protagonist, who used to be the measure and yardstick for the literary materials that a writer conjured up. The pressure of modern life, which produces the very weak egos who are in turn exposed to the pressure, makes it necessary to forego identification with just one figure, or with the inner processes of the soul, or with theoretical ideas and values.

Thus the classical situation of literary consumption, in which the reader shares the solitude of choice or fate with the solitude and uniqueness of the one and unrepeatable work of art, may be replaced by collective experience of well-organized activity in the direction of adaptation and the acquisition of the tricks of self-manipulation. More and more studies are making source materials available,[34] but their systematic sociological exploration remains to be done.

The Writer's Attitude

What the reader is looking for in literary communication is one thing; what the author delivers beyond the conscious awareness of the reader is something else again. The case of Knut Hamsun illustrates this kind of problem.

Whether and to what extent opinions and attitudes are influenced by the literary avalanche depends not only on its manifest content but also on its latent implications. It is true, to lift them from their formulated content is a task to be undertaken with untried tools. Nevertheless, an extremely inexpensive social laboratory might be suggested where no living beings need be interviewed with all the paraphernalia of money-and-time-outlay. More or less consciously, usually less, the author is a manipulator who tries to get over certain messages that reflect his own personality and personality problems. To find out where he stands, it might be worth while reviving him and the figures of his imagination with artificial respiration and subjecting them to questions and psychological experiments on the most advanced level.

With the help of standardized ideological questionnaires, for example, we might scan through a well-chosen sample of mass literature and find out about the author's attitudes, about his points of view on human nature, on group tensions, on historical and natural catastrophes, on sex, on masses versus great individuals, and so forth. We might then, in scoring the answers,

[34] See, e.g., Frank Luther Mott, *Golden Multitudes* (New York: The Macmillan Company, 1947); Alice Payne Hackett, *Fifty Years of Best Sellers* (New York: R. R. Bowker Company, 1945). Edward H. O'Neill, *The History of American Biography* (Philadelphia: University of Pennsylvania Press, 1935).

get a qualitative and quantitative yardstick with which to locate the social position of the writer and thus be able to make predictions about his behavior as a person and about the kind of production with which he will follow up work previously done. If we enlarge our sample sufficiently we might learn much about the self-identification of these agents of mass communication and of the potential influence of these hidden self-portraits on the readers.

Such a laboratory experiment could be implemented by analyzing the character structure of the protagonists in the fictional material. Recent work in social psychology has furnished us with a set of structure syndromes to be gathered from responses to ideological and projective interview procedures, by which we can diagnose with a high degree of reliability whether a person is authoritarian or antiauthoritarian in type. These findings have an obvious bearing on prognostications of political, moral, and emotional behavior. Surface descriptions are very often misleading and can be corrected by these new methods.[35]

Cultural Heritage

In studying the direct and indirect social content of popular literature the marginal media deserve far more attention than they have received so far, particularly the comics[36] and perhaps some other products the enjoyment of which is shared by adults and juveniles alike. A thorough-going content analysis of these materials should result in a number of valuable hypotheses on the continuing significance of ideas, values, and emotions stemming from situations that have become completely obsolete.

It would be necessary to study not only the obviously archaic and infantile motives of the fairy world of subhuman and superhuman serials, but also those materials in which, under the guise of everyday misery or everyday enjoyment, values become visible which were associated with earlier stages of modern society, and especially with the more serene style of life in the nineteenth century. Measuring such material against the ideological and emotional content of traditional and respectable fiction, we might gain added insight into the wavering of modern readers between the necessity of learning the mechanisms of adaptation and conformity and the daydreams of a happier, though unattainable or historically impossible, way of life. Taking "adult" and "preadult" contents together we might be able to develop hypotheses that would open up systematic exploration of likes and dislikes on levels of awareness, as well as of deeper psychological levels.

[35] See, e.g., T. W. Adorno *et al.*, *The Authoritarian Personality* (New York: Harper & Brothers, 1950).

[36] See, however, Coulton Waugh's *The Comics* (New York: The Macmillan Company, 1947). See also Chapter 1, footnote 5.

The Role of Social Environment

In the area description three aspects of social determinants of success were noted, two of which should be referred to here in order to clarify the type of research envisaged.

There is first of all the problem whether different stages of the economic and political cycle leave distinguishing marks on literary products. The research task would involve a modification of the studies in functional content mapped out earlier in this section. An inventory should be taken of a literary sample in times of depression and boom, of war and peace. This inventory would not be limited to an enumeration of fictional topics, but would be particularly concerned with emotional patterns which may safely be assumed to be closely tied up with the specific gratifications and frustrations of the readers. As a very tentative example, the hypothesis is ventured that the use of happy or not so happy endings is a point of difference. At the height of an economic depression, escapist identifications with lovely daydreams of unchallenged happiness may characterize the literary scenery. Today, however, a pseudo-tragic ending on a note of unsolved problems is by no means rare because the relative prosperity permits fictional experiences with a higher degree of reality and even some insight into our psychological and cultural shortcomings.

Many other situations may have to be selected before one can construct an index of content and motive preference for various over-all situations. A study comparing the two postwar booms and the two prewar depressions of the last forty-five years might actually lead to a point from which future predictions of preferences in fiction would be possible. Educational and professional inferences which could then be drawn are so obvious that they need not be gone into here.

In the field of technological determinants it would be worth studying the reading ability of the average man and the way it has been modified by his experiences with auditory and visual media. We know a lot about clinical reading disabilities but we know relatively little about intellectual selectivity in reading.[37] Similarly it would be interesting to study what is read and remembered and what is more or less slurred over or not read at all. A more precise knowledge about "content-reading" abilities and disabilities could become a labor-saving device for writers; as for sociologists, they would gain corroborating evidence to the findings of functional content analysis.

Blueprinting research tasks has all the shortcomings of any set of unfulfilled promises. The expert in communications research might, however, become interested in the troublesome achievements and tasks of a neighboring branch of study and its potential contribution to his own field.

I should like to conclude with a personal experience. A sociologist treating literature in the classroom is bound to encounter a divided reaction: Students will display an eager interest in a new scientific experience, but, as instruc-

[37] See Rudolf Flesch, *The Art of Plain Talk* (New York: Harper & Brothers, 1946).

tion goes on, some of them will protest against the analytical "dismembering" of poetic material. The students are eager for guidance in an uncharted sea since they never have been quite able to find out what is good and what is not so good. Somehow they look forward to getting possession of a foolproof formula that will set them straight once and for all regarding this vague and vast field situated somewhere between education and mere entertainment. What the students do not know is that their initial approach is already a manifestation of the particular stage at which sociological interpretation of literature still finds itself.

Index

Addison, Joseph, 59, 67–69, 76, 84, 88, 104, 107
  quoted, 68, 82–83, 88–89, 100, 102n.
Adjustment to society, 128–129
Adorno, Theodor W., 6n., 155n., 159n.
Advertising, 11
  of books, 60, 65
Albig, William, quoted, 24n.
Alison, Archibald, quoted, 106
Allen, B. Sprague, 69n., 74n., 87n., 94n.
Altick, Richard D., 56n.
Amelia, Fielding, 63
American Soldier, The, Stouffer, 9
Amusement, 105, 108
  (*See also* Diversion; Entertainment)
Ancestry, 119–120
Architecture, culture and, 38
Aristotle, xx, 6
Arnold, Matthew, 14, 32–33n., 97
  quoted, 29–30
Art:
  entertainment and, 14, 45–46, 48
  folk or "high," xx, 11
  function of, 23, 32
  genuine, versus popular culture, xix, 4–6, 23, 26–27
  higher, 42, 45–46
  literature as, xii
  mediocre, problem of, 27–28
  pleasure and, 26, 32
  popular, xvii, 42, 47–50
  and popular culture, debate over, 14–51
Art of Biography in Eighteenth Century England, The, Stouffer, 109n.
Art of Plain Talk, The, Flesch, 160n.
Artists, xvii
  biographies of, 112–113
  and the public, 18–42
  status problem of, 33–34
Aspects of Biography, Maurois, 135n.
Atkins, J. W. H., 67n., 107n.
Audiences:
  building of, in eighteenth century England, 55–65, 77–78, 90–91, 95
  imagination of, 23–24
  passivity of, 20
  restlessness of, 20
  (*See also* Public, the)

Augustan Satire, Jack, 72n.
Aurelia, Hoole, 71
Austen, Jane, 93n.
Authoritarian Personality, The, Adorno et al, 159n.

Bagehot, Walter, 14–15
  quoted, 30–31
Bateson, F. W., 78n., 96n.
Battle of the Books, Swift, 106
Beauty:
  appreciation of, 27
  art and, 46–47
  and the good life, 25–27
Bee, The, 75, 81n.
Beggar's Opera, The, 35
Behaviorism, 125
Benjamin, Walter, 155n.
Bentley, Eric, 144n.
Berelson, Bernard, 153n.
Bible Societies, 56
Biographies, 109
  function of, 114
  increase in, 111
  language of, 127
  lists of types of, 111–112
  modern, 114
    familiarity in, 134–136
    German, 130n.
    language of, 130–134
    in magazines, 109–140
    shortcomings of, 143
  in the 1920s, 112–113
  popular, xiv
Blackmore, Sir Richard, 67
Blair, Hugh, 99, 101
Bobbitt, Franklin, quoted, 135
Bon Ton, Garrick, 70
Book clubs, 57
Book publishers, 10, 56, 59, 61
Book reviews, 62–65
Books:
  advertising of, 60
  cost of, 60
  women and, 58, 68, 71
  (*See also* Literature; Reading)
Booksellers and bookselling, 58–62
Boswell, James, 61

SPECTRUM  PAPERBACKS

S-1 THE CAUSES OF THE CIVIL WAR, Kenneth M. Stampp, $1.75

S-2 IMMIGRATION AS A FACTOR IN AMERICAN HISTORY, Oscar Handlin, $1.95

S-3 PSYCHOANALYSIS AND PSYCHOTHERAPY—36 SYSTEMS, Robert A. Harper, $1.95

S-4 FALLACY—THE COUNTERFEIT OF ARGUMENT, W. Ward Fearnside and William B. Holther, $1.95

S-5 THE GREAT DEBATE—OUR SCHOOLS IN CRISIS, C. Winfield Scott, Clyde M. Hill, and Hobert W. Burns, $1.95

S-6 FREEDOM AND CULTURE, Dorothy Lee, $1.95

S-7 UNDERSTANDING TODAY'S THEATRE, Edward A. Wright, $1.95

S-8 GOLDEN AGES OF THE THEATER, Kenneth Macgowan and William Melnitz, $1.95

S-9 THE SEARCH FOR AMERICA, edited by Huston Smith, *paper* $1.95, *cloth* $2.95

S-10 THE GREAT DEPRESSION, edited by David A. Shannon, $1.95

S-11 WHAT PRICE ECONOMIC GROWTH? edited by Klaus Knorr and William J. Baumol, *paper* $1.95, *cloth* $3.95

S-12 SCARCITY AND EVIL, Vivian Charles Walsh, *paper* $1.95, *cloth* $3.95

S-13 JUSTICE AND SOCIAL POLICY, Frederick Olafson, $1.95

S-14 CONSTRUCTIVE ETHICS, T. V. Smith and William Debbins, $1.95

S-15 LONELINESS, Clark E. Moustakas, *paper* $1.75, *cloth* $3.75

S-16 KNOWLEDGE: ITS VALUES AND LIMITS, Gustave Weigel, S.J., and Arthur G. Madden, *paper* $1.75, *cloth* $3.75

S-17 THE EDUCATION OF TEACHERS, G. K. Hodenfield and T. M. Stinnett, *paper* $1.95, *cloth* $3.95

S-18 LITERATURE, POPULAR CULTURE, AND SOCIETY, Leo Lowenthal, $1.95

S-19 PARADOX AND PROMISE: ESSAYS ON AMERICAN LIFE AND EDUCATION, Harry S. Broudy, *paper* $1.95, *cloth* $3.95

S-20 RELIGION IN AMERICA: PAST AND PRESENT, Clifton E. Olmstead, $1.95

S-21 RELIGION AND THE KNOWLEDGE OF GOD, Gustave Weigel, S.J., and Arthur G. Madden, *paper* $1.95, *cloth* $3.50